I0018344

Perspectives on
Digital Comics

Perspectives on Digital Comics

Theoretical, Critical and Pedagogical Essays

Edited by
JEFFREY SJ KIRCHOFF *and*
MIKE P. COOK

Afterword by DREW MORTON

McFarland & Company, Inc., Publishers
Jefferson, North Carolina

LIBRARY OF CONGRESS CATALOGUING-IN-PUBLICATION DATA

Names: Kirchoff, Jeffrey SJ, 1984– editor. | Cook, Mike P., editor.
Title: Perspectives on digital comics : theoretical, critical, and
    pedagogical essays / edited by Jeffrey SJ Kirchoff and Mike P. Cook;
    afterword by Drew Morton.
Description: Jefferson, North Carolina : McFarland & Company, Inc.,
    Publishers, 2019. | Includes bibliographical references and index.
Identifiers: LCCN 2018060564 | ISBN 9781476671888 (paperback : acid
    free paper) ∞
Subjects: LCSH: Webcomics. | Comic books, strips, etc.—History and
    criticism. | Digital media.
Classification: LCC PN6714 .P47 2019 | DDC 741.5/9—dc23
LC record available at https://lccn.loc.gov/2018060564

BRITISH LIBRARY CATALOGUING DATA ARE AVAILABLE

ISBN (print) 978-1-4766-7188-8
ISBN (ebook) 978-1-4766-3515-6

© 2019 Jeffrey SJ Kirchoff and Mike P. Cook. All rights reserved

*No part of this book may be reproduced or transmitted in any form
or by any means, electronic or mechanical, including photocopying
or recording, or by any information storage and retrieval system,
without permission in writing from the publisher.*

Front cover illustration by Lana Stern/Shutterstock

Printed in the United States of America

McFarland & Company, Inc., Publishers
    Box 611, Jefferson, North Carolina 28640
    www.mcfarlandpub.com

JSJK:
To my family

To all the comic creators

MPC:
To my wife (Sara) and daughter (Sawyer)

To Jeff for countless conversations around comics,
both digital and otherwise

And to all the comics that got me through childhood
(and adulthood)

Table of Contents

• Global •

• Education •

Introduction

Digital Comics—Savior or Destroyer of a Medium?

JEFFREY SJ KIRCHOFF *and*
MIKE P. COOK

Anecdotally, we have found a wide range of reactions when we tell people we are editing a collection on digital comics. Some people react with extreme enthusiasm, excitedly remarking that a collection devoted to digital comics is far overdue. Others share a bit more skepticism, wondering why we would devote a collection to comics that may not be available for reading just a few weeks from now. And there is a third reaction that we get quite often—most often from colleagues not familiar with comics studies—that can effectively be paraphrased as "Digital comics? Is that a thing?"

Perspectives on Digital Comics is written for all three groups: the enthusiasts, the skeptics, and the uninitiated. We have been doing research with comics and digital comics for the last several years, and we continually noted that the scholarship on digital comics seemed scattered at best—an article in a scholarly journal here, a chapter in an edited collection there, and presentations sprinkled in at popular culture, rhetoric, composition, and comics studies conferences across the globe. The issue is certainly not the quality of scholarship—in fact, part of our inspiration for our collection stems from what has come before us on the subject—but rather that the scholarship remains so fragmented. We feel that as comics studies continues to grow and expand, the field would benefit from a collection devoted to a comic type that continues to develop at a seemingly exponential rate. While many fine collections exist offering varied perspectives on print comics, ours is the first edited collection to focus solely on the thriving digital comic market. We feel this is a needed collection, as the conversation on digital comics is diverse and robust; as one might expect, some believe digital comics to be the "future" and "savior" of print comics, while others argue vehemently that digital comics aren't comics at all. All of these perspectives are important and grow our understanding of comics—what it means to be a "comic," how to read a comic, interpreting comics as literature, and implementing comics into a classroom setting. Given that our collection is entitled *Perspectives on Digital Comics*, we find it wholly appropriate to offer three distinct perspectives on the highly controversial media known as digital comics.[1] By sharing these three respected scholars' distinct views, we hope to show the fertile ground for discussing this important medium while also introducing readers to the contentious debates that often surround digital comics.

Consider the viewpoint of Scott McCloud, oft considered to be one of the most accessible and engaging comic theorists. In *Reinventing Comics* (2000)—the second of McCloud's provocative trilogy that explicates the complexity of comic books in an accessible way—McCloud discusses the infiltration of comics into the digital world. He argues that, theoretically, the shift from print to digital comics will radically change the "shape" of creating, producing, and consuming comics. Specifically, he posits that the page is tethered only to the print medium—it need not be a function of the digital or web comic. He writes, "Once released from that box ... gradually comics creators will stretch their limbs and start to explore the design opportunities of an infinite canvas" (p. 222). McCloud's notion of infinite canvas encourages comic creators (particularly digital comic creators) to challenge the traditional structure of a comic book. Thus, he advocates digital comics to dabble in creating "a 500 panel story ... told vertically—or horizontally like a great graphic skyline" (p. 223). Put quite simply "In a digital environment, comics can take virtually any size and shape as the temporal map—comics' conceptual DNA—grows in its new dish" (p. 223). Though McCloud admitted that most online comics are "no more than 'repurposed' print at heart," he writes about infinite canvas comics with a hopeful verve, believing that digital comic creators would soon be productively challenging the boundaries of what it means to be a comic.

Contrast McCloud's optimism with Thierry Groensteen's healthy skepticism. In Groensteen's *Comics and Narration* (2015), he challenges the idea that digital comics are a liberating future for comic creators and even questions whether digital comics can (or should) be perceived as inherently "comic book" in form and structure. Much of Groensteen's argument is rooted in the idea that digitized versions of print comics and multimedia comics distort the "intended" comic book reading experience. In regards to digitized versions of print comics, Groensteen aptly notes that reading digital comics

> entails the loss of a very strong, affectively charged object relation: the physical handling of the book, which involves both arms, or even the entire upper body, is replaced by intermittent pressure on the mouse from the reader's index finger [p. 65].

Haptic interfaces that strive to mimic the action of turning a page is insufficient for Groensteen. He also asserts that digitized versions of print comics destroy the integrity of the printed page, as "A printed comic can be perceived as a collection of images spread out across the page, arranged according to a positional logic that is easy for the memory to retrieve" (pp. 65–66). In digital comics, he notes, pages replace other pages; moreover, while some digital comics allow for multiple pages to be seen at once, he suggests that the size of the screen—and definitely the size of the mobile device—impacts how this information is consumed. However, he saves his most scathing critiques for multimedia comics; he finds the addition of multiple media to be superfluous, arguing "there is … no need to 'bring comics to life,' since it is an art form that is already complete. Any reader looking at a comics page will imaginatively compensate, easily and spontaneously, for the absence of real motion or sound" (p. 70). Moreover, the addition of motion and animation disrupts the reader's chosen rhythm; Groensteen strongly believes that comic readers should choose points of entry in a comic book, but multimedia comics—and digital comics through guided view—often dictate points of entry for the reader.

Lastly, we turn to Aaron Kashtan, who offers a kind of middle ground between the extreme optimism of McCloud and the heightened pessimism of Groensteen. In "'And It Had *Everything* in It': *Building Stories*, Comics, and the Book of the Future," Kashtan (2015) notes that while digital comics have obviously borrowed from the narrative form and structure of print comics, print comics can—and should—borrow some of the distinct storytelling techniques of digital comics. He goes on to argue that Chris Ware's creative masterpiece *Building Stories*—a collection of fourteen comics that can be read in any order and that are all printed on different materials/media—liberally borrows characteristics of the digital comic, specifically how it "celebrates its own materiality" (p. 423) and how it "fragments" its story (p. 436). Thus, Kashtan implicitly argues that digital comics and print comics can learn from one another, be inspired by each other, and ultimately coexist—that is, the comic medium is large enough for both print and digital comics.

We open with these three disparate perspectives because it effectively gives a snapshot of the healthy debate that the emergence of digital comics fosters. The goal of our collection is to demonstrate the varied ways one can read, interpret, and view digital comics; we want to collect the valuable perspectives on many different facets of digital comics, including the history/evolution of digital comics, theories for understanding and reading digital comics, criticism and analysis of specific digital comic titles, and how digital comics can be used in educational settings. After reading our collection, scholars should better understand the landscape of digital comic scholarship, while hopefully adding to their knowledge of comic history, theory, criticism, and education. In short, this collection can work as an introduction to ways of seeing digital comics and can also help established (digital) comic scholars understand perspectives other than their own.

Collection Overview

Perspectives on Digital Comics aims to bring together comic scholars to discuss a variety of issues related to digital comics: theory, criticism, its global reach, and education. Through this collection, we aim to benefit a range of digital comic scholars, from novice, new to the field academics and pedagogues to those with significant experience in the digital comic realm. For those new to or relatively young within the field of digital comics, we offer multiple possible entry points into the current conversation. Through these essays, readers are given a glimpse into the range of existing scholarship in the field. We hope this range can serve a new digital comics scholar by providing an entry point into their own inquiry and application. Of specific benefit to those newer to the field is the "Theory" section, which offers a vocabulary for different ways to approach digital comics. Additionally, the essays in the theory section foster looking at and considering digital comics as a plural concept: database, infinite canvas, remediation, and so forth. First, Jayson Quearry's "Experiencing the Infinite: An Introduction to Digital Comics Phenomenology Through Marvel Infinite Comics" takes on the issue of how digital intermediaries such as Marvel Unlimited changes the reader's engagement with what he terms the "comics-object." Quearry pays particular attention to how the reader's body engages with digital comics differently from print comics, while arguing that that comic scholarship needs a consistent means to discuss the relationship between print and digital comics. Where Quearry's essay offers an optimistic outlook for reading digital comics, Jeffrey SJ Kirchoff's "Considering ComiXology's Guided View" takes a slightly different approach. This essay argues that ComiXology's guided view disrupts, rather than enhances, the reading practices associated with comic book reading. Using scholars such as Lev Manovich and Scott McCloud, this essay aims to show that Guided View distorts two distinct properties of the printed comic page: the database like nature of the page, which allows for significant reader flexibility in determining reading path, and the spatio-temporality of the comic page (specifically the panopticity of the page), which aides in comprehension and immersion.

In "Re-Theorizing the Infinite Canvas: A Space for Comics and Rhetorical Theories," Rich Shivener looks to reframe Scott McCloud's theory of infinite comics through the use of various digital rhetoric theories including

Edbauer Rice's affective ecologies, Ridolfo's rhetorical velocity, Gries' principle of vitality, and Helms's *Rhizcomics*. Shivener's goal is to develop a theoretical framework that can be used to study such expansive comics as Munroe's *xkcd* comic *Click and Drag*. Our final essay in the "Theory" section addresses documentary web-comics, or graphic narratives addressing real-world issues that are disseminated online. Johannes C.P. Schmid's "Documentary Webcomics: Mediality and Contexts" observes that documentary webcomics eschew the affordances associated with digital media (e.g. moving images, sound, interaction) but instead take advantage of the faster and cheaper circulation. Schmid specifically examines webcomics that serve as alternative media hubs and webcomics that work within institutions and facilitates education on specific topics.

Those contributing essays to the "Criticism" section create an opportunity for others to expand their initial thoughts on how they might study digital comics. For example, scholars entering the field may do so assuming they will only study and write about one aspect—e.g., form—and push another—e.g., literary criticism—to the back burner. The criticism essays in this collection remind us that digital comics are literary works in their own right by providing looks at how themes, ideas, and content are represented in and for these digital contexts. Recognizing that digital comics are more than a formalistic, structural novelty and are indeed powerful pieces of literature is one of the goals of this collection, and to that end, this section offers literary criticism of specific digital comics and digital comic creators. This section opens with Eden Lee Lackner's "It Came from the Woods (Most Strange Things Do): Emily Carroll's *Through the Woods* and Interactive Internet Reading" which closely examines Canadian comic artist and writer Emily Carroll's collection of illustrated stories, *Through the Woods*. Lackner pays particular attention to how Carroll is able to explore the boundaries of the medium in which she works. "Death's 'Friend Hug': Analyzing the Personification of Death in Three Webcomics," by Karis Jones, analyzes the representation and characterization of Death in three webcomics: *Cyanide and Happiness, Life and Death,* and *Mary Death*. Noting that few scholars have investigated the representation of death in webcomics, Jones posits that such an examination can reveal society's attitudes regarding death in the 21st century. Lastly, John Logie's "*MAUS* (W)HOLES: Reflections on (and in) the Digital Editions of Art Spiegelman's *MAUS*" discusses how sometimes, the digital format of a comic can work counter to the purpose of a text. In this essay, Logie points out how *The Complete MAUS*—a 1994 CD-Rom version of Spiegelman's critically acclaimed *MAUS I* (1986) and *MAUS II* (1991)—fails to capture the spirit and intent of the original text material.

The authors in our "Global" section offer all readers, but especially those less familiar with the breadth and scope of digital comics, a broad overview and a look at what has been and is being done around the world, including South Africa, francophone countries, and the United States. In "When Funding is *the* Issue That Prevents an Issue: Are Digital Comics the Logical Platform of Production in a South African Context?," Ray Whitcher shows readers how the South African comic market has, historically, been slow to develop. He further notes that based on the success of *Velocity: Darker Forces*, a digital comic distributed through ComiXology, that the digital comic platform may be a way for the South African comic industry to gain a stronger foothold. Chris Reyns-Chikuma and Jean Sébastien's "Digital Comics in Francophone Countries: Never Too Late to Be Creative" acknowledges that historically, francophone digital comics have lagged behind American digital comics in regards to quantity, diversity, inventiveness, and commercialization. However, they also show that in the last decade, francophone digital comics are beginning to catch up through very creative means and should not be overlooked.

Finally, through the "Education" section, readers (i.e., teachers) are given two ways to use digital comics in classrooms. Herein, the authors marry scholarship and pedagogy and offer theoretical positionings of digital comics in the context of instruction. These essays provide a range of how-to-style instructional methods for implementing digital comics in secondary classrooms for the purposes of information literacy and as mentor texts leading to digital composing. Teri Holbrook, Melanie Hundley and Bill Holbrook begin this section by arguing how digital comics can serve as mentor texts for students in their essay "Upwards and Backwards: Blurred Perspectives on Digital Comics as Mentor Texts." The authors select three texts to show how digital comics can be used to teach narrative writing and simultaneously help students learn how to compose with digital media. Similarly, Mike P. Cook and Luke Rodesiler use two titles to show how digital comics can serve as a powerful information literacy sponsor. In "Using Digital Comics to Support Information Literacy: 21st Century Research Skills and Authentic Composing," the authors demonstrate the importance of information literacy education in secondary classrooms before arguing that digital comics can be used to (a) teach information literacy skills and (b) disseminate student's own research projects.

For those readers who come to this collection as experienced digital comic scholars, we believe the essays herein offer utility to you as well. A reading of these essays offers a look at how the work being done parallels your own, especially as many of us tend to follow a relatively narrow line of inquiry. Likewise, this collection represents the breadth of the work being done around the world. An "Afterword" subtitled "Losing My Edge" concludes our collection with Drew Morton reflecting on the growth of digital comics scholarship over the last few years, while also considering a couple of possible directions the field might take on in the near future.

This powerful collection, as mentioned above, is intended for a broad audience—enthusiasts, skeptics, and those new to the field of digital comics—and compiled to add to the scant existing scholarship through the first edited collection focused entirely on, and giving adequate space to, digital comics. Curated into four sections, the authors discuss the history of, theories for, criticism and analysis of, and pedagogical uses of digital comics. Rather than looking to answer questions or to position digital comics as *the* next and best evolution in comics studies, we hope our collection raises additional questions in readers and fosters further inquiry, theory, and practical dialogue. The perspectives offered herein are intended to represent the breadth and rigor of contemporary scholarship on digital comics; that is, they simultaneously highlight the wonderful work currently being done and argue for the necessity of continued academic pursuits across all aspects of digital comics. And as readers and fans, we hope they offer you yet another digital comic for your "to-read" list.

NOTE

1. It is fascinating to note that there is even a highly contentious debate regarding the *naming* of this medium. Some, as we do, prefer the broad, umbrella term "digital comics." Others find it necessary to differentiate between digital comics—believing them to be digitized versions of print comics—and web comics, those comics made exclusively for consumption on a computer, tablet, or other mobile device.

REFERENCES

Groensteen, T. (2015). *Comics and narration.* Jackson: University of Mississippi Press.
Kashtan, A. (2015). "And it had *everything* in it": Building stories, comics, and the book of the future. *Studies in the Novel, 47*(3), 420–447.
McCloud, S. (2000). *Reinventing comics: How imagination and technology are revolutionizing an art form.* New York: HarperCollins.

Experiencing the Infinite

An Introduction to Digital Comics Phenomenology Through Marvel Infinite Comics

Jayson Quearry

My first memories of encountering "floppies" are paired with a hidden corner in a grungy convenience shop; like Dana Anderson (2013), my clearest childhood impression of comic books begins with "the spinner rack in the local store" (p. 67). Not only were the various sensations of the store associated with the comics, but they impacted the physical texture of the object itself; the pages of the issue would be bent or frayed due to the rigidness of the rack, adolescent fingerprint smudges were left behind on the pages like ghosts, and the cover had accumulated a perceptible coating of dust and grease. Over time, my comic buying habits evolved out of convenience store corners into direct market specialty shops—an environment with its own characteristics—but, either way, the "purchase context ... [set] the stage and ... [was] the first step in the encounter" with comic books (Anderson, 2013, p. 69).

Of course, in the contemporary comic book market, the brick and mortar context is often completely absent. Readers now regularly encounter the comics-object through digital intermediaries, like ComiXology or Marvel Unlimited. Even though these "purchase contexts" impact the reader's phenomenological engagement with the comics-object, they appear less pervasive than the musty smell of back issue bins or the indentions left by the spinner rack. Instead, the consumer is oriented directly toward an engagement with the digitized object. My intention here is to focus on that engagement: the phenomenological process of taking-in the digital comic. In that way, digital and print comics are, as other scholars have stated before, dissimilar. Where previous studies have emphasized their differences in terms of narratology and aesthetics, I will focus on how the reader's body encounters digital comics differently from print comics.

While scholars like Ian Hague (2014) have detailed how smell, touch, and even taste influence the reading process of print and digital comics, I am concerned with the exchange between comics-object, eye, and mind. Regardless of their oppositional methodologies, Scott McCloud, Thierry Groensteen, and Neil Cohn all foreground the reader's impartation of some form of completion or "closure" through a combination of sight and cognition. Similarly, for each of these theorists, that process is enabled by the interstice, "gutter," or cavity left open by the comic's aesthetic design, only to be filled by the participation of the reader. That gap, no matter the name, is where the phenomenological difference between print and digital comics exists; where print comics leave the filling of that gap entirely to the reader, digital comics initiate the process. In recent publications, Tom Gunning (2014) and Scott Bukatman (2016) have suggested that even print comics rely on exchanges of motion. If that is the case, I propose—just as Thomas Lamarre (2009) claims that "The interaction between manga and anime is a matter of *difference in motion*" (p. xviii; emphasis in original)—that the proprioception of digital comics is distinct from print due to a ramping up or throttling of visible, experiential motion. Aside from doing a portion of the work for the reader, that motion is often reminiscent of various cinematic movements, using the reader's familiarity with that medium to direct them through the process. Though motion comics may seem to be a logical example of filmic motion, they are closer to animation, where a form of digital comic, like Marvel Infinite Comics, fuses comic book-ish aesthetics with motion. In suggesting Infinite Comics as a heightened representative of all digital comics, my analysis of one specific miniseries, *All-New Captain America: Fear Him* (Hopeless 2015), will help to exemplify the kinetic nature of digital comics. While I will not provide a comprehensive study of the topic, I intend to begin a conversation—to create dangling plot threads, so to speak—meant to be continued by other scholars in "the next thrilling issue."

Defining Digital

The term "digital comics" likely calls to mind reading a comic on some form of screen, but as creators experiment with the possibilities provided by quickly advancing technology, the scope of the term begins to expand past that initial mental image. With that expansion comes questions about which criteria should be used to qualify what is and is not a digital comic.

Arguably the most widely read perspective on how to define digital comics comes from Scott McCloud's (2000) *Reinventing Comics*. McCloud, writing during digital comics' nascence, suggests that the "native soil" of the digital as unique medium yields a product that would never be possible within the medium of print (p. 203). The opportunities provided by the digital medium are endless, manifested in what McCloud calls the "infinite canvas" (p. 200). More than an endless receptacle for artwork, digitization provides a sort of purification. Borrowing language from Henry Jenkins, McCloud views the convergence of the old and new mediums as an opportunity to ignore the canvas and recognize the foundational concept of the art; digital is freeing, an arena where the essence of comics potentially shines through. He does, however, also allow for instances where the additive properties of multimedia distract from the "temporal map" (p. 209), or ability to represent time through space, which he views as the quality that binds comics across print and digital. Ideally, the "infinite canvas" is comics in their purest form, using digital not as a distinction from print, but as a method of clarifying what comics are and can be.

Dittmar (2012) both narrows and complicates that discussion. Specifically, he pursues how the digital medium shapes narrative, in the process aligning with McCloud in one respect by suggesting that digital comics rely upon access to particular technology across all aspects of production and reception. By prioritizing the technology responsible for the production and dissemination of digital comics within his definition, Dittmar relies upon the digital as medium, though he is less concerned with its potential and more with its necessity to the processes of production and reception. That specification leads Dittmar into an entanglement another digital comics scholar, Wilde (2015), argues for avoiding when studying comics.

The requirement of Internet access to read digital comics becomes part of how Dittmar distinguishes between web and downloadable comics as "subforms of digital comics" (p. 85). Noting web comics' inability to be downloaded, Dittmar (2012) does highlight a characteristic that separates them from digital comics sold online, but Wilde (2015) sees a greater benefit in studying the print/digital divide through the discursive need to create these distinctions. Both authors do find consensus in proclaiming a frequent feature of digital comics to be a malleability of form, but Wilde (2015) makes a valid case that isolating web comics from digital or any other segregating distinction only slows the discussion, ultimately muddying the goal of clarification.

Accepting Wilde's point, inspecting what McCloud's "infinite canvas" has yielded might be more worthwhile than renegotiating the web/digital split. Goodbrey (2013), for instance, believes that the digital can breakdown the sedimentation of format that decades of print have established, potentially creating "significant changes in the relationship between space and time within the medium" (p. 188). As Goodbrey and McCloud both admit, though, few creators or publishers have begun to use digital comics to demolish those barriers. Not often grouped under the digital comics heading, motion comic adaptations of popular comics series, like *Astonishing X-Men* and *Watchmen*, have possibly pushed against the restrictions of print the furthest, raising questions about their inclusion in digital comics discourse. Smith (2011) is one of the few scholars to have written about motion comics in detail, studying the form from an adaptation perspective. By detailing the production process behind specific scenes in a few major motion comic releases, Smith emphasizes the creators' attempts at consistency between the hypo- and hypertext, but that, ultimately, only showcases how aesthetically distinct the adaptation is from the source, further distancing motion comics from other digital or print comics. Drew Morton has pursued the subject further, attempting to create a taxonomy of the formal characteristics that have appeared across multiple prominent motion comics. Arguably Morton's (2015) most intriguing proposition is the category of the "motion book"—a merger of digital and motion comics—as a progression of the motion comic. Based on his description, what he considers "motion books" would include Infinite Comics. However, Goodbrey (2013) cautions that "Once animation has been introduced into a comic, the question arises … at what point a comic ceases to be a comic and becomes an animation," (p. 194) and, in the case of motion comics, the shift to animation has undoubtedly occurred. For me, then, the motion comic and the "motion book," occupy different spaces, especially in terms of sensation. I tend to agree with Goodbrey's (2013) suggestion that the reader's ability to determine the pace of the reading experience is paramount. Agreeing with that belief, I propose that digital comics—in all forms— have already managed a state where a core trope of print comics has been erased while reader control is still maintained.

That state has been reached through the inclusion of movement or bursts of movement, not fully autonomous animation. Located within the interstices of these comics—the gutter, the division between pages—and the panels themselves, these bursts of movement are brought about by reader interaction (clicking, swiping) but aid in the completion of the image in a way static print comics do not. In short, the motion is not imagined: it is perceived. In a print comic, the page housing the panels is what moves; the panels bend or ripple as the page is flipped forward or backwards. The digital experience incorporates motion directly into and between the panels. For example, in a web comic—even one with a single panel—the click of the mouse results in a shift of data as the webpage changes to the next screen, which serves as a literal movement of the panel information as it is replaced by new data. The same experience occurs in terms of the swipe, as the panels slide off the screen, replaced by the pixels and digital information of new panels. The movement of panel data, however, is the least obvious within digital comics. First, in terms of the Guided View, the programming recreates a movement that resembles a camera, drifting from panel to panel, isolating specific panels through black matting. Second is the actual movement of panels within the screen. In these instances, panels will dissolve or layer on top of each other, slide off the screen, or have other graphic elements appear or vanish on-screen.

As exemplified by the previous instances, the reader still controls a majority of the pacing (aside from bursts of directive motion), but the method—the click, the swipe—results in an alternative experience. Where Dittmar (2012) considers the mouse click to be similar to progressing through the pages of print comics, there is actually little sensory resemblance within the digital variant. Depending on the device being used, readers either click a mouse or swipe through screens when reading a digital comic; the former distances the reader from the tactility of touching the comics-object directly, while the latter alters the motion the hand traditionally follows when progressing through a comic. Either way, the dominant sensation is that of the device, not the comics-object, removing the unmediated interaction present in a print comic. More than just comics read on a screen, digital comics channel motion through a device in a way that creates an inherently different sensational experience from traditional comics. What, though, is the phenomenological experience of print that digital separates itself from?

Creating "Closure" Between Comics and Phenomenology

In *Understanding Comics*, Scott McCloud (1993) describes the act of "closure" as the "phenomenon of observing the parts but perceiving the whole" (p. 63). A gestalt process, this involves the reader cognitively completing the action between two or more panels, filling-up the blank space dividing the panels—dubbed "the gutter"—by cognitively picturing the action in motion. Considered a foundational mechanism of comics by McCloud (1993), "closure" enables the illusion of movement, temporality, and other sensations within a static art form, unifying "the visible and the invisible" within perception (p. 92). Intentional or not, McCloud's use of "visible" and "invisible" to describe the process of "closure" creates a fitting connection back to the phenomenological work of Maurice Merleau-Ponty.

Within Merleau-Ponty's (1986) unfinished final work, *The Visible and the Invisible*, he describes how during the act of perceiving "we situate ourselves in ourselves *and* in the things, in ourselves *and* in the other, at the point where, by a sort of *chiasm*, we become the others" (p. 160; emphasis in original). This exchange between who is seeing and what is seen depends upon interweaving mutual reflexivity. An engagement of perception, the process of taking-in a comics-object involves the same reflexivity; the artwork reaches toward the reader as the reader simultaneously gazes toward the artwork. That is, the seer reaches out through sight and is touched in return by the art-object. Within comics, that mutual extension finds a unity in the interstices of the page. The closest Merleau-Ponty ever got to describing such an interaction was writing about how classical painting and the seer participate in a similar interaction. In "Cézanne's Doubt" (1993) he contends that the painter's work should not only impart their concept but spark the same concept within the spectator through a memory of experience. The illusion of motion, for instance, becomes facilitated by the comingling of the spectator and the object; what is not represented, that which is invisible, then becomes visible.

Miers (2014) elaborates upon a similar, simultaneous process that occurs in relation to the linework within panels. He argues that comics readers participate in a process of imagination when taking-in the artist's line, where they "generate fictional truths" (p. 148) about the reality of the image they are looking at. Miers is describing a directly proprioceptive act. The experience of decoding linework inherently involves the mind using the body's sense recall to imagine, then attach the movement being represented, finding an experiential truth in fiction. Though writing in terms of painting, Dufrenne (1973) foreshadowed Miers when noting that "we go straight to the object and immediately reconstitute it. We behave in relation to it as we would before a real object" (p. 275). The comic, like the painting, relies upon that engagement between the spectator's body, as directed by cognition and the object.

The layout of the comics' page will often involve a similar response, specifically to how one engages with the flow and design of architecture. As Pérez-Gómez (1992) details within *Polyphilo or The Dark Forest Revisited,* the construction of a space often influences the temporal experience of the body traversing the space. Such is the temporal map as described by McCloud (2000), where the seer advances through time by taking-in the spatiality of the page. When illustrating the concept, McCloud uses the example of a finger running across adjacent panels, signifying the reader generating time via movement through space. As comics readers do not traditionally brush their fingers across a page when reading, the finger becomes a stand-in for the eye taking-in the comics-object. The hapticity of that phenomenon resembles Pérez-Gómez's description of architecture, where the spectator produces temporality by way of progression through a structure. Thus, how the eye is directed to traverse the page, in terms of how the layout is built or designed to support ebbs and flows in the gaze, impacts the duration of the action via the reading process.

Each of the experiences detailed to this point find a unity within Groensteen's (2007) notions of "general arthrology" and "braiding" (pp. 144–158). Groensteen's (2007) *The System of Comics* stresses the networked nature of comic books, but nowhere more than in these two concepts, emphasizing how the "structuration ... taking account of the breakdown and the page lay-out, defines a *series* within a sequential framework" (p. 146; emphasis in orig-inal). That is, the illustrative construction of the comics-object is designed with the intention of meaningful combination. Of course, where Groensteen is concerned with the semiotic value of such arrangements and structures, the important aspect here is that the reader locates the connection, the "braid-ing," through their gaze and cognition. As Groensteen (2007) notes "Braiding ... manifests into consciousness the notion that the panels of a comic con-stitute a network, and even a system," (p. 158) an important reference to the phenomenological process inherent in comics—the reaching out of the object to meet the extension of the reader's gaze and cognition. Cohn (2010) has questioned Groensteen's arguments, however, claiming that layout is not what causes readers to mentally recognize links between illustrations, but instead proposing an unconscious hierarchy of iconic understanding. In his words, "These principles feature the conceptualization of time and space not in a linear sequence, but in underlying hierarchic groupings" (p. 144). He provides a similar counter to McCloud's aforementioned temporal mapping, suggesting that the concept of time within comics does not only depend upon the jux-taposition of images/panels, but what is depicted within them and that the reader decodes those signifiers in a way that suggests temporality.

Regardless of whether Cohn's counterarguments of the unconsciousness or Groensteen's and McCloud's ontological proposals are favored, the consis-tency between them lies in the mental processes of the reader. To then determine whether any phenomenological difference occurs between print and digital comics, attention needs to be paid to the body's cognitive reaction to the mate-rial, which is precipitated by the eye's ingestion of the aesthetics, the *sensing of the sequential*. Where the emphasis within print comics is placed upon the equal, reflective exchange between the seer/reader and the seen/object, the process is augmented by the transition to a digital format. While digital and print comics share in this proprioceptive ontology, the latter complicates the process by regularly completing or "closing" the image without the aid of the reader. That redistribution of control—moving from the reader to the object—in turn alters the cognitive effects of taking-in the comic visually.

Moving Toward the Infinite

Announced at the South by Southwest festival on March 11, 2012, Marvel Infinite Comics—a slightly confused homage of McCloud's "infinite canvas" terminology—was promoted as part of Marvel's ReEvolution initiative (Esposito, 2012). Focused on merging comics with other forms of media, the ReEvolution marketing push positioned Infinite Comics as a step towards a new form of comic book. Marvel editor-in-chief Axel Alonso described them as "not print comics, but also not animation," playing coy about which audience they were directed at and what experiential pleasures readers could anticipate (as cited in McMillan, 2012, para. 4). Senior vice-president of the Marvel Digital Media Group, Peter Phillips, reiterated the same sentiment when speaking at SXSW, saying that Infinite Comics would be "taking advantage of modern technology while staying true to [the] [*sic*] medium's greatest strengths" (as cited in Esposito, 2012, para. 11). Those quotes are a fair description of what Infinite Comics would eventually deliver, but another unspoken intention motivated Marvel to pursue such an initiative: attaining a new readership off the success of a series of narratively interconnected film franchises called the Marvel Cinematic Universe. Only four years old when Infinite Comics was announced, the MCU had achieved record-breaking box office returns, reaching a mainstream audience that print comics had consistently failed to attract. Recognizing the potential for new comic readers, Marvel's publishing arm appears to have intended Infinite Comics, and other digitally oriented products, as a bridge between film and print comics.

Not only do comics face a social stigma that characterizes them as immature and childish, the formatting of the medium has often been viewed as difficult for the uninitiated to understand. Though Cohn has suggested that an unconscious, hierarchical awareness guides readers through sequential illustrations, an initial confusion and bias toward the medium's format by first-time readers often results in avoidance. The Marvel Digital Media Group saw ample benefit in a format that could break down those barriers and attract new readers. First, Infinite Comics avoided any social stigmas by being purchasable surreptitiously through online providers. Second, the product was viewable on devices associated with other popular apps, like Twitter, Facebook, and Instagram, creating a trendiness through association. Finally, the minimal animations that added movement to the illustrations lead the reader's eye by highlighting important panels, replacing panels with other panels, panning or tilting the "camera" across the screen, and having word balloons and dialog boxes appear only when they need to be read. The result is a product that still resembles comic book aesthetics, but directs the audience, creating a sensation that occasionally emulates cinema.

Though *Avengers vs. X-Men: Infinite* was the first Infinite Comics release, I have chosen to use *All-New Captain America: Fear Him* as a case study for a few reasons. One, the miniseries exemplifies the phenomenological overlap between cinema and the movement of digital comics. Specifically, the series repeats three motion techniques throughout its six issues that are used frequently within Infinite Comics. Two, *Fear Him* was released further into the existence of the Infinite Comics brand, providing time for the creators to understand the potential of the format. Finally, I have access to personal insight into the creative process provided by co-author Dennis Hopeless. Recorded during a phone conversation conducted with Hopeless in February of 2016, these comments illuminate how the consideration of motion occurs throughout the comics' creation.

Along with Hopeless, the miniseries was co-written by prolific Marvel mainstay, Rick Remender. Remender's role was primarily advisory in nature, collaborating with Hopeless to plot out the story as a semi-prequel to the Captain America solo series he was scheduled to launch shortly after *Fear Him*'s release (Richards, 2014). Due to the inclusion of movement, the illustrative duties for *Fear Him* and other Infinite Comics are disseminated between a primary penciler and graphic artists who apply motion effects to the linework of the penciler. Hopeless (personal communication, February 11, 2016) penned a two-page script for each issue—resembling an outline that highlighted key narrative beats. By his own account, Hopeless was cognizant of the difference in format, attempting to write action and narrative turns that favored how readers "clicked" through panel changes rather than page turns. Once Hopeless completed his script, he would email it to Szymon Kudranski who provided the initial pencil and ink illustrations. Kudranski, in turn, would send his linework to the team of Mast and Geoffo who would create what Hopeless called an "animatic"—referencing a process used in the pre-production of numerous films—that incorporated a majority of the transitions between panels and screens. Hopeless would then provide a lettering draft that would be incorporated into the animatic, with him later polishing dialog to better suit the artwork and transitions. Following the release of the digital version of *Fear Him*, the six installments were translated into four print issues. The contrast between each version is striking, as the layouts, word balloon order, sound effect graphics, and number of panels are noticeably reorganized, suggesting the sizeable difference the motion effects have on pacing and spatiality.

All-New Captain America: Fear Him, for its standard superhero-versus-supervillain plot, is still a contemporary comics narrative, which means that it builds upon a web of narrative continuity. A brief synopsis will help to avoid confusion. At the time the miniseries is set, the original Captain America, Steve Rogers, had lost his powers and passed the mantel to his former partner, Sam Wilson, previously codenamed The Falcon. With Rogers out of action, Wilson is joined in the field by Rogers's adopted son, Ian, under the moniker of Nomad. The plot of the miniseries follows Wilson and Ian, with Rogers coaching from the sidelines, tracking a supervillain named Scarecrow into the sewers, where they discover a population of kidnapped children.

Since there are technically two characters that could be referred to as Captain America within the story, I will be using "Cap" to refer to Sam Wilson, instead of Steve Rogers.

Experiencing the Infinite

Infinite Comics, like all digital comics, can be read on various devices, but most commonly laptops, smartphones, and tablets. Each device has the potential to produce a slightly different phenomenological reaction for the reader, as the screen sizes and interface will differ in minor ways. Going forward, my analysis will concern the tablet version of Infinite Comics, as the screen dimensions are averagely sized, and readers advance through using touchscreen technology—a directly haptic interaction, as opposed to a mouse-click. Unlike most digital comics, Infinite Comics are formatted in landscape; that is, they are designed to be read horizontally. If the reader turns the tablet vertically, the comic can still be read, but black bars (akin to the letterboxing of films) will appear at the top and bottom of the screen. Given that those bars compress the image and hamper the experience, the design of Infinite Comics favors the horizontal orientation, a formal choice that immediately associates them with the aspect ratio of cinema. Additionally, the programming of Infinite Comics removes a few of the standard options digital comics readers have at their disposal. Commonly, digital comics interfaces allow zooming, the choice for one or two pages to appear on-screen, and the option of Guided View. The reader is locked out of these options by the Infinite Comics program, a design choice that forces the reader into an experience that, once again, resembles cinema.

Those orientation preferences cause me to use "screen" rather than "page" when discussing Infinite Comics. In that respect, I am agreeing with Goodbrey (2013), who distinguishes the digital comics window in contrast to the comic page. Like other authors who have studied digital comics, Goodbrey is examining them from a narrative perspective, but notes how an unrestricted space—due to the expansive possibilities of the screen versus the page—spurs the creator to explore new avenues in terms of panel relations. While the printing costs and page borders associated with traditional comics may no longer be a restriction within the "infinite canvas," the concept of endless, expansive space is somewhat of a misnomer. Goodbrey (2013) pointedly qualifies his comments by noting that digital comics "retains the concept of the page as a grouping of panels.... Importantly however, it does not treat the content of each page as being fixed" (p. 190). A key distinction to make here is that the borders of the screen still serve the same framing purpose as page borders, but unlike print comics, the panels within those borders are mutable. I will add that even though the possibilities of the "infinite canvas" allow a publisher to break from standard page lengths (current print issues are on average twenty-one pages in length), Infinite Comics are consistent, with each issue of *Fear Him* comprised of, on average, sixty screens. Considering that rigid boarders and semi-mandatory lengths still exist within the current iteration of the "infinite canvas," the application of motion to the content within and between the screens is where the difference in sensation is felt.

That sensation is noticeable through three affordances provided by the motion-oriented capabilities of digital comics. First is what I will call the *faux-camera*, an evolution of ComiXology's Guided View. Used to recreate familiar camera movements, like pans and tilts, the faux-camera regularly acts as a transition from one screen of panels to another. As I will discuss, these faux-camera movements are frequently associated with panels depicting characters in action, using the transition to simulate the sense of direction and force. Second is the technique of *panel layering*. A staple of Infinite Comics, panel layering exploits the mutability of digital data to have panels dissolve over other panels within a screen, either replacing them altogether or partially covering them. Lower layer panels will often become desaturated, drawing the eye to the colored, top layer through contrast. At times, panel layering is even used to resemble a camera zooming or moving in relation to a subject. The third technique I am proposing is *figural animation*. In these instances, the same panel placement and composition of characters is maintained, but minor illustrative differences occur as the reader progresses forward. Figural animations become the active, digital comics equivalent to McCloud's (1993) moment-to-moment panel storytelling. These slight changes provide the suggestion that the character is moving and, thus, that time is passing, completing the act of closure for the reader with a dissolve. Each of these techniques appear repeatedly throughout *Fear Him*, but I have chosen exemplary instances from three issues to focus on.

Issue Three—An Introduction

Beginning in the first third of the issue (the Infinite Comics interface designates it as "page fifteen," a remnant of print comics), this section sees Nomad protecting three sewer-dwelling children from Scarecrow's flock of murderous crows in a decommissioned subway train. The screen is comprised of three panels in two rows, with the top two panels depicting (1) a close-up of Nomad and (2) a fuller shot of Nomad bisected by the panel border. Below these is a smaller panel showing two of the three children. Across the next four screens, these rows of panels operate on a back-and-forth rhythm that leads the reader's eye using the movement techniques of Infinite Comics.

Progressing to the next screen, the reader's gaze is directed upwards from the lower panel as the formerly bisected panel of Nomad expands left, covering over the previous close-up panel. An instance of panel layering, the replacement of the close-up panel by the other half of the bisected panel operates on an interchange between space and movement; as the top right panel expands to the left, overtaking the space of the previous panel, the expansion paired with the motion of a dissolve implies the sensation that Nomad's body is moving. Even though the illustration is not *literally* moving, the reader's eye perceives the reveal of Nomad's other half as the suggestion of his arm extending. The fictional truths of Miers' (2014) theory are partially at play, with the imagination of the reader generating the idea of bodily movement, but unlike a print comic, the literal movement of the panels' digital data takes over from the reader's cognitive input.

When looking at the same section within the print version of the issue, the difference in sensation becomes apparent. Rather than depicting the bisected panel next to the full panel, the print version *only* shows the full panel. To Miers' point, the reader's cognition must create the entire sensation of Nomad pointing and speaking. As a result, the amount of time the reader expends looking at the panel is longer, which, in turn, effects the sensation of diegetic time. The Infinite Comics version reaches out more aggressively to aid the reader in completing the action. The unconscious process that Cohn (2010) describes is, similarly, assisted. Instead of the reader relying upon an unconscious recognition of the hierarchical ordering of the images, the added motion directs the reader toward the proper sequencing. With the eye darting between two rows of panels on the same screen, there is far less demand placed upon the unconscious to assemble the chronology of the illustrations; instead, the cognitive work is akin to a shot-reverse-shot exchange within film.

On the next screen, the use of the faux-camera directs the reader further. A new version of the top panel is overlaid onto the previous version, depicting the same image, but closer. That slight alteration paired with a dissolve resembles the motion of a camera pushing-in, using the faux-camera to remind the reader of a cinematic movement that suggests an approximate sensation of time passing. Essentially, the technique is a rudimentary version of the compositing Lamarre (2009) describes in his introduction to *The Anime Machine: A Media Theory of Animation*. Though Lamarre's book concerns itself specifically with Japanese anime, the author's discussion of that artform's production process overlaps with the animatic nature of Infinite Comics, while his larger theories resonate with the idea of digital comics technology altering reader's perception of the content.

Writing about the way anime "thinks technology"—or becomes a representation of the technology that produced it as well as a vehicle for contemplating technology—Lamarre (2009) sees a unification between the "machines" that enable the creation of anime and speed, itself. Instead of viewing the artist's renderings as the source of motion in anime, Lamarre (2009) draws the reader's attention to the "animation stand" (pp. xxiii–xxiv) creators use to organize layers of illustrations that insinuate movement when viewed together. No longer requiring an animation stand, the programming technology behind Infinite Comics still relies upon similar compositing principles, especially within the previously described faux-camera and panel layering examples. That similarity is not entirely surprising, however, as these are basic strategies of animation. Where Lamarre's (2009) ideas become relevant is in "how technologies affect thought," (p. xxiv) or alter cognition from artform to artform. Not arguing for a complete differentiation, Lamarre sees these changes as variances in speed, a throttling up or down of motion that coincides with technological advancement. The comparison between print and digital comics can be understood in a similar way, as recognition of similar principles being altered at the level of cognition by the incorporation of new technology.

Returning to *Fear Him*, a swipe to the next screen sees the top panel replaced with one featuring Nomad in the same composition as the previous screen, but with his arms at his side and his mouth shut. The bottom panel also changes, both expanding to the left, revealing a third child, and altering the eye illustrations of the other children. In the case of both panels, figural animations occur. Like a rudimentary form of film, the dissolves between these panels are perceived as the movement of the figures. The reader's eye takes-in the minimal illustrative changes through the relation of the previous panel to the new one, both literally seeing and figuratively sensing the movement of Nomad and the kids. For Lamarre (2009), those "invisible interstices between layers," (p. xxix) the fraction of time where the layers overlap, is where motion is perceived. In a traditional print comic, and, indeed, in the print version of this Infinite Comic, the interstices would commonly be McCloud's gutter, where the reader would provide the sense of movement. During the figural animation of Nomad and the children, the gutters have been replaced by dissolves, effectively removing the burden of supplying motion from the reader and inserting it within the Infinite Comic itself.

What I have not mentioned thus far is how the placement and erasure of word balloons within these panels supplements and impacts the reader's sense of progression through time. In the same way that panels will be replaced or layered over with other panels, dialog—either in the form of word balloons or dialog boxes—will often undergo a similar change. In some cases, balloons will be part of the panel's artwork—dissolving with the rest of the panel—while in other cases balloons are separated from the panel artwork—dissolving independently. During the aforementioned section of the issue, both methods occur. For instance, the bisected panel of Nomad contains two word balloons that are erased completely when the panel expands to the left. Though the bottom panel featuring the two children remains unaltered during the first three screens, the word balloons emanating from the children do change. Beginning inside the confines of the panel, the balloons featuring the dialog of the two boys move outward as the reader progresses. The placement of the word balloons, that is the movement of the dialog outside of the panel and closer to Nomad's word balloons, suggests a speed of exchange between the characters, while the erasure and replacement of the dialog creates a sense of time passing. Where dialog persists within print comics, never completely vanishing from the reader's periphery, the erasure of word balloons within Infinite Comics becomes a more perceptible suggestion of time. Not only does the reader experience a length of time by reading the words, they sense time moving forward through the elimination of the dialog on the page. The disappearance of the dialog from the screen is cognitively perceived in a similar way to the ephemerality of spoken words—the lingering sense of what was said, but a feeling that time moves on as new words are spoken/seen. Having established the three basic techniques of the faux-camera, panel layering, and figural animation in Infinite Comics, I wish to examine each in greater detail as their limits are tested within future issues of *Fear Him*.

Issue Four—Moving Through Time and Space

All the previously described techniques collide within the fourth issue of *Fear Him* for a particularly proprioceptive sequence of transitions. During the scene, Cap, inhibited by Scarecrow's fear toxin, is immobilized as a flock of crows swarms the children. Across the screens comprising the scene, Cap regains his composure, ultimately commanding the crows to disperse by way of a psychic link he has with avian creatures.

On the first screen, Cap is depicted in color and positioned in the foreground, with a monochromatic version of the panels from the previous screen placed in the background (see Figure 1). The reader enters the scene in a moment of stillness. With Cap layered over the panels from the previous screen, the sensation is that of simultaneity. Using the ability to spatially layer panels, rather than only spatially relate them on a page, this screen relies upon Infinite Comics' suggestion of temporality through a depth of panel accumulation. The perception of time slowing in the face of Cap's impaired mind segues into the next series of four screens.

Upon swiping forward, the same illustration of Cap from the previous screen gradually shifts to the right as a new background of three panels layers over the previous monochromatic panels (see Figure 2). The figural animation

Figure 1: All-New Captain America: Fear Him #4; Cap layered over previous panels (Marvel).

of Wilson's body is possibly a mistake of the programming—an unintentional shifting of the illustration—but provides the sensation of movement to the reader. Ever so slight, Cap's shifting appears as an off-kilter, disoriented repositioning of the body. The same suggestion would be difficult in print comics, as subtle compositional changes are harder to notice in adjacent panels. Contrasted with Cap's stillness in the foreground, the layering of the three background panels generates a nearly explosive sensation of activity. Not only is the presence of color in relation to the previous monochrome taken-in by the eye as a rush of movement (facilitated by the actual movement of the panels onto the screen), but so is the appearance of a cluttered arrangement of word balloons and sound effect graphics; overlaid on top of each other and appearing simultaneously, these graphics are initially too chaotic for the eye to perceive individually. As the reader's gaze attempts to parse through the images and dialog that has appeared, the persistence of Cap on-screen furthers the notion of his catatonia.

Progressing to the next screen becomes a release of tension as Cap's illustration alters, as he strains against the cacophony by covering his ears.

Figure 2: All-New Captain America: Fear Him #4; "movement" between screens (Marvel).

A prime instance of figural animation, the individual images—Cap standing still, Cap covering his ears—become a singular motion of his body through the added movement of the panels between screens. Hidden in the interstice of the dissolve between screens is the perceptible suggestion of his arms raising and his face contorting. Within that same transition, the illustrations within the background panels zoom-in. By enlarging the image within each individual panel in tandem with the added movement of the transition, the reader perceives a version of the faux-camera zooming-in simultaneously on each panel. Due to the foregrounding of Cap's figural animation, the sensation of zooming that occurs behind him, while perceived as movement by the reader, is not consciously registered. Arguably more than previous examples, this transition grasps at the true phenomenological potential of Infinite Comics and, thus, digital comics. Here the reader's body—namely the interchange between eye and mind—senses diegetic movement as facilitated by the non-diegetic movement of the digital information. The sensation only ratchets further upon progressing to the next screen, with the background images enlarged enough that the blackness of the crows threatens to overtake the screen. Zoomed-in to the point that the illustrative details of the birds become indistinct, the reader senses less a movement of the crows and more a general sensation of space being actively filled.

The reader's body receives a release from that spatial compression in the final screen of the series. Having repeated the same background panels and only two illustrations of Cap over the last four screens, artist Kudranski provides a single panel (taking up the entire screen) of Wilson throwing out his arms and screaming "Stop it!" Though the difference between illustrations of Cap are not subtle enough to be considered figural animations, the consistency of Wilson within the center of the screen still manages to impart an exaggerated bodily movement to the reader. The throwing up of his arms and a widening of the framing is perceived as a fluid action and a swift zooming-out, respectively. Temporally, the reader experiences a release from the stalled moment lingered on in previous screens. No longer repeating the same three background panels nor the foreground illustration of Cap, the reader senses a swift advancement of time—a sizable progression forward in diegetic time as created by non-diegetic panel movement. Though the composition of the crows does not line-up between this screen and the last, the nondescript blackness of the crows' bodies remains, though now dispersed throughout a single background image. The result of the dissolve between the screens is effectively perceived as an explosion of motion.

The faux-camera, panel layering, and figural animation operate together within the latter sequence to convey spatial and temporal changes in ways that temporal map of traditional comics could not. In that respect, a defining feature of print comics—the suggestion of time through space—has been augmented and altered through the use of motion.

Issue Five—
Pushing the Boundaries of Digital Motion

To conclude, I wish to look at two examples of applied motion from the penultimate issue of *Fear Him*. During the issue, Cap—still drugged—hallucinates Nomad as an armor-clad knight resembling a crow. Misinterpreting Nomad as his enemy, the two exchange blows across the entirety of the issue, until Nomad debilitates Wilson. Given the kinetic focus of the issue, the motion techniques I have enumerated to this point are applied in ways that push the limits of the current Infinite Comics technology.

Appearing immediately after the issue's credits screen, the first example sees Cap running from Nomad across a curved surface that serves as a representation of both the diegetic ground and the gutter separating the top and bottom panels. On the first screen of this series, Cap is positioned screen-right against a black background, juxtaposed against a left-aligned panel depicting Nomad trailing behind him. As the reader swipes forward, the illustration of Cap progresses further along the curved gutter, until he is positioned along screen-left; an extra tactile dimension, the direction of the reader's swipes mirror Cap's movement, conflating one motion with another. Due to a combination of minor figural animations (not only is the figure repositioned across the screen, but the illustration of his bodily orientation is altered as he "runs"), the reader receives a sense of motility within Cap's limbs as well as a suggestion of forward progression; each dissolve facilitated by the swipes is paired with a limited cognitive input by the reader to imply Cap's kinetic motion. Aiding in that sensation is a transitioning of word balloons, which generates the sensation of temporal progression as balloons vanish only to be replaced by new balloons. With the transition to the final screen, Cap's body is seen to pivot, destabilized by his mental state, as the background panels are layered over with a black and yellow filter. Optically, the reader takes-in the transition, experiencing the moment as a jarring shattering of the environment through the motional shift of the aesthetics. Three "KSSSH" sound effect graphics, placed to the right of the screen, herald the next screen, depicting the floor falling out from under Cap's feet as shards of glass trail his falling body.

That screen is a transition to a new series, where Cap is shown to be descending deeper and deeper into an unknown darkness. An immediate sense of downward motion is imparted upon the reader by a faux-camera tilt that transitions the reader to the next screen. The literal motion of the previous screen (depicting the start of Cap's fall) notably does not match Cap's trajectory, as the illustration of his body slides upwards, but the downward sensation imparted to the reader by the tilt ends up cognitively implying descent. Additionally, Cap's body shrinks as the reader progresses, an illustrative technique that supplements the faux-camera motion, causing the reader to feel the character's gradual distancing from the perspective point. Two tilts carry the reader through the series of three screens, until a fourth screen showing Cap flying upwards toward the reader's perspective is layered over the third screen of him falling. While the appearance of that screen is facilitated by a dissolve, the sudden closeness of the character in relation to his previous distance creates the burst of motion needed to imply his redirection. Enhanced by the transition to the next screen, another faux-camera tilt up and right matches the character's path of flight. Here the motion of the faux-camera is parallel to the direction of the character, which completes the sensuous experience of his movement for the reader.

Finally, in the last section of the issue, Nomad puts Cap in a headlock to render him unconscious in an especially proprioceptive use of the Infinite Comics' motion techniques. Using minor figural animations, the illustration of Nomad's body is steadily blurred across three screens. Subtle to the point of possible imperceptibility, the transition between the first and second screens in the series only sees Nomad's outline soften slightly. The reader registers that the illustration has changed, but—barring a swipe back to the previous screen—will likely only do so unconsciously. The transition to the third screen, however, is distinctly taken-in by the eye, as Nomad's outline has softened drastically. In tandem with the blur effect, a minor figural animation "closes" Cap's eyes, while the other, previously adjacent, panel is erased along with all graphics save for a single word balloon. The cumulative sensation across the three screens is one of the reader's own vision distorting. An inventive use of Infinite Comics capabilities, the figural animated movement is used to imply the blurring of vision to impart a sensation of slipping into unconsciousness. The final screen capitalizes on that sensation, by using panel layering to snap the reader into Nomad's perspective (no longer depicted as the Crow Knight). Overlaying the previously black backgrounds with a detailed illustration of a concrete wall and a matching composition of Nomad and Cap from the last screen causes a shock to the reader's vision, emphasizing Cap passing into unconsciousness and a shift to Nomad's perspective. By phenomenologically examining the latter selections from issues three, four, and five of *Fear Him*, I hope to have provided an indication of how to discuss and explore the unique proprioceptive experience of movement within Infinite Comics as a way of understanding what digital comics do differently from print.

Continued Next Issue!

While certain long-time comics readers bemoan the rise of digital (I have done my fair share in the past), the format is here to stay and will likely match or eclipse print readership in the future as newer generations replace the old. For that reason, comics scholarship needs a consistent, reliable means of discussing the dichotomy between print and digital. Here I have suggested using phenomenology as a means of understanding how print and digital comics can be differentiated by spectator experience. With Scott Bukatman (2016) suggesting comics as "a moving-image medium," (p. 149) building off Tom Gunning's (2014) efforts to connect comics with pre-cinematic movement experiments, it is clear traditional comics produce a degree of motion in tandem with the reader. However, the inclusion of animatic motion within digital comics shifts the dynamic between object and reader, producing a greater degree of visible motion within the comics-object, itself. Importantly, that motion begins to resemble familiar cinematic movements, used, especially in the case of Infinite Comics, to appeal to an amateur comics readership.

While I have explained how those motions—in the form of the faux camera, panel layering, and figural animation—are present within a specific instance of digital comic, these same elements need to be further explored across the growing, diverse world of digital comics. Though I have touched on it only briefly here, putting the sensations of those forms in relation to motion comics, building upon the work of Smith and Morton, to establish a clearer distinction between them may also prove fruitful. Of course, expanding phenomenological work on digital comics also requires that the study of the phenomenology of traditional comics grows, as well. Finally, a project over how cinematic comic adaptations recreating the sensations of their source material relates back to digital comics emulating cinematic sensations would aid in completing the phenomenological circle.

When comics readers hold a tablet versus a "floppy," look at a screen versus a page, or see a superhero's ascent into the sky rather than imagine it, the body's processing of these engagements changes. The comics industry is still at the cusp of exploring how the infinite canvas enables that contrast in experience. As the industry moves beyond the spinner rack of the local store, venturing into the animatic realm of the digital, comics scholarship should follow.

REFERENCES

Anderson, D. (2013). The experience of the superhero: A phenomenological definition. In R.S. Rosenberg P. Coogan (Eds.), *What is a superhero?* (pp. 65–70). New York: Oxford University Press.

Bukatman, S. (2016). *Hellboy's world: Comics and monsters on the margins.* Oakland: University of California Press.

Cohn, N. (2010). The limits of time and transitions: Challenges to theories of sequential image comprehension. *Studies in Comics, 1*(1), 127–147.

Dittmar, J.F. (2012). Digital comics. *Scandanavia Journal of Comic Art, 1*(2), 82–91.

Dufrenne, M. (1973). *The phenomenology of aesthetic experience.* Evanston, IL: Northwestern University Press.

Esposito, J. (2012). What is Marvel infinite comics? [Website] Retrieved from http://www.ign.com/articles/2012/03/12/what-is-marvel-infinite-comics.

Goodbrey, D.M. (2013). Digital comics—New tools and tropes. *Studies in Comics, 4*(1), 185–197.

Groensteen, T. (2007). *The system of comics* (B. Beaty N. Nguyen, Trans.). Jackson, MS: University Press of Mississippi.

Gunning, T. (2014). The art of succession: Reading, writing, and watching comics. *Critical Inquiry, 40*(3), 36–51.

Hague, I. (2014). *Comics and the senses: A multisensory approach to comics and graphic novels.* New York: Routledge.

Hopeless, D., Remender R., Kudranski, S., Mast, & Geoffo. (2014). *All-new Captain America: Fear him infinite comic.* [Digital comic] Retrieved from https://comicstore.marvel.com/All-New-Captain-America-Fear-Him-Infinite-Comic/comics-series/30565.

Lamarre, T. (2009). *The anime machine: A media theory of animation.* Minneapolis: University of Minnesota Press.

McCloud, S. (1993). *Understanding comics: The invisible art.* New York: HarperPerennial.

McCloud, S. (2000). *Reinventing comics: How imagination and technology are revolutionizing an art form.* New York: Perennial.

McMillan, G. (2012). Marvel announces digital-only "infinite comics" imprint and "augmented reality" app at SXSW. [Website] Retrieved from http://comicsalliance.com/marvel-infinite-comics-digital-imprint/.

Merleau-Ponty, M. (1968). *The visible and the invisible* (A. Lingis Trans.). In C. Lefort (Ed.). Evanston, IL: Northwestern University Press.

Merleau-Ponty, M. (1993). Cézanne's doubt. In G.A. Johnson (Ed.), *The Merleau-Ponty aesthetics reader: Philosophy and painting* (59–75).

Miers, J. (2014). Depiction and demarcation in comics: Towards an account of the medium as a drawing practice. *Studies in Comics, 6*(1), 145–156.

Morton, D. (2015). The unfortunates: Towards a history and definition of the motion comic. *Journal of Graphic Novels and Comics, 6*(4), 347–366.

Pérez-Gómez, A. (1992). *Polyphilo or the dark forest revisited*. Cambridge, MA: MIT Press.

Richards, D. (2014). SDCC: "All-new Captain America" fights fear in Hopeless' infinite comic. [Website]. Retrieved from http://www.cbr.com/sdcc-all-new-captain-america-fights-fear-in-hopeless-infinite-comic/.

Smith, C. (2011). Motion comics: Modes of adaptation and the issue of authenticity. *Animation Practice, Process & Production, 1*(2), 357–378.

Wilde, L.R.A. (2015). Distinguishing mediality: The problem of identifying forms and features of digital comics. *Networking Knowledge: Journal of the MeCCSA Postgraduate Network, 8*(4), 1–14.

Considering ComiXology's Guided View

Jeffrey SJ Kirchoff

Introduction

Much of the current scholarship on digital comics discusses the affordances digital comics provide comic creators, focusing specifically on how digital comics offers opportunities to do something different and new with the comic medium. Perhaps the most well-known and oft-cited example of this scholarship is McCloud's (2000) assertion in *Reinventing Comics* that digital comics offer creators endless design possibilities; specifically, he advocates for comic creators to challenge the traditional structure of a comic book by instead utilizing an infinite canvas form—comics that are not restricted by the notion of a comic "page"; he suggests that "in a digital environment, comics can take virtually any size and shape as the temporal map—comics' conceptual DNA—grows in its new dish" (p. 223). The result of this exploration, McCloud says, could be stories ranging from "500 panel[s]" to a story "told vertically—or horizontally like a great graphic skyline" (p. 223).

While many have taken issue with McCloud's underlying argument that digital comics are the future of the comic medium, his line of thought has inspired similar exciting research discussing the potential of digital comics. For instance, scholars have alternatively explored the notion of integrating motion in digital comics, sound in digital comics, multicursality in digital comics, and animation in digital comics (see, among others, Dittmar, 2015; Goodbrey, 2013, 2015; Kirchoff, 2013; Smith, 2012, 2015; Zanfei, 2008). Digital comics in this vein—from infinite canvas to multicursal comics—are what Josip Bataníc (2016) terms "enhanced webcomics," those that "refer to all these different varieties of webcomics which are 'enhanced' by the use of digital properties, tools, and effects" (p. 81). Understandably, comic scholars are interested in the power and possibility these kinds of enhanced webcomics offers readers, creators, and theorists alike.

There is no doubt that the aforementioned scholarship on enhanced webcomics is exciting and represents some of the strongest research in comic studies. However, one form of digital comic—a form that does not neatly fall under the umbrella of enhanced comics—could be discussed at greater length. Specifically, little scholarship has been produced on what I call remediated comics—digital comics that recreate (as accurately as possible) their print-based counterparts; that is, the anatomy of the traditional print-based comics are found in an identical form in the digital universe. What scholarship exists on remediated comics tends to focus on economics (Allen, 2014; Johnston, 2017), how remediated comics impacts collecting (Steirer, 2014; Stevens & Bell, 2012; Wershler, 2011), and the limitations and perceived problems of remediated comics (Groensteen, 2015). This chapter speaks very specifically to the last aforementioned focal point: Groensteen's concerns with remediated comics.

In Groensteen's (2015) *Comics and Narration,* he questions whether digital reproductions of printed comic books through applications such as ComiXology can be (or should be) perceived as inherently a *comic book* in form and structure. Much of Groensteen's argument is rooted in the idea that digitized versions of print distort the "intended" comic book reading experience. In regards to digitized versions of print comics, Groensteen aptly notes that reading digital comics "entails the loss of a very strong, affectively charged object relation: the physical handling of the book, which involves both arms, or even the entire upper body, is replaced by intermittent pressure on the mouse from the reader's index finger" (p. 65). Haptic interfaces that strive to mimic the action of turning a page is insufficient for Groensteen. He also asserts that digitized versions of print comics can destroy the integrity of the printed page, as "a printed comic can be perceived as a collection of images spread out across the page, arranged according to a positional logic that is easy for the memory to retrieve" (pp. 65–66). In digital comics, he notes, panels replace other panels, making it difficult to regularly see multiple panels at once; moreover, while some digital comics allow for multiple pages to be seen at once, he notes that the size of the screen—and definitely the size of the mobile device, if that is what a reader is using—impacts how this information is consumed (p. 66).

This chapter, then, speaks to Groensteen's issues by closely examining how one remediated comics' platform—Amazon's ComiXology—changes, and possibly complicates, the reading practices of print comics. While I do not focus on the affective reading practices described by Groensteen—Ian Hague (2014) has already discussed this with great success—I am interested in exploring how ComiXology as a platform responds to two features that have become inherently associated with the comic form: the database nature of the comic page and the spatio-temporality of comics. I pay particular attention to ComiXology's (2014) tool of Guided View, which advertises itself as being able to help novice comic readers traverse the comic page while simultaneously mimicking the "natural motion" of the user's eye and reading path. My analysis reveals how Guided View moves away from the database logic of the comic page and revises the spatio-temporality of comics impinges on a reader's ability to comprehend and immerse themselves in a comic narrative.

ComiXology Overview

Created in 2007 by David Steinberger, John D. Roberts, and Peter Jaffe, ComiXology (which was purchased by Amazon in 2014) is a marketplace that facilitates the sale of digital comics from over 75 publishers, while allowing independent comic creators to publish their own work. Available through ComiXology.com, Kindle Fire, the App store, Google Play, and the Windows store, ComiXology boasts over 75,000 total comics, along with a wide selection of graphic novels available for purchase. While it is free for readers to create a user-name and password, which is required in order to access any ComiXology comics, most of the product available costs money. Newer comics are most often available for the list price, while older comics and graphic novels are usually available for a discounted price. ComiXology also offers several free comics, which are usually comics that represent a jumping on point for new readers. In 2016, ComiXology offered a new ComiXology Unlimited service; offered at $5.99 a month, ComiXology Unlimited offers readers unlimited access of roughly 10,000 titles, including select titles from Marvel Comics, Dark Horse Comics and Image Comics (among others). According to Gregory Steirer (2014), ComiXology accounts for over 76 percent of all digital comic sales.

The interface is fairly user-friendly, as it allows readers to search by title, publisher, genre, or creator. Browsing for comics is also relatively easy, as you can browse through categories such as new comics, top sellers, free comics, series, publisher, and more. ComiXology is perhaps best known, though, for their unique Guided View feature. This tool allows a reader to "cinematically shift from panel-to-panel at your own pace." According to ComiXology's website, each comic's Guided View is "handcrafted by a comic lover to make sure you have the best possible adventure" in an effort to allow readers to "view a comic on a panel-by-panel basis … in a way that mimics the natural motion of the user's eye through the comic" (ComiXology, 2014). The notion of mimicry suggests that ComiXology is striving to create as authentic a reading experience of the print-based comic as possible. Put differently, ComiXology seemingly looks to preserve the integrity of the printed comic page and the printed comic reading experience. Additionally, ComiXology couches Guided View as a tool designed to help novice comic readers navigate a complicated comic page. Anecdotally, though, I know several avid comic readers and established comic creators who utilize the Guided View regardless, simply because they appreciate the tool and the new reading experience.

Reading Comics: Print Comics vs. ComiXology

Despite the prevailing societal perception that comics are a simple, ephemeral form of communication, comics are, in fact, exceedingly complex texts making use of multiple semiotic affordances that require a great deal of skill and work to decode. This lends credence to Versaci's (2001) claim that creating meaning from words and images (essentially comics, a kind of multimodality) is a complicated, nuanced task. On the surface, it is quite apparent that comics are an example of a multimodal text as most comics, particularly mainstream comics, consistently make use of images juxtaposed with text (usually in the form of speech balloons, captions, or sound effects). However, this understanding of comics—a combination of text and image— grossly oversimplifies the semiotic complexity of this medium. Jacobs (2014) argues that readers of print comics are asked to shape meaning not only from words and images, but also "spatial layout, gutters, sound effects, panel composition, body language, facial expression, emanata [lines to indicate a character's surprise], and other comics elements" (para. 4); here, then, Jacobs extends the idea readers of comics only interpret images and alphabetic text by highlighting other semiotic affordances readers must negotiate. Another affordance (not mentioned by Jacobs specifically) readers derive meaning from is perspective. Schwartz (2006) notes that comics gives readers the opportunity to better understand how angles and points of view can affect narrative interpretation; to that end, Bongco (2000) notes that perspective can "manipulate and produce various emotional states in the reader" (p. 59).

Additionally, another affordance not discussed by Jacobs is color and, similarly, the boldness/thickness/delicacy of lines. These affordances can help depict emotion and tone of a character, place, time, or even an extended scene. In short, then, readers need to be comfortable examining not only *what* the characters are doing, but also *how* they are depicted doing that particular action. Given this, we can see that the reading of comics—specifically, the interpretation of meaning from a comic text—is far from a simple task, instead requiring readers to interpret a number of signs and symbols while undergoing a variety of reading processes. This section, then, seeks to highlight how two aspects of reading comics—an already complex process—is further complicated by ComiXology's tool of Guided View. Specifically, I discuss how the database-logic informing the flexibility of the comics' page and the spatio-temporality of the page is disrupted by Guided View. I moreover posit that the database logic that informs the comic page and the spatio-temporality of the page are key elements in helping a comic reader—novice or otherwise— make meaning from a comic; thus, when ComiXology disrupts these two elements, it potentially hinders a reader's ability to interpret the narrative of the comic book.

Database

There is no correct way to read print comics—the printed comic page lends itself to multiple reading strategies. The layout of print comics—that is, how the panels are organized in a specific way on the comic page—gives readers a tremendous amount of freedom in how to traverse the narrative put before them. As Bongco (2000) notes, comic books can be read by "looking at individual panels, a sequence of panels, at one full page, or a double-page layout" (p. 60). While Cohn and Campbell (2015) assert that most readers consume comics in a Z-path (see Figure 1), they do not account for the database nature of a comic page. That is, the way a comic page is organized, as Bongco notes, gives readers a significant number of options to traverse the narrative, including re-reading (and reading differently) any panels and pages. Perhaps Gunning (2014) articulates this phenomenon the best, when he suggests that "comics offer simultaneously two alternative regimes of reading: an overall one that grasps the page as a total design and a successive one that follows the order of individual frames at one time" (p. 44). Bongco and Gunning's ideas can be seen through a brief analysis of the first page of Zalben and Kenfield's (2013) *Detective Honeybear* (see Figure 2). Readers might first glance through the entire page, examining all the panels at once. Or, perhaps readers might start with the top panel, reading the text ("No Leads?") and then examining the images of the detectives accompanying the text. The reverse (examining the images of the detectives before reading the text) could also hold true. However, it is equally possible that an individual might study all the word balloons on the page first—that is, only looking at the balloons before going back and examining the images. Again, the reverse could also hold true. And of course, any combination of these options is a possibility—no two panels need to be read the same way twice, and a reader can change his/her habits and practices mid-page, and indeed, mid-panel. In this way, the structure of the printed comic book allows a great deal more flexibility than a more traditional printed narrative (though some readers have been known to read the last page of a novel before starting the novel

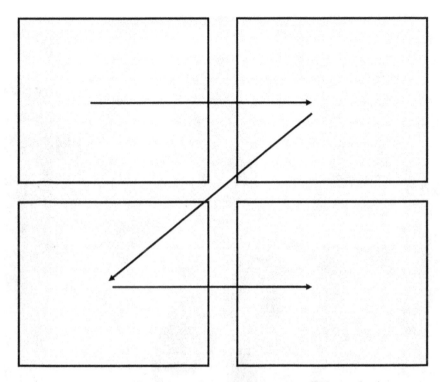

Figure 1: Z-Path reading of comics (image created by author).

proper). This reading path flexibility is a unique marker of the print comic text.

In this way, then, the printed comic page follows a kind of database logic. Manovich (1999) defines databases as "collections of individual items, where every item has the same significance as any other" (p. 80). Within the database, a user must be free to "view, navigate, search" (Manovich, 2001, p. 219) the components that comprise the database. Manovich (2013) later writes that "even when a user is working only with a single local media file ... the experience is still only partly defined by the file's content and organization. The user is free to navigate the document, choosing both what information to see and the sequence in which to see it" (n.p.). While the printed comic page cannot wholly function as a database—for Manovich (2001), a database is often endless with no boundaries, and a comic has a finite beginning and end—it follows the logic of databases, as the comics' page does not privilege, inherently, any one item (e.g. speech balloons, captions, images, motion lines, etc.) that is collected on the page. All semiotic affordances are needed and privileged equally by the comic creator and reader—all are needed to craft any kind of meaning. Certainly, the design of the comic encourages a specific

Figure 2: Alex Zalben and Josh Kenfield's *Detective Honeybear* (creator owned, 2013).

kind of reading (and a certain interpretation of the narrative)—but there is nothing inherent about the elements and the way they are presented on the page that overtly privileges one *affordance* over another when it comes time to *navigating* the comics' page. Because no one affordance is privileged, it allows readers to pick their own narrative path—they aren't coerced or persuaded into reading one kind of affordance first. That is, readers can "search" the page for any item they wish to start their "navigation" of the comics' page, whether that item is an image, a caption, a word balloon, or something else entirely. Again, there may be logical ways to read a comics' page—and certainly, experienced comic readers will have certain strategies they routinely use—but the page gives the reader significant autonomy and freedom to choose their own navigational path. By giving readers the freedom to navigate the page in any way they see fit—and by not privileging any singular aspect of the comic—a printed comic book page utilizes, in part, Manovich's database logic. There are multiple ways to read the comics' page which offer many possibilities for re-reading, as the reader can always re-sequence how s/he navigates the contents of the page.

In ComiXology, the reader is given the choice to consume the comic more traditionally—that is, following the same database logic as the printed page—or using the Guided View option. Most frequently, the Guided View utilizes the familiar Z-Path that Cohn and Campbell note to be the most common reading pattern. While this may be logical for a standard 2 × 3 comics' page, complex layouts do not always neatly adhere to a traditional Z-Path. The Guided View option given to Benitez's (2014) *Lady Mechanika* #0 (see Figure 3) offers a particularly instructive look at how Guided View can be used to peruse a complex comics' page. The Guided View begins with an extreme close-up of the blow dart found in the top-left panel. As this panel functions as a panel within a panel (that is, it overlaps another panel), the extreme close-up does show the secondary panel underneath it—but only partially. Specifically, you can see the dart itself and the accompanying sound effect ("Shnkt"). When the reader advances to the next frame, we get an extreme close-up of Lady Mechanika's prey—the Demon of Satan's Alley. However, due to the extreme nature of the close-up, readers are no longer able to see the full sound effect caused by the dart—rather, we can only make out "nkt." As the reader progresses to the next frame, they may be surprised to see the image size shrink—where the first two extreme close-ups fill the entire screen, the third frame only takes up a third of the screen—there is now quite a bit of black-space on both the left and right side of the frame. And, even more interestingly, the reader is not looking at one panel, but two—Lady Mechanika exclaiming "SHAITE!" and the Demon of Satan's Alley crying "WHAHH!" No sound effects are obscured in this shot: readers can clearly make out the "Cha-Chink" of the dart-gun being reloaded and the

"Ffft" of the dart missing the demon in the next panel. We get a more "traditional" transition to the next frame, which focuses on Lady Mechanika and the demon doing battle. Part of the demon's claw falls out of frame here, though most of the battle is clearly seen; the clarity of image is helped by returning to a full screen view, as the image fills up the entirety of the screen. The last two transitions take us to the bottom of this comics' page. First, the Guided View zeroes in on the demon, which is on the far-right side of the bottom panel. In this frame, we get a close-up of Lady Mechanika's punch landing and the Demon reacting it to it ("Wrahh!"). The final transitions move us back to the left of the page—negating the traditional Z-Path—as we finish reading this page by seeing Lady Mechanika throw the punch and mutter "Feisty Little Bugger." In this frame, Mechanika is partially cut off—we don't see the top of her head.

Here, Guided View no longer follows database logic and, as such, makes it impossible to truly "mimic" the comic readers' eye motion and reading path, as Guided View is ostensibly trying to accomplish. While the collection of individual items—that is, the icons, the captions, the sound effects, speech bubbles, etc.—are all identical to its print-based counterpart, the Guided View (presented in a style akin to how one might traverse a Prezi Presentation), by nature of where the "camera" or "lens" is placed, favors certain affordances of the comics' page. In this particular case, the images are very much so privileged by way of using extreme close-ups for the icons (e.g. Lady Mechanika, the Demon of Satan Alley, etc.). Moreover, the *freedom* that the reader has in traversing the comics' page—that is, the ability to freely *navigate* the page, such an important aspect of database logic, is removed. That is, choice is replaced by a singular path. This becomes a more egregious issue with so-called complex page layouts (those that do not follow a simple 2 × 3 grid), as the more complex a layout, the more choices exist for traversing and navigating the comics' page. Thus, with each page that increases in complexity, the more assumptions ComiXology will be forced to make about the reader when they craft their Guided View for each comic.

Reading this comic using the Guided View option eschews database logic in favor of what Manovich might call algorithmic logic. In his *Language of New Media*, Manovich (2001) uses computer games to describe algorithms:

> In a game, the player is given a well-defined task—winning the match, being first in a race, reaching the last level, or attaining the highest score.... Often the narrative shell of a game ... masks a simple algorithm well familiar to the player [p. 222].

For Manovich (1999), games follow algorithm logic because "while proceeding through them, [players] must uncover the underlying logic—the algorithm"

Opposite: Figure 3: Joe Benitez's Lady Mechanika #0 (Benitez Productions, 2014).

(p. 85). Poian (2015), borrowing from Manovich's ideas of algorithm, ultimately argues,

> an algorithm is defined as a procedure that permits to obtain a certain result, executing, in a particular order, a series of simple steps or actions. A series of finite instructions that lead to a result and are materially executable and not ambiguous [p. 2].

ComiXology's Guided View exemplifies this definition adroitly. It is a *procedure* designed to obtain a universal result—all readers will traverse the comics' page in the same order. The Guided View allows readers to execute the steps of reading the comic in a particular order—it becomes a simplified series of steps. The goal of ComiXology's Guided View, then, is to provide readers with an unambiguous reading experience.

Spatio-Temporality

The layout of print comics not only provides readers with a tremendous amount of freedom in terms of reading the narrative, but it also gives readers a unique way of how to interpret *time* in the comic narrative. McCloud (1993) explains this idea of time in reading comics thusly: "In every other form of narrative that I know of, past, present, and future are not shown simultaneously—you're always in the now ... comics is the only form in which past, present, and future are visible simultaneously" (p. 104). As such, readers can—with a glance of just a single page—simultaneously view several moments in time. Bartual (2012) elaborates, noting:

> In comics, the reader can watch a considerable number of events at the same time within the frame of the page. A glance to the page is often enough to relate one image to the others without fear of losing any of the information contained in the discourse [p. 52].

The layout also helps the reader go back and forth between two moments in time, inviting a kind of unique re-reading. It is only when beginning to read a single panel that you dive into one singular moment of time. In an interview with Hilary Chute (2007), McCloud goes on to note that "You're [the reader] looking at panels, which, if you're reading panel two on page two, then to its left is the past, and to its right is the future. And your perception of the present moves across it" (n.p.). Peeters (1998) suggests that when we see one panel on a page, we really see all the panels on the page, which informs our understanding of the current panel. Bartual (2012) also discusses this notion, noting

> when we read a comic we are not always aware of the fact that we can perceive different temporal units at the same time, but it has very well argued that when we read a panel, we are being influenced by the contents of the panels that precede and succeed it, and also by the way panels are organized on the page [p. 52]

Bartual (2012) notes that this phenomenon has been called peri-champ by Benoit Peeters, panopticity by Jacques Samson and tabularity by Pierre Fresnault-Deruelle. Moving forward, I will use Samson's panopticity to describe this effect.

Given that ComiXology (2018) touts its Guided View as "an incredible Cinematic experience," it is unsurprising that ComiXology's Guided View disrupts the panopticity of the comic page. Indeed, by negating the panopticity that defines the spatio-temporality of the printed comics page in favor of privileging singular moments rooted in the present, it becomes clear that Guided View is closer to the realm of cinema than comics. By showing only one image—often a panel, or part of a panel—at a time, the reader is no longer able to see past or future events, which is a hallmark of the spatio-temporal map of the (printed) comics' page. Simply put, with ComiXology's Guided View, the comic reader can no longer assess a series of moments in time all at once, but are instead mired solely in the present. This forces the reader to more thoroughly engage their short-term memory when trying to construct the narrative. Granted, a reader is able to use navigational arrows to move back and forth between frames, but unless the reader leaves Guided View, the reader can only examine one moment in time. While this may not seem like a major issue, it mitigates the chances of prior or future panels influencing our perception of the current panel the reader is experiencing. Put differently, the reader has fewer semiotic clues to help inform and interpret the comic narrative. This in turn, theoretically, can impact reader comprehension.

By removing the panopticity of the comics' page, Guided View also severely disrupts the presence and utilization of the gutter, which is defined as the empty space between the panels. McCloud (1993) writes, "Nothing is seen between the two panels, but experience [and common sense] tells you something must be there" (p. 67); Bukatman (2012) elaborates by suggesting "the gutter demands that the reader … simultaneously grasp the continuities and discontinuities that connect panel A and panel B…" (p. 134). As such, narration in comics rely on "the interaction among various panels of the work" (Lefevre, 2011, p. 26). McCloud (1993) argues that the gutter is one of the most important aspects of comics; this is an understandable and logical argument given that the gutter, though often unconsciously overlooked by the reader, helps establish the spatio-temporal movement of the sequence. That is, the reader mentally constructs what happens between panels and, similarly, how long the events from panel to panel take; this mental construct is based on how well panels interact with, or build on, one another.

While the artist certainly gives the reader visual cues (and the writer, if applicable, verbal cues), the gutter is the space that forces—or allows, depending on the viewpoint—the reader to make a seamless narrative from image to image. However, by removing the panopticity of the comics' page, the gutter also disappears. The Guided View of ComiXology focuses, in turn, exclusively on singular panels or parts of a singular panel, and the result is omitting the white space between panels. Thus, readers no longer rely on the *interaction* of the panels, but rather must make meaning after examining panels individually and in isolation.

Additionally, as Wolk (2007) notes, the gutter plays a large part in the comic reader's immersive experience. He writes

> There's more to the immersive experience of comics than what's visible in their panels and what specific actions happen between them. A lot of the pleasure in reading comics is filling in *all* the blank space beyond each panel, as far as it can go in both space and time, with the drawing on the page as a guide or a set of hints [p. 132].

Thus, not only does the elimination of panopticity disrupt the reading practices that comic readers would be accustomed to, but moving back and forth between panels using navigational arrows (and bypassing the gutters) threatens to remove the reader from the immersive world of the narrative. A byproduct of this, then, might also be to disrupt the reader's ability to seamlessly make meaning from the narrative. Put differently, when focusing on one panel at a time, the relationships between panels become less and less clear. Given that the reader's ability to comprehend a multi-panel comic is indelibly tied to the interaction of the panels, seeing only one moment in time limits the reader's ability to comprehend the narrative.

Moreover, by only showing one panel at a time, readers using Guided View are not able to see the rhetoric of the entire page. As Peeters (1998) notes, the comics page can often be designed with a purpose—with a certain aesthetic or "*mise en page*" (para. 15, emphasis original)—in mind; to that end, Peeters emphasizes that understanding how a work benefits from the page layout is a fundamental question to understanding a comic; he writes "the panel and the page are no longer autonomous elements; they are subordinated to a narrative which their primary function is to serve. The size of the images, their distribution, the general pace of the page, all must come to support the narration" (para. 19). As Peeters is noting, the page works *with* the panels. By separating the two, some of the intended rhetoric and aesthetic is lost. This in turn can interfere with reader comprehension; at the very least, it reduces the number of semiotic cues available for a reader to interpret.

Conclusion

In this essay, I have highlighted how ComiXology's Guided View—touted as a tool helping the (novice) comic reader navigate the comic page while also striving to provide an experience that mimics reading a traditional print comic—disrupts two distinct properties of the printed comic page: the database logic of the page, which allows for significant reader flexibility in determining reading path, and the spatio-temporality of the comic page (specifically the panopticity of the page), which aides in comprehension and immersion. In this way, then, I ultimately support Groensteen's (2015) assertion that the shift from print to digital necessarily changes the comic reading experience. Given Guided View's privileging of a singular reading path and the emphasis on present moments, it seems that ComiXology's Guided View is closer to providing a cinematic experience and less the experience of reading comics. While I will leave it to other scholars to debate the merits of how successfully ComiXology's Guided View provides an immersive cinematic experience, I will note briefly here that it is problematic that ComiXology simultaneously markets Guided View as a cinematic tool and a tool capable of mimicking the reading of a print comic—the two ideas are wholly incompatible. Beyond this incongruity, my analysis suggests that ComiXology's Guided View is a disruptive tool—one that could significantly alter reading practices of readers, reader immersion, and reader comprehension.

I recognize, of course, that reading practices are changing as we increasingly become a digital-based culture as opposed to a print-based culture. As we move from print to digital, does it not make sense that the reading practices will change as well? As I've noted elsewhere (Kirchoff, 2013), it seems impossible to recreate the reading experiences found in print comics, so perhaps experimentations in digital comic reading practices—even those of remediated comics—should be expected and even lauded. Additionally, Johnston (2017) ardently argues that ComiXology should not try replicating the reading process of a print comic book, but instead think about the way comics function. Moreover, I openly acknowledge that on some mobile devices—such as a smartphone, for instance—reading a comic one panel at a time might be necessary to accurately view and read the icons and alphabetic text on the comics page and subsequent panels. That is, there may be reading situations where viewing one panel at a time is the only realistic option to traverse a narrative. Based on my analysis, though, I would argue that the rigidity of the Guided View takes away something inherently unique to the comic reading experience: reader autonomy and flexibility. Many scholars have argued that comics are control (see Barber, 2002; Goodbrey, 2013; Hammond, 2009; Magliano, Loschky, Clinton, & Larson, 2013; Rabkin, 2009). That is, one of the charms of the (printed) comic is for readers to control the pacing of the comic; this control, these scholars contend, is highlighted by an ability to dictate reading path and the flexibility in moving back and forth between past, present, and future. In turn, this kind of control leads to a strong immersive experience for comic readers. Guided view, while well-intentioned and an interesting tool, does eliminate the database-reading structure of the comic (reading path) and does significantly alter the spatio-temporal map of the comics page—two elements that, as I have demonstrated in this essay, are integral to the comic reading experience. Given that ComiXology is touted as a tool to help novice comic readers, it does seem troubling that readers would lose out on two aspects that make the medium of comics wholly unique: database and spatio-temporality.

ComiXology is not without its positives, of course, chief among them its ability to make so many comic titles available to readers of all ages, and Gavaler (2017) suggests that ComiXology has helped the comics' industry gain new readers. This essay is not designed to discredit the work of ComiXology, but rather aims to highlight how Guided View might prove to be problematic for comic readers, novice or otherwise. Thankfully, ComiXology does give the reader *some* control—the reader can opt out of Guided View altogether. Based on my analysis, it seems that if a comic reader is intent on maintaining the so-called integrity of comic reading, this may be a rational and encouraged choice in order to maintain an authentic comic-reading experience.

References

Allen, T.W. (2014). *Economics of digital comics.* USA: Indignant Media.

Barber, J. (2002). *The phenomenon of multiple dialectics in comics layout.* (master's thesis). London: London College of Printing.

Bartual, R. (2012). Towards a panoptical representation of time and memory: Chris Ware, Marcel Proust, and Henri Bergson's "pure duration." *Scandinavian Journal of Comic Art, 1*(1). Retrieved from http://sjoca.com/?page_id=114.

Batanic, J. (2016). "Enhanced webcomics": An exploration of the hybrid form of comics on the digital medium. *Image and Narrative 17*(5). Retrieved from http://www.imageand narrative.be/index.php/imagenarrative/issue/view/82.

Benitez, J. (2014) *Lady Mechanika #0.* Retrieved from https://www.ComiXology.com/Lady-Mechanika/comics-series/24606.

Bongco, M. (2000). *Reading comics: Language, culture, and the concept of the superhero in comic books.* New York: Routledge.

Bukatman, S. (2012). Online comics and the reframing of the moving image. In D. Harris (Ed.), *The new media book* (pp. 133–143). London: British Film Institute.

Chute, H. (2007). [Interview with Scott McCloud, author of *Understanding comics*]. *Believer 5* (3). Retrieved from https://www.believermag.com/issues/200704/?read=interview_mccloud.

Cohn, N., & Campbell, H. (2015). Navigating comics II: Constraints on the reading order of page layouts. *Applied Cognitive Psychology, 29.* Retrieved from http://www.visuallan guagelab.com/P/NCHC_pagelayouts2.pdf.

ComiXology. (2014). What is ComiXology's guided view? Retrieved from https://support.ComiXology.com/customer/portal/articles/768035-what-is-ComiXology-s-guided-view™-technology_____.

ComiXology (2018). Welcome to ComiXology. Retrieved from https://www.comixology.com/new-to-comixology.

Dittmar, J. (2015). Digital comics. *Scandinavian Journal of Comic Art, 1*(2). Retrieved from http://sjoca.com/wp-content/uploads/2013/01/SJoCA-1-2-Forum-Dittmar.pdf.

Gavaler, C. (2017). *Superhero comics.* London: Bloomsbury.

Goodbrey, D. (2013). Digital comics—New tools and tropes. *Studies in Comics, 4*(1), 185–197.

Goodbrey, D. (2015). Game comics: An analysis of an emergent hybrid form. *Journal of Graphic Novels and Comics, 6*(1), 3–14.

Groensteen, T. (2015). *Comics and narration.* Jackson: University of Mississippi Press.

Gunning, T. (2014). The art of succession: Reading, writing, and watching comics. *Critical Inquiry, 40(3),* 36–51.

Hague, I. (2014). *Comics and the senses.* New York: Routledge.

Hammond, H. (2009). *Graphic novels and multimodal literacy: A reader response study* (Doctoral dissertation). Retrieved from the University of MN Digital Converancy, http://hdl.handle.net/11299/48560.

Jacobs, D. (2014). Webcomics, multimodality, and information literacy. *ImageText, 7*(3). Retrieved from http://www.english.ufl.edu/imagetext/archives/v7_3/jacobs/.

Johnston, H. (2017). ComiXology and the future of the digital comic book. *The iJournal, 2*(2). Retrieved from http://www.theijournal.ca/index.php/ijournal/issue/view/1864/showToc.

Kirchoff, J.S.J. (2013). It's just not the same as print (and it shouldn't be): Rethinking the possibilities of digital comics. *Technoculture: An Online Journal of Technology in Society, 3*(1). Retrieved from https://tcjournal.org/drupal/vol3/kirchoff.

Lefèvre, P. (2011). Some medium specific qualities of graphic sequences. *SubStance, 40*(1), 14–33.

Magliano, J.P., Loschky, L.C., Clinton, J.A., & Larson, A.M. (2013). Is reading the same as viewing? An exploration of the similarities and differences between processing text and visually based narratives. In B. Miller, L. Cutting & P. McCardle (Eds.). *Unraveling the behavioral, neurobiological, and genetic components of reading comprehension* (pp. 78–90). Baltimore, MD: Brookes Publishing Co.

Manovich, L. (1999). Database as symbolic form. *Millenium Film Journal, 34.* Retrieved from http://www.mfj-online.org/journalPages/MFJ34/Manovich_Database_FrameSet.html.

Manovich, L. (2001). *Language of new media.* Cambridge, MA: MIT Press.

Manovich, L. (2013). The algorithms of our lives. *Chronicle of Higher Education.* Retrieved from https://www.chronicle.com/article/The-Algorithms-of-Our-Lives-/143557.

McCloud, S. (1993). *Understanding comics.* New York: HarperCollins Press.

McCloud, S. (2000). *Reinventing comics.* New York: HarperCollins Press.

Peeters, B. (1998). Four conceptions of the page (J. Cohn, Trans.). *ImageText, 3* (3). Retrieved from http://www.english.ufl.edu/imagetext/archives/v3_3/peeters/.

Poian, C. (2015). Investigating film algorithm: Transtextuality in the age of database cinema. Paper presented at the Gradisca Spring School.

Rabkin, E. (2009). Reading time in graphic narrative. In S. Tabachnik (Ed.) *Teaching the graphic novel* (pp. 36–43). New York: MLA.

Schwartz, G. (2006). Expanding literacies through graphic novels. *English Journal, 95*(6), 58–64.

Smith, C. (2012). Motion comics: Modes of adaptation and the issue of authenticity. *Animation Practice, Process & Production, 1*(2), 357–378.

Smith, C. (2015). Motion comics: The emergence of a hybrid medium. *Writing Visual Culture, 7.* Retrieved from http://www.herts.ac.uk/research/centres-and-groups/tvad-theorising-visual-art-and-design/writing-visual-culture/volume-7.

Steirer, G. (2014). No more bags and boards: Collecting culture and the digital comics marketplace. *Journal of Graphic Novels and Comics, 5*(4), 455–469.

Stevens, J.R., & Bell, C.E. (2012). Do fans own digital comic books? Examining the copyright and intellectual property attitudes of comic book fans. *International Journal of Communication, 6,* 751–772.

Versaci, R. (2001). How comic books can change the way our students see literature: One teacher's perspective. *English Journal, 91*(2), 61–67.

Wershler, D. (2011). Digital comics, circulation, and the importance of being Eric Sluis. *Cinema Journal, 50,* 127–134.

Wolk, D. (2007). *Reading comics.* Philadelphia, PA: De Capo Press.

Zalben, A., & Kenfield, J. (2013). *Detective Honeybear 1.* Retrieved from https://www.ComiXology.com/Detective-Honeybear-1/digital-comic/37896.

Zanfei, A. (2008). Defining webcomics and graphic novels. *International Journal of Comic Art, 10*(1), 55–61.

Re-Theorizing
the Infinite Canvas

A Space for Comics
and Rhetorical Theories[1]

RICH SHIVENER

> Comics must be approached as rhizomes with middles
> everywhere and no center to be found. This project attempts
> just that...—Jason Helms, *Rhizcomics*

"I just didn't expect it to be so big."

I am looking at a rectangular panel that depicts a stick figure floating high above the ground, a balloon in hand and a view of a sprawling landscape. While this is the fourth and final panel of the webcomic, the story is far from over. I start clicking and dragging to reveal more of the panel. Clicking. Dragging. Clicking. Dragging. That clicking and dragging doesn't seem to end, and neither does the panel, for that matter.

In this essay, I treat *xkcd* webcomic series creator Randall Munroe's (2012) production *Click and Drag* as a productive space for juxtaposing theories of digital comics[2] and digital rhetorics. The webcomic accords with what digital comics theorists and practitioners have called the "infinite canvas," or a comic that experiments with form and content in a seemingly infinite space. The infinite canvas implicates comics theories and theories that imagine rhetoric as a distributed and public event with diverse actors (Edbauer Rice, 2005; Gries, 2015; Helms, 2017; Ridolfo & DeVoss, 2009). Put differently, *Click and Drag's* expansive composition calls for a revised theoretical framework for analyzing digital comics, a framework that partners theorists such as McCloud and Gries. Indeed, Munroe's webcomic stretches theories of a comic's space, time and movement, as I explicate later in this essay.

This essay also aims to make a significant contribution to the study of comics within rhetoric and composition. While the body of scholarship on digital comics—namely, the infinite canvas—has accounted for ways in which comic practitioners experiment with long-held reading and composing practices, it has yet to engage deeply with theories of digital rhetoric that trace entities—such as remixes and new compositions—beyond the initial composer and digital comic itself. Theories on digital and visual rhetorics are useful for analyzing *Click and Drag*, a rhizome, but perhaps also an ecology and vital force that give ways to new works. With an extended framework, one with McCloud's comics theories as a foundation, I start in the infinite canvas and follow the reaches of *Click and Drag*. I account for its composition as well as what readers and networks do when they leave it, transform it, distribute it, and circulate it. Rather than starting with theoretical orientations, I start inside Munroe's infinite canvas and work my way out to theories of digital comics and digital-visual rhetorics. I use a practitioner case to critique and build on theory, forming new partnerships between disciplines and fields—between comics and rhetoric and composition studies.

Inside Click and Drag

Since 2005, Munroe has been self-publishing comics and illustrations through his website and eponymous series *xkcd*, referred to as "a webcomic of romance, sarcasm, math, and language" (Munroe, 2012). To date, Munroe has published hundreds of works, and his ideas on the aforementioned are often depicted with stick figures and line drawings. They are revered for their smart humor and illuminations on such topics as global warming, vodka, and musical artist M.C. Hammer. Munroe publishes new works three days a week. He publishes what he finds interesting, always surprising readers. According to the *xkcd* "About" page, his early invention strategies included looking back at illustrations in his high-school era notebooks. (Munroe, n.d., para. 7). As he told Megan Garber in a story for *The Atlantic*, "I think, if anything, it's noticing the things that make me laugh and grabbing onto them and figuring out how to write them down" (Garber, 2012, para. 40). Constructed with stick figures and line art, *xkcd* appears simple on the surface, but a closer look at Munroe's work illuminates its innovation and rhetorical power.

When Munroe composed *Click and Drag* in 2012, he delivered a webcomic in which the fourth panel spans 165,888 by 79,872 pixels (Plafke, 2012), and it was praised because of its scale and because of the motion required to navigate its wondrous pop culture references. As a reader, I'm free to explore by clicking and dragging on the image and dragging my mousepad. Much clicking and dragging is required in order to find character dialogues and items inside the panel. From my point of view, the image quite literally seems to go on and on and on, with many solid black and white spaces complemented with illustrations of the sky, landscapes, and underground passages. The image is a world. It seems new every time I refresh my browser. Every time I visit the panel, my navigation process changes. Just recently I followed characters walking along the hilly landscapes that stretch from end to end of the panel. I encountered parked cars, conversations about swimming and business, and a tire swing, among other items. If I had navigated toward the sky, I might have again encountered a plane, a floating jelly fish, and a man atop a tower and singing lyrics from "Flagpole Sitta" by Harvey Danger. And had I navigated below, I might have seen an X-Wing plane. Thus, it is impossible to see *Click and Drag's* fourth panel all at once. It is rhizomatic and affective insofar as readers are left to decide where to click and drag, embodying their wonder—and wandering—about the panel. The panel does not have a beginning or an end—at least one that isn't in plain sight.

Comics and rhetoric and composition ought to engage with a new, interdisciplinary framework to look critically at the spatial dimensions and content of *Click and Drag*. Both fields have advocated for experimental, non-linear composing practices in digital environments and welcomed innovative productions that disrupt publishing traditions. Drawing from theories of digital comics and rhetoric, scholars can look, perhaps with wide eyes, at Munroe's massive work, later turning to more compositions that accord with definitions of the infinite canvas. McCloud's theories of space and time in comics can be extended—and perhaps supplanted—by rhetorical theories.

As McCloud (1993) noted in the oft-cited *Understanding Comics: The Invisible Art*, when panels organize image and text in deliberate sequence, they often convey the passage of time. That is, sequential spaces are snapshots in time. "As readers," he noted, "we are left with only a vague sense that as our eyes are moving through space, they're also moving through time—we just don't know how much!" (p. 100). Put differently, the pace at which time passes in a comics narrative is dictated by what is depicted in a sequence of panels. Furthermore, according to McCloud, panel sizes manipulate time. He illustrated his point by depicting a square panel of a man talking, followed by a rectangular panel of his friend sleeping, followed by a square panel of the friend. The rectangular panel adds time to the story. Panels, in a way, function like paragraphs on a page. The denser a paragraph is with words and sentences, the longer one's read might be. Because *Click and Drag's* final panel is so large, it adds a significant amount of time to the story, assuming the reader pursues various drawings and words inside it. In a way, time is turned over to the reader, who can navigate the panel at the reader's own pace—the rate at which the reader wishes to click and drag.[3]

While *Understanding Comics* is a heuristic for understanding the spatiotemporality of *Click and Drag*, a turn to McCloud's more recent scholarship further illuminates Munroe's work. Writing in 2009, McCloud returns to his theory of the infinite canvas, something he first imagined in *Reinventing Comics: The Evolution of an Art Form* (2000), a hopeful look at the potential of comics, computers, and the World Wide Web. McCloud (2009) posited that the infinite canvas has implications for how comics creators conceptualize pacing, spatial ranges, panel distances, flow, and the identity of the medium. Table 1 outlines McCloud's key terms. Discussing the range of an "expanded canvas," McCloud (2009) suggested:

> Just as music allows for a wide range of volume, comics artists can vary panel size and shape for dramatic effect and they frequently do so in both print and online comics. On a single large canvas, those variations can again follow the needs of the story, but when a fixed page is involved, every decision about the size and shape of one panel restricts the size and shape of the next one [para. 7].

McCloud's comments implicate the size and volume of Munroe's *Click and Drag*. The last panel, as large as it is, is quite loud, and it does not have a "next" panel to answer to. It can therefore not be labeled as restrictive; it is, in fact, building, in a massive way, on the relatively tiny panels that precede it. The panel encompasses McCloud's position that expanded canvas comics shape the identity of digital comics. Rather than trying to gesture toward other multimedia forms, expanded comics' "emphasis on a single unbroken reading line and uninterrupted single mode of presentation can also provide what readers want most from any storytelling medium: a seamless, transparent window into the world of the story" (McCloud, 2009, para. 11). *Click and Drag's* window, then, is wide open and calls for readers to step inside and look around. Its reception also calls for scholars to critique McCloud's keywords and definitions of the infinite canvas.

Table 1. McCloud's (2009) Keywords and Definitions on the Infinite Canvas, Also Defined as the Expanded Canvas Approach

Pacing	"On an expanded canvas, he or she can add or subtract "beats" until the sequence feels right...."
Dynamic Range	"...when a fixed page is involved, every decision about the size and shape of one panel restricts the size and shape of the next one...."
Distance = Time	"...in a medium that measures time using space, readers will feel a slowing of the action as panels drift apart ... and a quickening when they run closer."

Flow	"…most page implementations online are clumsy hybrids of printed page shapes and a smattering of scrolling and clicking that distract from the reading experience."
The Z-Axis	"Introducing a third dimension doesn't have to be just a novelty … it could be used for other storytelling purposes including layered narratives, flashbacks, and tonal variation."
Identity	"…its emphasis on a single unbroken reading line and uninterrupted single mode of presentation can also provide what readers want most from any storytelling medium: a seamless, transparent window into the world of the story."

Going Infinite

For a *Composition Studies* special issue on comics, Bahl (2015) posited that comics "give voice to an alternative mode of meaning-making that … embraces a sense of wonder, discovery, and delight in the messy process of knowledge creation…" (p. 180). Comics and its theorist-practitioners, including McCloud and Munroe, hold promise for rhetoric and composition studies. Recent scholarship highlights such a promise. Like Bahl, scholars situated at the intersection of rhetoric and composition studies and comics have examined the medium through the lenses of literacy, genre, media, narrative and materiality (see Carter, 2007; Jacobs, 2014; Kashtan, 2015; Scanlon, 2015). To date, scholars in and outside rhetoric and composition studies have addressed McCloud's theory of the infinite canvas, but scholars have forged an extensive partnership between McCloud and rhetorical theorists. In addition, scholars have not looked widely at Munroe's work or treated it as a significant case study that illuminates McCloud's theory. This brief section, then, articulates my intervention, one that draws on rhetorical theories and *Click and Drag* to critique and build on McCloud's theory.

Digital comics scholarship is vast, no doubt due in part to McCloud's speculations in his 2000 book *Reinventing Comics*. Shedd (2005), Goodbrey (2013; 2015)[4] and Batinic (2017) are among scholars who have questioned what digital comics do (or should do) that print comics do not, asking about extents to which they implicate the long-held, aforementioned format. The aforementioned scholars' works are useful to me because they place value on McCloud's infinite canvas vision and digital comics criteria as a heuristic for experimenting with media and space. Whitson and Salter (2015), and Martin (2017) have deemed Munroe's *Click and Drag* as emblematic of an experimental digital comic and the infinite canvas. Because of its spatial dimensions and range of illustrations, it was controversial (Whitson & Salter, 2015) and "doesn't exactly obey the same codes as the printed strip" (Martin, 2017, para. 34). In both texts, neither McCloud's work or Munroe's *Click and Drag* are the central object of study, but they are framed as important texts that implicate print comics' capacities.[5] Nevertheless, like the aforementioned contributions, Whitson and Salter's and Martin's works occasion future studies of the infinite canvas.

However, there is a notable example of a scholar making extensive use of McCloud's theory of the infinite canvas to study digital comics and signal theoretical partnerships. Kirchoff (2013) examined digital comics such as *Nawlz* by Stuart Campbell and Marvel Comics' *Avengers vs. X-Men: Infinite* series as exemplary possibilities for digital comics' innovations. *Nawlz* is a panoramic digital comic complete with music, interactive pages, and more; Marvel's *Avengers vs. X-Men: Infinite* makes use of dissolving panels and some motion; these are part of Marvel's *Infinite Comics* series. Examining such comics, Kirchoff (2013) posited that

> one possibility for digital comics is to offer the reader multiple possibilities for how to navigate (and thus interact with) the narrative. Like *Nawlz*, a text could offer readers the opportunity to search, scroll, point, and click, but it could also give readers the chance to interact with the text using voice commands and movement [p. 17].

Kirchoff worked from McCloud's theory and intertwined it with theories of ergodic literature and hypertextuality to make his claim that digital comics should not remediate print comics' forms and navigation traditions. Digital comics ought "to continue evolving by exploring aesthetic, material, and interactive possibilities" (p. 23). I find Kirchoff's theoretical orientations significant because they illustrate that McCloud's theory is enriched—and perhaps, challenged—when partnered with theories outside of comics studies. Partnered theories help scholars see new possibilities for comics. Indeed, I follow Kirchoff's approach by partnering McCloud's key terms with those of recent rhetorical theories that concern digital and visual texts. In other words, I extend and merge ways of seeing and analyzing digital comics, partnering comics and rhetoric and composition studies. As Sealey-Morris (2015) argued in the comics issue of *Composition Studies*, the fields have a lot to offer in pedagogy and production, for both fields have commitments to digital and visual media. I add to Sealey-Morris' claims by engaging with rhetorical theories. Comics and rhetoric and composition, after all, are underdog disciplines, according to Kirtley (2015); they "share a focus on interdisciplinarity, which makes the fields exciting, innovative, and difficult to locate within institutions" (p. 172). In the next section, I highlight that interdisciplinarity and difficulty by synthesizing rhetorical theories that have been partnered with theories of affect, actor-network, new materialism, and more.[6]

Infinite Rhetorics

Having reviewed McCloud's work and situating my aims in digital comics scholarship, I now move to a discussion of rhetorical theories that could stretch the infinite canvas and McCloud's key terms on the format. I put to work theories such as Edbauer Rice's "affective ecologies" (2005), Ridolfo's "rhetorical velocity" (2009), Gries' "principle of vitality" (2015) and Helms's *Rhizcomics* (2017). By putting such theorists in conversation, I surface their key terms and show their common ground—that they are interested in the instability of fixed meaning and movement of texts. Ecology, velocity, virality, rhizomatic—these key terms account for movement and are thus interrogated in connection to Munroe's infinite canvas and McCloud's key terms.

Affective Ecologies

For Rice (2005), Lloyd Bitzer's oft-cited theory of the rhetorical situation was not enough to account for the public consumption and circulation of texts. As theorized by Rice, examining a text within "rhetorical and affective ecologies" decenters the rhetor and original text, and instead calls attention to "ways in which rhetorical productions are inseparable from lived encounters of public life" (p. 21). Her primary case study concerns the "Keep Austin Weird" slogan that was distributed and circulated in response to the city's commercial and big-box projects. The slogan's rhetorical work and affective energy—that of weirdness—flowed through stickers, T-shirts and advertisements, at times counter to the original rhetor.[7] For Rice, "we find ourselves engaging a public rhetoric whose power is not circumscribed or delimited. We encounter rhetoric" (p. 23). Her thinking can be extended to *Click and Drag's* affective energy—even energies—beyond the *xkcd* website and to its fan remixes and responses. As Whitson and Salter (2015) and Plafke (2012) noted, one website recoded *Click and Drag* into a zoomable Google Map, one in which a user could zoom out to see the entire fourth panel in its wondrous glory. In this case, the *Click and Drag* ecology expanded, the map serving as a dynamic and public iteration of Munroe's work. At the same time, Munroe's original work and the Google map were highlighted by scholars and online critics. Like "Keep Austin Weird," *Click and Drag's* command flowed and moved people across digital environments and tools. However, unlike Rice's object of study, *Click and Drag's* ecology is perhaps more permanent, as copies and impressions circulate in digital spaces and not the material. In this case, its digital ecology is a collection of living, affective encounters, less impacted by material conditions.

The digital ecology doesn't stop there. Another programmer transformed

Click and Drag into a massively multiplayer online (MOO) game, complete with a chat system. Extending Rice's theory again, I argue that *Click and Drag* MMO is within itself a living ecology, with viewers and composers encountering each other as well as Munroe's illustrations. This case also elides the original illustrator and coder of the comic—Munroe. Neither the map or MMO game were of Munroe's doing but were rather products of user encounter. Nevertheless, I can't ignore the fact that Munroe was, in part, responsible for the text's movement and the coders' respective agencies. A turn to Ridolfo's theory of rhetorical velocity (Ridolfo & DeVoss, 2009) highlights Munroe's contributions.

Rhetorical Velocity

For more than 10 years, Jim Ridolfo's work has redefined and extended the fifth canon of rhetoric—delivery—in studies of rhetors and digital texts. Ridolfo and DeVoss' (2009) application of Ridolfo's theory of rhetorical velocity concerns the appropriation of a text as well as the rapidity of its circulation after initial distribution. This is somewhat of an echo of Rice's (2005) work, but Ridolfo and DeVoss are more concerned with rhetors who compose for recomposition, meaning a text is appropriated, edited or re-distributed by third parties. As Ridolfo and DeVoss (2009) ask readers, "What document format should a file be sent in for certain types of future remixing? What resolution should images be released in if they are to be reprinted in a print publication?" (para. 2). Since asking those questions, Ridolfo has investigated authors' distribution strategies, third-party appropriations, and circulation speeds related to press releases, websites, and activist projects. When I situate Munroe's *Click and Drag* in this context of rhetorical velocity, I notice that Munroe's text is public and held under a creative common license (Munroe, n.d.). That means he published it and opened it to interpretation and transformation. Furthermore, examining *Click and Drag* through the lenses of rhetorical velocity means inquiring about the goals of the comic, the resolution of the fourth panel, the code used to store and transmit the data, even the material work Munroe did prior to the completion of the text. It also means studying *Click and Drag's* positive, neutral, and negative appropriations (Ridolfo & DeVoss, 2009). Simply put, their spectrum of appropriation accounts for transformations that accord with, and run counter to, a rhetor's goals.

In terms of *Click and Drag*, it is not a stretch to note that appropriations have been positive. For a bit of a flashback, recall that Rice's (2005) work calls attention to reception, of which scholars and online critics helped its ecology grow. Griggs (2012), Plafke (2012), May (2012), and McMillan (2012) and are among several writers and bloggers who resized or cited *Click and Drag*. Such bloggers embodied positive appropriations, as many provided more notice about the release and used their respective spaces to label the comic along the lines of "something wonderfully immersive and oddly disorienting ... as well as somewhat addictive" (McMillan, 2012, para. 3). Also positive were the aforementioned game and Google map made available for free. They should be free, in fact, if they are following Munroe's creative common license to the letter. Web searches do not show any, if at all, violations of the license, such as reprints sold in digital or material forms (e.g., a poster) outside of the *xkcd* website. Violations might fall under negative appropriation. However, that does not mean rhetors—human actors—are solely responsible for its potential misuse, as the next theorist demonstrates.

Vitality

With theories of mobility and circulation gaining traction in rhetorical studies, Laurie Gries has kept pace through her investigation of the Obama Hope image, first designed by artist Shepard Fairey. In *Still Life with Rhetoric*, Gries (2015) approached the image through the lenses of new materialism and actor-network theory (see Gries' work on Jane Bennett, Bruno Latour, and many others), arguing that a text such as the Obama Hope image moves in public with its own vitality, a capacity to act and be acted upon. For Gries, rhetoric is "a virtual-actual event that unfolds with time and space as things—whether they be images, pictures, books, movies, rocks, trees, animals—enter into material relations with humans, technologies, and other entities" (p. 39). Thus, the Obama Hope image took on a life of its own, in relation with other vital forces, with Fairey not solely responsible for its wide circulation. Gries puts her theoretical orientations to work by tracking the material and digital manifestations of Obama Hope—from Zombie Obama to Pope Obama. Like Rice, she de-centers the original rhetor and text and instead pays close attention to human-nonhuman "actants" that make rhetorical production possible.

With Gries' framework, I consider the magnitude of *Click and Drag's* final panel and its potential effects on networks and servers that have hosted the original and subsequent iterations. On the *xkcd* site, Munroe's final panel is not one large image but a collection of graphic tiles, all of which are downloadable. Programmers who have created maps and remixes of the final panel have taken apart the tiles and reassembled them into one large image, all the while keeping file sizes small. Along with studying image sizing, I might also study quite rigorously its circulation via news media and digital networks and communities, such as Reddit and the Explain *xkcd* wiki pages, embodying Gries' (2015) "iconographic tracking" method (p. 88). Gries' method accounts for actancy, or things moved to action. Are there any physical manifestations?

If so, where, and what materials, bodies and networks assembled as they came into being? In short, Gries' work considers not only *who* composes but also *what* makes a composition vital. In a way, Gries' theoretical orientation converges Rice's and Ridolfo's previous contributions, attempting to capture the dynamic, living entities that spawn from a distributed text. I admit here that her work occasions an ambitious future study, for its difficult to sense when digital entities stop moving. Nevertheless, her work remedies the digital media concerns I shared when discussing Rice.

Rhizcomics

Of the four theorists I draw from here, Helms is the only one who engages directly with comics theory and the medium, putting the likes of McCloud and French comics theorist Thierry Groensteen in conversation with philosophers such as Jacques Derrida and Gilles Deleuze. In *Rhizcomics*, Helms (2017) argued that "comics must be approached as rhizomes with middles everywhere and no center to be found" (para. 7). As explained in the section "Comics, Differend, Synthesis," comics and writing scholars ought to "rhizcompose … to find new ways to write and to be written, and [to compose] not a destination but a becoming" (para. 16). Helms' theory is useful for analyzing *Click and Drag* because it emphasizes the fourth panel, an unstable reading experience, one that opens readers to unique connections inside the panel. The panel's so-called middle might be the initial presentation of the image, but even if that is the case, consider that the stick figure holding the balloon is not at the center of the panel. Readers begin off-center and are hard-pressed to find a center, let alone a conclusion.

Thinking about Helms's (2017) visual rhizome, I ask at what point are we finished reading and embodying *Click and Drag's* final panel, and what leads us to that decision—if at all? There are infinite ways of navigating the panel and leaving it, so it does not "end" in a uniform way for all readers. Helms' contribution is noteworthy in relation to the *Click and Drag* MMO game, an ecology that was becoming and taking on new bodies (i.e., stick figures), rhetorics, and meanings thanks to participants. It was always "becoming" amid networks or ecologies of digital media. As examined through the lenses of Rice (2005), Ridolfo (2009), and Gries (2015), I suggest that *Click and Drag*-as-becoming is also contingent on archives and search engines, contributions from fans, hyperlinks coded by bloggers, and the like. What's more, *Click and Drag* doesn't stop becoming when Munroe deletes it and reader activities "end." In a world where most digital files are rigorously archived by search engines and databases, *Click and Drag* has a seemingly infinite lifespan. It is an infinite rhizome, perhaps forever open to relations that give way to new stocks and roots—in this case, remixes, copies, and hyperlinks. To borrow from Michele Knobel and Colin Lankshear (2008), it is subject to media hybridization and endless remixing. The authors wrote, "In the sense that each new mix becomes a meaning-making resource for subsequent remixes, there is no end to remixing" (p. 26). Quite simply, the Internet is a fertile ground for the *Click and Drag* rhizome.

Extensive Agency

Considering rhetoric and media, the aforementioned theorists and their key terms prompted me to conduct a case study of *Click and Drag* to analyze composers and things beyond the infinite canvas. They also prompted me to critique McCloud's (2009) criteria for the infinite canvas, as I do in this section. Considering ecology, velocity, vitality, and rhizcomics, I don't think any of the key terms can be situated alone among McCloud's key terms. *Ecology* locates the rhetorics, affective energies, and disparate objects that follow a text, eliding the human. *Velocity* embraces a human's rhetorical delivery strategies and the speed at which texts circulate. *Vitality* and *rhizcomics* are good theoretical partners but pay less attention to the affective work and rhetorical production of human actors. Nevertheless, after putting such key terms to work on *Click and Drag*, I expose what McCloud's criteria has elided—that of reader and media activities that surround the text. Adding another term to McCloud's criteria might enrich it, thereby accounting, in some way, for the dynamic surround of digital comics. Perhaps we need a term that encompasses all of the aforementioned—a term that unites all and that has value across theoretical orientations and agendas.

Ideas of agency cut across all previously discussed theories by Rice, Ridolfo, Gries, and Helms, and thus might serve well as an add-on to McCloud's criteria. When I am talking about agency, I am talking about "an act of change that arises from an entanglement of human and nonhuman entities and other environmental factors" (Gries, 2015, p 70). In terms of digital comics, acts of change, then, arise from readers, various audiences, and nonhuman participants (code, avatars, networks, and the like). Acts of change, of movement, are critical in McCloud's previous discussions. In a view that channeled Marshall McLuhan, McCloud said comics are a participatory medium, meaning that the reader is required to make some cognitive moves and jumps as she reads (1993). His primary point on such participation centers on what he calls closure. As mentioned earlier, panels can be conceptualized as snapshots of time, and those snapshots are divided by the gutter, or the white space that break panels. In the gutter, McCloud (1993) theorized that a reader is "a silent accomplice" in a story's action, "mentally construct[ing] a continuous, unified reality" (pp. 66–68) between panel breaks and bringing closure to the event, plot point, etc. In other words, a reader completes the murder in her mind, or so the theory goes.

While *Click and Drag's* fourth panel lacks gutter space, it does ask the reader to participate in the closure of the story. It does not show us, for example, where the man floating with the balloon ends up (Hint: He's there somewhere! Just keep clicking and dragging...). As mentioned earlier, this generates a sense of wonder, a question of his location. Furthermore, there are two reoccurring characters in the massive panel, indicating that Munroe composed a still image while trying to convey motion. Thus, it seems fair to contend that motion is possible in the massive panel because the reader is presumed to click and drag away from the previously seen segments of the panel. Motion, then, is an act of bringing some closure to the comic. It is also an act of change in a typical comics' reading experience, asking a reader to motion through the panel by clicking her mouse, dragging it, and reading. It's a refreshing entanglement between reader, media tools, and the comic itself. It's no question that such an act of change to the typical comics reading experience gave rise to the *Click and Drag* Google map and MMO game.

Furthermore, theories of agency and closure informed McCloud's (2009) writings on the infinite canvas, about which he argued that the experimental approach calls for a more "reader-related philosophy," as discussed here:

> The only way the infinite canvas approach can ever come of age is if the readers' needs come first. Advancing from one panel to the next should be as easy as hitting a spacebar or tapping the screen. Bookmarking locations for return reading should be as easy as, well ... a bookmark. If all-in-one downloads would be convenient, readers should have that option [para. 18].

McCloud's ideal philosophy and theory partners well with the rhetorical theories on which I draw here; each offer valuable insights about a text's growth and transformation as well as agency it manifests. Like his rhetorical counterparts, McCloud's words infer that agency emerges from an assemblage of human and nonhumans, composers and their tools, audiences and their web resources, with no end or beginning in sight once a text circulates in digital environments. Thus, I propose that *extensive agency* joins McCloud's criteria for the infinite canvas. Agency is about the capacity to do things with a text. A term like extensive agency might help account for the varying ways composers, readers, and entities do work with digital comics—work such as downloading, reprogramming, editing, rescaling, redistributing, and circulating, all of which happen at varying speeds and locations. Extensive agency encompasses the initial composer and the living, moving, digital actors that do things to and with a text, namely a digital comic. For *Click and Drag*, the term occasions such questions as: What did Munroe do to make future changes possible—to make the fourth panel a living document for change?

What changes came as a surprise, or an unexpected change for a reader, algorithm, or network? To what extent did a participant or entity create new possibilities for action? In what ways do their changes and actions sustain the digital comics and its interactions? Questions like these echo those posed by the rhetorical theorists under discussion in this essay, converging their key terms to underscore a productive partnership with McCloud.

Participatory Media

Besides extending McCloud's work and those of rhetorical theorists, there are of course infinite ways of analyzing *Click and Drag*, but I do not have infinite space here to do as such. Still, before closing this essay, I cover additional insights that extend ways of seeing Munroe's comic. While this is a digression from my essay's scope, it nevertheless looks to open new entries to Click and Drag, and it reinforces my argument that the webcomic is a massive map for theoretical exploration.

Theories on reader participation and motion (i.e. clicking and dragging) might partner well with Frank Serafini's (2012) concept of the four reader roles of multimodal texts: navigator, interpreter, designer, and interrogator. Reader as navigator, he contends, involves navigating the orientation of print-based text; it also involves constructing meaning from such non-sequential texts as websites and advertisements. The navigator role precedes the role of interpreter, with which the reader draws "upon a wide range of experiences with other images and texts during their act of interpretation" (p. 156). In the case of *Click and Drag*, the navigator role is most vital, for not assuming that role negates the rich experience to be had with comic's fourth panel.

Click and Drag's emphasis of the navigator role in a reader aligns with theories concerning audience. Lisa Ede and Andrea Lunsford (1984) contend that rhetors address and invoke audiences when composing a text. When audiences are invoked, they write, "the writer uses the semantic and syntactic resources of language to provide cues for the reader—cues which help to define the role or roles the writer wishes the reader to adopt in responding to the text" (p. 160). While their theory is more than 30 years old, it still holds up in connection to Munroe's work. By the title alone, *Click and Drag* invokes audiences by asking them to commit the acts of clicking and dragging. It is not simply a lecture or narrative in comics form, like McCloud's *Understanding Comics* (1993), in that the creators explicates his comics theory to audiences. In *Click and Drag*, audiences are not addressed; they are moved to action. As mentioned earlier, audience interaction—really, navigation—is a centerpiece of *Click and Drag*.

More recent works on audience are needed, though, for a richer understanding of reader navigation and audience interaction toward *Click and Drag*—and the infinite canvas, in general. Media theorist Henry Jenkins has written extensively about the participatory culture of media. In *Confronting the Challenges of Participatory Culture*, Jenkins, Purushotma, Weigel, Clinton, and Robison (2009) describe the new media literacy "play," which is indeed bound up with audience invocation. While he considers play in the context of games and learning, comics like *Click and Drag* apply. *Click and Drag* is indeed playful. "On the basis of the available information," Jenkins et al. (2009) write,

> the player poses a certain hypothesis about how the world works and the best ways of bringing its properties under their control. The player tests and refines that hypothesis through actions in the game, which either fail or succeed. The player refines the model of the world as he or she goes [p. 24].

Click and Drag invites a kind of play because, as mentioned, the fourth panel is so massive and it warrants action. Clicking and dragging, though, wasn't playful enough for some readers of Munroe's ambitious comic. Enter the Google map and MMO game discussed earlier in this chapter. Jenkins, Green, and Ford (2013) would label such reader efforts as part of *Click and Drag's* "spreadable media" (p. 3). In *Spreadable Media*, the researchers contended that audiences play an active role in spreading content, whether as a link with an annotated or a remix of sorts. "In this emerging model," they argued, "audiences play an active role in 'spreading' content rather than serving as passive carriers of viral media: their choices, investments, agendas, and actions determine what gets valued" (p. 21). *Click and Drag*, once uploaded by Munroe in 2012 and linked by various blogs shortly thereafter, took on new lives once audiences transformed—and spread—the fourth panel in the aforementioned ways. For Jenkins, Green and Ford (2013), "this continuous process of repurposing and recirculating is eroding the perceived divides between production and consumption" (p. 29). To wit: audiences ignore the dividing lines; or rather, active audiences stand on both sides of dividing lines. Upon consuming *Click and Drag*, audience members found agency in the click-and-drag function, and, perhaps in attempts to demystify the reading process, they took it upon themselves to remix the fourth panel. These audience members are what Jacqueline Rhodes and Jonathan Alexander (2014) and others have called a "prosumer" (p. 70), who consume and remix texts in public spheres, sometimes for disruptive purposes. I do not mean to suggest that the audience uptake of *Click and Drag* is disruptive to Munroe's work. The "prosumer" drive that circulated *Click and Drag* opened potentially unseen views to the fourth panel's exhaustive content.

Navigating, invoking, playing, spreading, prosuming—these are actions that audiences can take in relation to a digital comic. From a critical perspective,

I see them as actions that have limitless potential in analyses of *Click and Drag*. As long as *Click and Drag* remains a living text, the aforementioned actions might inform new theoretical partnerships.

Infinite Screens

As discussed in earlier sections of this essay, Randall Munroe's *Click and Drag* webcomic has seemingly infinite angles to approach and exploit; it does not end simply—nor does the work that spawns from it. *Click and Drag's* unique design and circulation, then, warrants a theoretical framework that merges comics studies and rhetorical scholarship. The new framework I present in this essay is a way to address a passage from Sousanis' *Unflattening*, a graphic meditation in which the comics scholar invites us to open our senses to interdisciplinary possibilities. "If we have a superpower," Sousanis (2015) mused, "it's the capacity to host a multiplicity of worlds inside us. All of us do. Frames of references from which to see the same world differently. To make the familiar strange" (p. 96). In this essay, by drawing on several frames of references, I aim to make McCloud's oft-cited theories strange. *Click and Drag* and rhetorical theories on mobility and circulation help cultivate that strangeness.

Like Kirchoff, my aim is not to disassemble McCloud's infinite canvas criteria, but rather to build on his significant and widely cited contribution to comics theory. My aim is also not to expose the flaws of any one theory under discussion. As mentioned in the previous section, a term like extensive agency would forge productive partnerships between the theories of the "underdog disciplines" (Kirtley, 2015, p. 171), accounting for the infinite possibilities for action in and outside of the massive canvas. By situating McCloud with Rice, Ridolfo, Gries, and Helms, I encourage readers to consider extensive agency cultivated by Munroe and *Click and Drag*. Munroe's webcomic is multi-faceted—at once a rhizome, ecology, and assemblage of vital entities that take on varying branches and speeds of transformation.

As I look back on my time with *Click and Drag*, I hope future researchers will look to Munroe's other contributions as well as infinite canvases not mentioned in this essay. The rhetorical theories I cite could indeed be applied to an array of digital comics. The same goes for media theories I discuss in the previous section. Any one of such theories drive an extensive investigation. Single theoretical applications work well, but they often times trap researchers into a narrow scope, or what Burke (1966) calls a terministic screen. Less critically, I'm saying that at times we need multiple terministic screens in order to study dynamic digital comics like *Click and Drag*. McCloud's infinite canvas criteria and *Click and Drag* hold more weight when extensive agency is introduced because the term calls for screens that reveal more human and nonhuman contributions to a production. The social field and dynamic surround of a digital comic comes into view, and we can expect it to be so big.

NOTES

1. This essay was inspired by my presentation at the 2017 Conference on College Composition and Communication in Portland, Oregon. I'm grateful to Molly J. Scanlon, Susan Kirtley, and Dale Jacobs for helping me develop this idea.

2. I'm using the term digital comics as an umbrella term for multimedia comics, online comics, and webcomics. Whether appearing on an app, site, or CD, such comics are appearing in digital environments.

3. I acknowledge that some readers might simply click away from the comic after reading the seemingly static fourth panel.

4. In fact, Shedd and Goodbrey are practitioners. Goodbrey has a long history of experimenting with comics in digital environments. McCloud has cited Goodbrey's Tarquin Engine, a tool for creating infinite comics.

5. Whitson and Salter's article introduces a *Digital Humanities Quarterly* special issue on digital comics. They have citations and links to publics that responded to Munroe's *Click and Drag*. Again, their work occasions a more extensive study.

6. That said, I focused on their contributions, paying little attention to the theorists that informed their work.

7. For example, as Edbauer Rice writes, "Keep Austin Weird" was appropriated as "Make Austin Normal."

REFERENCES

Bahl, E.K. (2015). Comics and scholarship: Sketching the possibilities. *Composition Studies, 43*(1), 178–182.

Batinic, J. (2017). "Enhanced Webcomics": An exploration of the hybrid form of comics on the digital medium. *Image & Narrative, 17*(5), 80–91.

Burke, K. (1966). *Language as symbolic action: Essays on life, literature, and method.* Berkeley: University of California Press.

Carter, J.B. (2007). *Building literacy connections with graphic novels: Page by page, panel by panel.* Urbana, IL: National Council of Teachers of English.

Edbauer Rice, J. (2005). Unframing models of public distribution: From rhetorical situation to rhetorical ecologies. *Rhetoric Society Quarterly, 35*(4), 5–24.

Ede, L., & Lunsford, A. (1984). Audience addressed/audience invoked: The role of audience in composition theory and pedagogy. *College Composition and Communication, 35*(2), 155–171.

Garber, M. (2012, September 2012). A conversation with Randal Munroe. *The Atlantic.* Retrieved from https://www.theatlantic.com/technology/archive/2012/09/a-conversation-with-randall-munroe-the-creator-of-xkcd/262851/.

Goodbrey, D.M. (2013). Digital comics—New tools and tropes. *Studies in Comics, 4*(1), 185–197.

Goodbrey, D.M. (2015). Distortions in spacetime: Emergent narrative practices in comics' transition from print to screen. In R. Pearson & A. Smith (Eds.), *Storytelling in the media convergence age* (pp. 54–73), New York: Palgrave McMillan.

Gries, L. (2015). Still life with rhetoric: A new materialist approach for visual rhetorics. Boulder, CO: Utah State University Press.

Griggs, M.B. (2012, September 19). The best bits of xkcd's really, really big comic. *Smithsonian.* Retrieved from https://www.smithsonianmag.com/smart-news/the-best-bits-of-xkcds-really-really-big-comic-43101254/.

Helms, J. (2017). *Rhizcomics: Rhetoric, technology, and new media composition.* Ann Arbor:

University of Michigan Press. Retrieved from https://www.press.umich.edu/7626373/rhizcomics.

Jacobs, D. (2014). Webcomics, multimodality, and information literacy. *ImageTexT: Interdisciplinary Comics Studies, 7*(3). Retrieved from http://www.english.ufl.edu/imagetext/archives/v7_3/jacobs/.

Jenkins, H., Ford, S., & Green, J. (2013). *Spreadable media: Creating value and meaning in a networked culture.* New York: NYU Press.

Jenkins, H., Purushotma, R., Weigel, M., Clinton, K., & Robison, A.J. (2009). *Spreadable media: Creating value and meaning in a networked culture.* New York: NYU Press.

Kashtan, A. (2015). Materiality comics. *Digital Humanities Quarterly, 9*(4). Retrieved from http://www.digitalhumanities.org/dhq/vol/9/4/000212/000212.html.

Kirchoff, J.S. (2013). It's just not the same as print (and it shouldn't be): Rethinking the possibilities of digital comics. *Technoculture: A Online Journal of Technology in Society, 3.* Retrieved from tcjournal.org/vol3/kirchoff.

Kirtley, S. (2015). The Underdog disciplines: Comics studies and composition and rhetoric. *Composition Studies, 43*(1), 171–173.

Knobel, M., & Lankshear, C. (2008). Remix: The art and craft of endless hybridization. *Journal of Adolescent & Adult Literacy, 52*(1), 22–33.

Martin, C. (2017). With, against or beyond print? Digital comics in search of a specific status. *The Comics Grid: Journal of Comics Scholarship, 7.* Retrieved from https://www.comicsgrid.com/article/10.16995/cg.106/.

May, M. (2012, September 20). Xkcd's "Click and Drag" creates entire world for readers to explore. *Comic Book Resources.* Retrieved from https://www.cbr.com/xkcds-click-and-drag-creates-entire-world-for-readers-to-explore/.

McCloud, S. (1993). *Understanding comics: The invisible art.* New York: HarperPerennial.

McCloud, S. (2000). *Reinventing comics: How imagination and technology are revolutionizing an art form.* New York: Paradox Press.

McCloud, S. (2009, February). The "infinite canvas." Retrieved from http://scottmccloud.com/4-inventions/canvas/.

McMillan, G. (2012, September 19). Xkcd creates a whole new world to explore with sprawling "click to drag" comic. *Comics Alliance.* Retrieved from http://comicsalliance.com/xkcd-click-to-drag-webcomic/.

Munroe, R. (n.d.). Click and drag. *xkcd.* Retrieved from https://xkcd.com/1110/.

Munroe, R. (2012). Click and drag. *xkcd.* Retrieved from ttps://xkcd.com/1110/.

Plafke, J. (2012, September 19). Everything you need to know about today's *xkcd* comic, "Click and Drag." *The Mary Sue.* Retrieved from https://www.themarysue.com/xkcd-click-and-drag-comic/.

Rhodes, J., & Alexander, J. (2014). *On multimodality: New media in composition studies.* Urbana, IL: National Council of Teachers of English.

Ridolfo, J., & DeVoss, D.N. (2009). Composing for recomposition: Rhetorical velocity and delivery. *Kairos: A Journal of Rhetoric, Technology, and Pedagogy, 13*(2). Retrieved from http://kairos.technorhetoric.net/13.2/topoi/ridolfo_devoss/intro.html.

Scanlon, M.J. (2015). The work of comics collaborations: Considerations of multimodal composition for writing scholarship and pedagogy. *Composition Studies, 43*(1), 105.

Sealey-Morris, G. (2015). The rhetoric of the paneled page: Comics and composition pedagogy. *Composition Studies, 43*(1), 31.

Serafini, F. (2012). Expanding the four resources model: Reading visual and multi-modal texts. *Pedagogies: An International Journal, 7*(2), 150–164.

Shedd, A. (2005). *No borders, no limits: The infinite canvas as a storytelling tool in online comics* (master's thesis). University of Idaho, Moscow. Retrieved from http://www.alyciashedd.com/folio/writing/sheddthesis.pdf.

Sousanis, N. (2015). *Unflattening.* Cambridge, MA: Harvard University Press.

Whitson R.T., & Salter, A. Introduction: Comics and the digital humanities. *Digital HumanitiesQuarterly, 9*(4). Retrieved from http://www.digitalhumanities.org/dhq/vol/9/4/index.html.

Documentary Webcomics

Mediality and Contexts

Johannes C.P. Schmid

Documentary Drawn into a Changing World

Throughout the 1990s and around the turn of the millennium, the advent of the digital age has sparked high hopes towards a medial and cultural renaissance. As Ritchin (2010) puts it, "From digital images to mobile phones to the World Wide Web, media have become, in their easy transcendence of previous limitations of time and space, nearly messianic for us" (p. 10). Accordingly, early scholarship on webcomics has envisioned the affordances of the new digital sphere as a paradigm shift for graphic storytelling. In *Reinventing Comics: The Evolution of an Art Form*, which is advertised on its back cover as "the seminal new century manifesto on the many futures of comics art," McCloud (2000, back cover) claims the digital sphere will bring about "absolute access to absolutely everything" (p. 230), a fair and egalitarian marketplace that in which the consumer's interests are served directly, and a new maturity to the medium of comics as a whole, thusly "saving" print comics, as well. The Internet has been hailed as a space where the power of the capitalist mainstream media can finally be challenged in favor of more democratic news media "generating a new culture that is critical, selective, and participatory" (Curran, 2013, p. 227). In the second decade of the new millennium, though, this enthusiasm towards digitalism has waned considerably (cf. Kukkonen, 2014; Ritchin, 2013). At the same time, digitalization has given rise to a renewed skepticism towards documentary media in the conventional sense: photographs and film footages that traditionally have laid claim to representing reality through an indexical connection towards their subjects now face mass-awareness of their malleability by means of editing software. The problematic status of camera-made images as evidence is of course not a new insight; for decades, scholarship on visual culture has argued against a naïve conception of photography as a "window upon reality" and all camera-made images have included selective, subjective, and often-times even manipulative aspects (Bourdieu, 1990; Sontag, 1977; Sturken & Cartwright, 2001; Tagg, 1988). But only with the advent of new digital technologies has this skepticism taken hold in larger audiences. Scholars like M. Rosler (2004) and F. Ritchin (2013) therefore even consider the current era to be *post-documentary* and/or *post-photographic*. In turn, as trust in camera-based documentary media has waned, to certain niche-readerships comics has become more and more accepted as a means to represent reality (Chute, 2016; Mickwitz, 2016; Vanderbeke, 2010). Hand drawn images on a printed page can be thought of as a countermovement towards digitalization and the comic book, including graphic novels, caters to an interest in manifest artifacts that visibly bear traces of their creators. Documentary webcomics, now, continue to employ hand drawing and the attached connotations, yet change the way these comics are delivered; they close the circle by bringing documentation through hand drawings back into the digital sphere. These comics employ the affordances of digital environments for the publication of nonfiction graphic narratives that report on events and occurrences in the real world and encompass both the skepticism and new possibilities that the advent of the digital age entails. They react to the crisis of representing reality by choosing the medium of comics, specifically webcomics, which allows for different forms of production and distribution. Documentary webcomics react to the historical changes of digitalization, its media skepticism but also its new possibilities, and thus aspire to become a form of *alternative media* (Atton, 2006; Mattoni, 2016) as this essay will outline. To delineate them as a medial phenomenon, the mediality of webcomics, the contexts that they are published in, and how they are thusly framed will be described.

Comics as Documentary

As pointed out above, the digital age has raised widespread concern towards the capacity of media to represent the world truthfully. The following essays will explore the sociopolitical and media-historic of digitalization and describe the position of comics as a hand drawn medium within this context.

Post-Truth Politics and Digital Evidence

While the term *post-truth* was coined somewhat earlier (Keyes, 2004), in the context of recent elections it has become especially prominent. In a widely noted 2016 article, *The Economist* describes post-truth politics, especially with regard to Donald Trump, as "assertions that 'feel true' but have no basis in fact" (The Economist, 2016, para. 2). While lies certainly do not constitute a new phenomenon in politics or the media, post-truth demarcates the phenomenon "that truth is not falsified, or contested, but of secondary importance" (The Economist, 2016, para. 5). While lies and deception have consistently been part of political discourse, "what seems new in the post-truth era is a challenge not just to the idea on *knowing* reality but to the existence of reality itself" (McIntyre, 2018, p. 10). *The Economist* attributes this development partly to digitalization and "the fragmentation of news sources," (para. 9) but also to a well-intentioned pursuit of fairness in journalism that may bolster dubious voices and to a larger democratic spirit of questioning institutions. The waning of belief in the truth-telling through camera-based media certainly augments this phenomenon. As outlined above, a tradition of postmodern deconstructions of photography has in recent decades converged with a new understanding of malleability of digital image and video files. As photographs have largely ventured into the digital sphere their evidential capacity is, hence, questioned even more forcefully. Ricciardelli (2015) even asks whether "digital images [can] be used to 'reveal' truths about reality, or rather the concept of digital evidence sounds like an oxymoron" (p. 54).

But while the idea of *digital evidence* raises skepticism towards established media institutions and companies, amateur content that documents events of public interest becomes increasingly influential and a major driving force of public perception, with consequences that both strengthen and undermine belief in the veracity of images. As "the average person [has] gained more power to affect social discourse ... digital media have also blurred the distinction between author and user, knowing subject and object known" (Ricciardelli, 2015, p. 51). One phenomenon that follows from this development is the rise of so-called "citizen-journalism" (Ritchin, 2013, p. 28). As Ritchin writes, "the very subjectivity of nonprofessionals, their transparent self-involvement and lack of financial incentive, can be reassuring—many viewers may empathize with the motivations of these ordinary citizens, which are possibly similar to their own" (p. 11). While in relation to photography, amateurishness was not a hindrance regarding its veracity even in analog times (cf. Bourdieu, 1990); the Internet has provided distribution channels that grant access to vast archives of supposedly evidential photographs. At the same time, this form of distribution unfortunately also allows for the rapid spread of faked images that receive the same form of authentication, blurring the boundaries between what is by professional journalistic standards objective, what provides the subjectivity of the amateur as authentication, and what is purposefully misrepresented. But so far in the discussion of whether digital images can constitute evidence, only camera-made images are taken into account.

From Digital to Drawn—and Back

Webcomics display a vastly different approach to providing evidence online—but although they generally do not exhibit amateurishness, subjectivity is their central element. In contrast to digital photography, which may generate evidence instantly by pressing the button of the omnipresent smartphone camera, comics as a craft demands practice and commitment and is therefore time-consuming to learn as well as to carry out. Producing comics with pen on paper or on a graphics tablet clearly entails a mode of production that is entirely different from technologies, which create instantaneous digital images. As a vessel for documentary, the medium of comics indeed, "challenge[s] the tacit assumption that a documentary mode of address is dependent on recording technologies" (Mickwitz, 2016, p. 31). While, as Bruzzi (2006) claims, documentary per se entails "a perpetual negotiation between the real event and its representation" (p. 13), and the constructedness and self-reflexivity of comics pushes this negotiation to the forefront. Comics as a decidedly subjective and self-reflexive medium shifts the burden of authentication from the image itself to its producer who inscribes her or himself so visibly in the graphic style of the work (cf. El Refaie, 2012). Furthermore, in contrast to photographs which put forth evidential claims, "[c]omics texts … eliminate the question of 'staging' entirely: they are evidently staged, built, made images as opposed to 'taken' ones" (Chute, 2016, p. 21). Thus, in an environment of constant perceptual overload through digital photographs that may or may not be manipulated, comics present a form of documentary that authenticates its claims by the medially inherent disclosure of its limitations. Hatfield (2005) calls this strategy "ironic authentication," which he defines as "the implicit reinforcement of truth claims through their explicit rejection" (p. 125). This authorial gesture thus serves to consolidate trust in him or her as a person and less so in the text itself.

The Comics Reportage: Documentary or Journalism?

While nonfiction comics are still primarily defined by the immense success of graphic memoirs starting from the 1970s, they somewhat later also turned towards reportage and documentary, with the pioneering work of Joe Sacco in the 1990s. In recent decades, a more diversified body of documentary comics has been produced, including Guy Delisle, author of *Pyongyang: A Journey in North Korea* (2007) and the recent *Hostage* (2017); Josh Neufeld, author of *A.D.: New Orleans After the Deluge* (2010); and Sarah Glidden, author of *How to Understand Israel in 60 Days or Less* (2011) and *Rolling Blackout: Dispatches from Turkey, Syria, and Iraq* (2016a). In contrast to graphic memoirs, these comic reportages do not focus on the author's own life but rather seek to represent the experiences of others. Specifically, these authors travel into regions of crisis with the agenda to give voice and visibility to those whose plight has been overlooked by the mainstream media.

This genre has been addressed as *graphic journalism* or *comics journalism* as popularized by Joe Sacco (cf. 2012) and echoed by others (e.g., Vanderbeke, 2010; Weber & Rall, 2017). Yet, as Woo (2010) convincingly argues, the term "journalism," if narrowly defined, is somewhat misleading since these comic books work differently from news journalism. The authors have not been hired by news organizations, and instead their works are released through comic book publishers—a quite different institutional background. Furthermore, comic books can hardly lay claim to delivering "news" as comic books are notoriously slow to produce, both the manuscript as well as the printed book (Mickwitz, 2016; Woo 2010). Additionally, the ideal of objectivity that is central to news journalism does not sit well with the very subjectivity that comics entails. Documentary, in turn, as Nichols (2001) claims, "may represent the world in the same way a lawyer may represent a client's interests: they put the case for a particular view or interpretation of evidence before us" (pp. 3–4). Thus, rather than stating the facts in an overtly balanced manner as a news report ideally would, "they more actively make a case or argument; they assert what the nature of a matter is to win consent or influence opinion" (pp. 3–4). Accordingly, documentarians privilege the document and their "responsibility is to society," whereas "for journalists ... the most crucial thing is to protect the professional status of the practitioners and the practice itself through the establishment of 'objectivity'" (Rosler, 2004, p. 226).

Of course, this narrow definition of journalism is fixated on news reporting, to which comics and other subjective forms, as outlined above, are somewhat incompatible. Also, it has to be taken into account that most authors and publishers in this field explicitly call their work comics journalism. The notion of objectivity presents an ideal that in reality is often thwarted and, in addition, journalism encompasses explicit opinion pieces that include personal commentary. In this sense, comic images complicate this notion regarding their potential to be objective yet might serve as opinion pieces. After all, in graphic narrative the exclusion of personal opinion is hardly conceivable. Nevertheless, the works subsumed under the label of documentary comics certainly do not just present personal opinion but rather detailed accounts of actual occurrences as well as their implications and causes—and their focus is oftentimes on the experiences of the people encountered. Discussing the difference between photojournalism and documentary photography,

Rosler (2004) acknowledges that the same photograph may in reality function both in journalistic and documentary context. In contrast to photographic practices, though, the intention of most authors of comic reportages does not seem to be to supplement other forms of reporting, but rather to offer an alternative on several levels. Still, portions of their work might be published by newspapers and others as books. Authors of documentary comics oftentimes apply journalistic practices in their information gathering and fact checking. Therefore, their work could be subsumed as journalism—if very broadly defined, which might include all practices of methodical and at least semi-professional mediated transmission of information that relates to events and occurrences in the real world. Yet, the more precise term for book-length comics that present personally motivated factual accounts of actual events, which seek to present observations and testimonies and therefore exceed the scope of mere opinion pieces, is documentary. Below in this essay this discussion will be continued with specific regard to the publication contexts of webcomics.

Comics in Digital Contexts

Documentary webcomics, in the next step, need to be differentiated from other forms of digital comics and be described with regard to their specific mediality. Chute (2016) stresses that documentary comics as "a visual-verbal narrative documentary form" is "significantly … also a print form" (p. 14). Accordingly, Chute discusses comic books specifically as a means of "materializing history" through the marks on the page, which "gives it a corporeality, a physical shape…" (p. 27). The materiality of the printed book as a manifest artifact, indeed, serves as another instance of authentication with the publishing house as gatekeeper and social prestige attached to it. Likewise, the publication of documentary comic books presents an obvious counter-movement to the flood of digital images, privileging the anachronism of the slower form. So, what do documentary comics gain by being published as "pure information," as McCloud (2000, p. 203) would have it? Before this question can be answered, though, further aspects that characterize webcomics have to be taken into account.

Towards a Definition of Webcomics

Comics themselves are quite hard to define (Groensteen, 2007; Hatfield, 2005) and, unsurprisingly, so are webcomics. In the perhaps most basic definition, "Web comics are comics (primarily) published on and distributed through the Internet" (Kukkonen, 2014, p. 521). Fenty, Houp, and Taylor

(2004) even exclude those works that have an "originary print version" (p. 6). Dittmar (2012), furthermore, differentiates between "webcomics" and "digital comics" (p. 85), which are not read online but to be downloaded—both of course sharing the aspect of being read on various digital screens. Besides distribution online, the question arises whether webcomics include inherent medial qualities, specific to their digital makeup, such as interactivity or hypertextuality. As Kukkonen (2014) describes, "some, but by far not all, of these comics make use of the affordances of digitalization." (p. 521) Yet there is, as Mickwitz (2016) describes, a certain expectation being raised. She writes:

> Often, the suggestion is that a webcomic can, and should, involve an increased inter-active and participatory experience…. Certainly, there is a sense of expectation that "new" media platforms not only offer, but demand, an emphasis on innovation. To merely transcribe, store, and circulate print-based comics, or digitally create comics that for all intents and purposes look and work much like their print counterparts, falls short of the promise and potential of comics in a digital environment [p. 148].

Kirchoff (2013), for instance, warns that "producing digital comics that reprint print comics limit the potential and future of digital comics and as such … may become a 'retro' technology" (p. 25)—one that becomes increasingly irrelevant to society. Other scholars still stress the "new possibilities" for storytelling that digital environments enable (Dittmar, 2012; Kukkonen 2014). One of the central arguments appears to be that webcomics that simply emulate the print form "lose" something of the original experience (Kichoff, 2013, p. 10) and therefore need to employ their own unique medial assets to become or remain relevant.

Webcomics, Hypercomics and Interactive Documentary

Most documentary webcomics are fairly close to print comics and seldom engage in experiments in digital storytelling. Therefore, it seems appropriate to differentiate them from "interactive documentaries" that are built around the aspect of user agency and let the user navigate to some extent freely through hypertext or three-dimensional environments (Gaudenzi, 2014). Indeed, some comics artists also produce interactive documentaries, perhaps most prominently Dan Archer who created works like *The Nisoor Square Shooting* (2011) and *Ferguson Firsthand* (2015), which let users explore the depicted events in a nonlinear fashion and, in the case of the latter, even include virtual reality environments (see Mickwitz, 2016; Schlichting, 2016). Whereas these works do integrate comics as one mode of documentation, they are vastly different from the majority of documentary webcomics and demand research of their own. Mickwitz (2016), following Goodbrey, therefore differentiates between "webcomics" and "hypercomics," which "enable enhanced interactivity, choice, and multiple narrative paths by means that are specific to their digital form" (p. 148). While there is certainly overlap between these categories, documentary webcomics have become a format of its own—one that is decidedly close to print comics in that it seldom employs inherent interactive or nonlinear elements.

The Page, the Screen and Comics Framing

Many conventional practices of graphic storytelling are predefined by the affordances of the book or other printed artifacts in that the panel frames have to be arranged within the specific material units (Dittmar, 2012). Documentary comics, therefore, are set apart from other forms of documentary by presenting its reportages in the comics grid instead of the continuous flow of moving images or the distinctness of the photograph. As Chute (2016) writes, "Comics makes a reader access the unfolding of evidence in the movement of its basic grammar, by aggregating and accumulating frames of information" (p. 2). Groensteen (2007), respectively, conceives of comics as a "multiframe" in which the individual panels and pages as lower order frames are arranged, interlock, and create interdependent meaning. Contrary to paintings or photographs, the comic panel is not "unique and global" but instead part of a larger "system of proliferation" (p. 5). Therefore, readers experience the panels on the page as spatially co-present, and each moment of the story that is framed within the panel is thus constantly framed and reframed within this system as the reader progresses through the narrative. Readers thus constantly revisit and reevaluate the information presented to them, being able to take their own time in the reading process.

Webcomics Frames

While in comic books the page is one of the most important instances of framing, termed "hyperframe" by Groensteen (2007, p. 34), webcomics according to the same author (2013), "are characterized by the removal of content from a surrounding context [so] when a comic is read on the screen, as each page succeeds the next it also replaces and effaces it, precluding the mental retention of the arrangement of panels" (p. 67). What this statement overlooks, though, is the fact that websites or "web-pages," too, include a system of frames that like book or magazine pages organizes content and assigns functions to specific designated areas on the screen—both facilitate spatial composition and layout (Bateman, Wildfeuer, & Hippala, 2017; Kress & van Leeuwen, 2006). Furthermore, webcomics oftentimes do not break up the system of proliferation into single panels, but either purposefully create page-like units of their own that correspond to Groensteen's hyperframe or let users scroll through a continuous layout that McCloud (2000) has labeled "infinite canvas" (p. 222). In any case, the co-present elements of a website that frame the webcomic have to be taken into account as carrying semantic weight. In this manner, these website elements are similar to the *paratext* of printed, alphabetic literature (Genette, 1997). As Hickethier (2010) discusses, the hypertext structure of web pages produces a system of paratexts that, diverging from Genette's book-centered concept, relate to and frame different primary texts. Yet, they share the aspect that they provide distinctly pragmatic spaces that categorize and influence the reception of the main text.

It is, thus, imperative when addressing (documentary) webcomics to take the medium-specific system of proliferation into account as well as the surroundings of the website or platform that the comic is framed by. In this regard, it is also important to acknowledge that different devices, settings, and browsers may lead to different resolutions and screen sizes and affect the reading experience (Dittmar, 2012).

As part of these different possible contexts, various forms of interaction are possible, which leads Fenty, Houp, and Taylor (2004) to claim, "webcomics facilitate communication between readers and webcomic artists" (p. 19). While it is undoubtedly true that webcomics greatly simplify this sort of communication by employing systems to read and publish that in most cases enable communication with the authors, publishers, or other readers without switching devices, the interaction possibilities that websites integrate indeed do vary. While some websites, as shall be described below, incorporate forums and comment sections, others put much less emphasis on direct communication. For nonfiction comics stemming from a political impetus, possibilities of interaction with a community and functions to share and spread these comics comprise an asset that printed formats distinctly lack. Therefore, the digital affordances need to be taken into account not only regarding the comics per se but also the environments and platforms they are published on.

Documentary Webcomics as Short-Form

Another important factor would be the length, both in terms of the production and reception, of individual works. The difference between the print and the webcomic format is strikingly exemplified by the works of Sarah Glidden. Her book *Rolling Blackouts: Dispatches from Turkey, Syria, and Iraq* (2016a) describes events taking place in 2011—before the Syrian civil war and the rise of the IS militia—and was released after the country had descended into chaos. In contrast, the webcomic by Glidden called *Spoiler: On the Campaign Trail with Jill Stein* (2016b) posted August 8th 2016, which will be discussed in more detail below, portrays a candidate in the then ongoing United States presidential race, thus providing time-sensitive information towards readers eligible to vote in the U.S. Of course, *Rolling Blackouts* is a massive volume of over 300 pages, whereas *Spoiler...* is much shorter (even though it is considerably long for a webcomic). Mickwitz (2016) therefore describes documentary webcomics specifically as "short-form documentary webcomics" (p. 43), claiming

> a diverse body of documentary work that, when compared to the long-form work privileged by print publication according to a "graphic novel" model, can be differentiated as predominantly short-form webcomics. This shorter form also offers a sympathetic fit with practices of online reading, viewing, and browsing that tend to be characterized by shorter bursts of attention [p. 145].

Thus, not only does the shorter form cater to the more succinct publication process, but as Mickwitz points out, also to the reading habits online and the shorter attention span.

Documentary Webcomics: Genealogy and Medial Context

The following section will now explore underground comics as well as pre-digital alternative media traditions as predecessors of documentary webcomics. Furthermore, documentary will be contextualized as a countermovement to medial power structures.

Webcomics and the Underground

In one of the earlier scholarly articles on webcomics, Fenty, Houp, and Taylor (2004) delineate webcomics in the tradition of the underground comix movement that started in the United States in the 1960s. These comics introduced more radical content that was formerly repressed by the infamous Comic Code Authority, which was made possible by new means of distribution, namely selling self-printed "zines" and underground newspapers in headshops rather than the mainstream newsstands. By alleviating the pressure to make a comics publication financially viable for the mainstream public, this allowed topics and themes to be included that were aimed at a much smaller target audience. Fenty, Houp, and Taylor (2004) in this regard draw a parallel between underground comix and webcomics, which also include topics oftentimes originating from geek culture that "would have difficulty within the mainstream" (p. 5). Rather,

> The web allows webcomic creators to write comics with content which is outside of the acceptable bounds for typical mass-released comics. Not all of them would appeal to a wide audience, but there are a number of high quality webcomics on the internet that are produced for very specific and large, yet distributed audiences [p. 3].

The authors, therefore, attest the "ability to explore new possibilities in making comics" to webcomics that "are unhindered by the standard production costs associated with color and format, and the standard restrictions in terms of comics themes and narratives" (p. 22). Also, similarly to underground comix, these works introduce "an ethical dimension" (p. 22). All this applies, indeed, to documentary webcomics in particular; through webcomics, authors are able to report events that established print formats would not be able to, as production costs demand higher circulation volumes. As Mickwitz (2016) describes, documentary webcomics "offer a way of drawing attention to material and events that might be subject to summary of peremptory treatment, or outright ignored, in mainstream news reporting" (p. 146). Here, another link to underground comix can be found, whose "strongest and most consistent element … is the anti-authoritarian theme" (Duncan & Smith, 2009, p. 56).

Documentary Webcomics as Alternative Media

Coincidentally, in the same time-frame as underground comix, more diversified means of production and distribution gave rise to "alternative media" that were circulated in similar ways, such as DIY-zines (Atton, 2006). Run by activists meaning to create spaces that challenge the mainstream news media, "alternative media is a field of social interactions, communication, and mediation with an intrinsic transformative power directed toward the realms of media, society, and culture" (Mattoni, 2016, p. 221). Mattoni thus defines "alternative media" as

> channels of communication, existing in places, situations, and contexts different from the realm of mainstream and corporate media, which spread content opposed to the dominant system of meanings and whose creation is sustained through face-to-face interactions and/or computer-mediated communication among nonmedia professionals [p. 221].

Documentary webcomics oftentimes do precisely that; they employ the Internet to target audiences aside from the mainstream to influence public opinion and transform society, thus presenting an effort in media activism. In this sense, documentary webcomics publishers may seek to present themselves as legitimate alternatives to established news media.

Financing Dissent: The Question of Money

Before addressing the question of journalism once more, the question of corporate sponsorship that is included both in the labels "underground" and "alternative" needs to be discussed. Fenty, Houp, and Taylor (2004) claim outright that webcomics, per se, have "no corporate sponsorship" (p. 6). Kukkonen (2014) concurs that webcomics "are usually individual and nonprofessional efforts, and even though larger infrastructures exist, no web comics industry comparable to the print comics industry has emerged" (p. 521). Mickwitz (2016), at the same time, points out that webcomics have also been integrated into larger transmedia franchises and can thus "hardly be defined in terms of their intrinsic remoteness from corporate publication" (p. 145). While this point is undeniably true for fictional webcomics, documentary webcomics are largely characterized by this very resistance to overt commercialization. Still, with regard to project-based documentary webcomics that will be described in more detail below, cooperation with established media companies is not uncommon. The prime example would be O'Neill and Momtaz's (2016) project *Madaya Mom*, which was produced by ABC News and Marvel. Platform-based documentary webcomics at the same time make a specific effort to provide alternative channels.

Webcomics as Reportage: Documentary or Journalism?

At this point, the discussion of how "documentary comics" differ from "comics journalism" needs to be revisited. As we shall see below, some of the outlets discussed in this essay explicitly portray themselves as journalism and, indeed, webcomics may have more weight in their claim to journalism. Exchanging the printed page for the diverse screens of web-enabled devices with the accelerated production cycles this entails might then, of course, indicate capability to report actual news. While this notion appears tempting, it is nonetheless misleading. Even if webcomics are considerably "faster" than print comics, nevertheless, very few people will use them as a first source of information on current events—the sheer rapidity and omnipresence of commercial camera-based news reporting would indeed be hard to compare to. Documentary webcomics, rather, present a different angle on events that readers will already be familiar with and that are not "news" to them—or address topics that are either historical or outside the focus of mainstream media. The concept of documentary, furthermore, as described above, caters to the aspect of political activism and the challenging of pervasive narratives, already firmly entrenched through mainstream reporting. Documentary webcomics instead seek to provide evidence that counter these narratives—and certainly do so with much faster reaction time than print publication—but cannot assert to fulfill the function of actual news reporting. In this regard, for documentary comics platforms, the medium of comics poses limitations that separate them from mainstream media, even if to some extent they are alleviated through the digital form. Hence, documentary webcomics can be conceived as a form of *alternative* media in the sense of a counter effort but not a viable replacement.

In the following sections, these two primary channels for the distribution of documentary webcomics will be described in more detail regarding the framing of their presented comics and interactive functions that they put forward towards their readerships. Further possible categories could include the author's own websites or social media profiles. Webcomics, of course, are also commonly shared. Social networks such as Tumblr, Imgur, Reddit, and Facebook include a wide array of groups, sites, and individual users that re-post webcomics to share them with a community. What is more, interpersonal communication through messaging services enters the picture as well. These forms of distribution, too, demand further research of their own as a mode of reading comics. This essay will focus on the websites that post documentary webcomics as "original content." This is not to say, though, that these websites are the only, or even primary, location to read these comics. But for the sake of conciseness, these two categories shall be investigated as the most relevant examples of syndicated and professionalized efforts to publish a continuing stream of original documentary webcomics.

Platform-based Documentary Webcomics

The first category would be platform-based documentary webcomics, which are posted on quasi-professional publishing platforms such as Cartoon Movement (www.cartoonmovement.org), The Nib (www.thenib.com), or the now-defunct Symbolia Magazine (www.symboliamag.tumblr.com). These platform sites allow a large number of different authors from all around the world to submit their nonfiction comics or political cartoons. These then have to be approved and are curated by an editorial team. Mickwitz (2016) locates documentary webcomics specifically with these digital platforms—and indeed, they have a high output in publications and fast publication cycles. The Nib posts new content daily and Cartoon Movement "at least 4 times a week" according to their FAQ (VJ Movement, 2010). Publishing platforms very straightforwardly aim to establish themselves as alternative media institutions and distinctly present themselves as professional (Mickwitz, 2016). Both platforms portray themselves strongly as journalism, which exhibits a drive to address current events but also a demand to be taken seriously as a professional media outlet. Most pieces published, though, that address events in the news cycle are cartoons that are very short in length and present opinion and commentary, rather than background information. In the next sections, both The Nib and Cartoon Movement shall be described in more detail.

The Nib

The Nib is part of the company First Look Media (firstlook.media) sporting the slogan "We Will Not Be Silent" and the describing itself as "We embrace the agents of change—the journalists who hold the powerful accountable…." Besides The Nib, First Look Media's portfolio includes the investigative journalism website The Intercept (theintercept.com), co-founded by Glenn Greenwald and which focuses on "fearless, adversarial journalism" (The Intercept, n.d.), the entertainment studio Topic (topic.com), and the documentary film site Field of Vision (fieldofvision.org) that "produce[s] cinematic work that tells the stories of our world from new perspectives" (First Look Media, 2013). Their entertainment business, according to their website, supports their nonprofit journalistic efforts. The Nib describes itself as follows: "We run political cartoons, journalism, essays and memoir about what is going down in the world, all in comics form, the best medium" (First Look Media, n.d.).

The proclamation that comics is "the best medium" (First Look Media, n.d.) is reflected in their website presentation, as well. The comics themselves are presented infinite canvas-style with almost no additional framing. On the right side of the comics, a foldout-navigation is placed and on the left side, the user finds a bar with the options to share on Facebook, Twitter, via E-Mail, or to copy the link. This bar is the most prominent of the already very few paratextual elements that frame the comics, thus emphasizing that readers are urged to spread the story. Below the comics this bar is repeated, followed by a field to sign up for their newsletter, paired with the slogan "Rise and Shine. The World is Doomed. The Nib, delivered to your inbox every a.m." (First Look Media, n.d.). Together with the claim that comics is "the best medium," a slogan like this can also be understood as a nod towards alternative audiences and away from professionalism. The Nib thus balances both the claim to be a professional media institution and the trust attached to it with an alternative edge and a specific activist political outlook.

Below the user can scroll to further comics and a link to a webshop (topatoco.com/collections/the-nib) that, for instance, sells stickers that attack Donald Trump. Furthermore, the website contains an "Authors" section (First Look Media, n.d.) in which all contributors are listed with individual pages dedicated to them. These include links to their web appearances and to the cartoons and comics they have published on The Nib. There is significantly no comment-section, forum, or other dialogical set-ups; rather, the reduced layout emphasizes the comics themselves, as well as on their distribution via social media by the readership. The array of comics published can, of course, not be comprehensively described in the scope of this essay. Most documentary comics published on the platform that exceed the length of very short cartoons, still qualify as what Mickwitz (2016) labels "short-form," as though they vary in length, never coming close to book-length, and serial formats do not seem to play a major role. Furthermore, as part of this survey, I have neither come across integration of further media, such as photographs, animations, or video, nor interactive elements. The Nib, therefore, appears to take its comics machismo seriously and caters to an audience that seeks to read nonfiction comics and cartoons, which are clearly politically motivated and seek to establish an alternative to and question the medial mainstream.

SPOILER: ON THE CAMPAIGN TRAIL WITH JILL STEIN

Sarah Glidden's *Spoiler: On the Campaign Trail with Jill Stein* (2016b) may serve as an example of The Nib's approach and its aspiration. This piece is somewhat longer than the average comics on The Nib, but it adheres to the norm on the platform in that it does not include any inherent elements that make use of digital affordance, save for the infinite canvas. But content-wise the difference to a printed format might, of course, be the relation to the then ongoing election and the temporarily limited in the person Jill Stein. In an interview with the *Washington Post*, The Nib-editor Matt Boers claims that the piece was intended to resemble "a good magazine profile" and show that they do "ambitious journalism" that "can stand next to work from 'words people'" (Cavna, 2016). In this quote, the aspiration to journalism that the platform harbors becomes clear once more. Yet, the comic described here also shows the limits of what the platform can do. Sarah Glidden travelled for several months around the country with Jill Stein, who according to Boers then had "very little press coverage" (Cavna, 2016). To date, this effort towards a single piece remains extraordinary and also the intention to influence political discourse is clear here. The Nib chose and had to choose just one candidate to report on in such detail, instead of, if only for the sake of objectivity, presenting an overview of different candidates. The ambition to journalism can in this regard also be conceived of as an authentication strategy, yet the piece shows that The Nib does not present comprehensive information on the presidential race, but only particular aspects of it. The social prestige of comics alone, one may speculate, might prevent a comics reporter from gaining such intimate access to the mainstream candidates.

Glidden created reportage about her time with Stein that employs a highly subjective approach to Stein as a person and includes Glidden's own feelings towards her. Large parts of the comics consist of interviews with Stein, her supporters, as well as potential voters. Many of the people are drawn in upper body frames, popular from television interviews. This approach entails that Glidden draws a large variety of portraits of Stein, showing here from different angles and exhibiting a range of feelings, from determined to angry and also worried. Glidden also includes renditions from campaign artifacts such as buttons, one of them prominently displayed as the opening panel. After the reportage on the campaign trail ends, Glidden takes some space to document the workings of U.S. voting system and interrogates its fairness. Thus, the comic not only serves to portray Jill Stein but also to educate and make a point about a larger political mechanism. The comic ends with a final three-panel column in which Glidden talks to her "progressive friends" about Jill Stein: "[T]hey say that they like her ideas ... but just not right now. Not this election." Glidden then concludes,

> Many of us ARE voting against the candidate we fear the most, rather than the one we most agree with.... Maybe if we had a system that allowed smaller parties and other voices to participate more fully, we wouldn't have gotten to this point in the first place [Glidden, 2016b].

This conversation of her with two female friends, one of them holding an infant child, frames and thus finally evaluates what she documented on the campaign trail. The "us" that Glidden writes seems to include average voters from her social circle that would potentially encompass the implied reader as well, thus suggesting that "normal people" like Stein's ideas but would not vote for her. Hence, the piece does not comprise an active endorsement but rather a documentation of an underreported campaign. At the same time, Glidden makes no secret out of her own subjective position towards the issue; ending with the opinions of her personal friends as stand-in for the larger public blurs the distinction between occupation and private sphere and clearly marks the piece as a documentary effort that is overtly based on Glidden's personal convictions.

The choice of an anti-establishment candidate to profile certainly exhibits The Nib's effort to counter mainstream reporting. Also, comics as a vessel for reportage certainly mirrors the unconventional ideas that Stein proposes, yet the piece itself also shows the platform's ambition to professionalism and the attached authenticity.

Cartoon Movement

Cartoon Movement, too, posts cartoons and comics, but involves a quite different layout. Here, the comics are presented as "pages" of various sizes within the surrounding website frame with the navigation visible at all times, and the reader has to click on the page to move forward. The top banner of the website includes, besides the navigation, the claim of being "The Internet's #1 publishing platform for high quality political cartoons and comics journalism" as well as the website logo containing the slogan "There is more than one truth" (VJ Movement, 2010). This slogan aligns with the name that presents the organization as a movement in that it positions itself against a prospective commonly accepted mainstream truth. The motto is shared with its mother organization, the non-profit Video Journalism Movement, "an organization dedicated to the promotion of video journalism and press freedom" (VJ Movement, 2010). As a business model, Cartoon Movement licenses their publication to other media outlets, offers "on demand cartoons" (VJ Movement, 2010) and also includes a web shop that sells licenses to their content, as well as t-shirts with the cartoons printed on them (cartoonmovement.shop). The comics themselves all include a comment section in which the readership indeed has the chance to get in touch with the cartoonists. While Cartoon Movement also includes social media functions, the emphasis here is much more on interaction within its online community. In their own words, "for the community" they, accordingly, claim to "offer a platform where you can discuss cartoons, and vote on the cartoon ideas submitted by our international network of professional editorial cartoonists" (VJ Movement, 2010). In their Newsroom section, users can vote four times per week regarding which cartoons should be published. As Cartoon Movement publishes the work of a large number of authors, the styles are fairly different. Like on The Nib, most comics are created in a style resembling print-publications. There are exceptions, like the above-mentioned *The Nisoor Square Shootings* (2011) by Dan Archer, which is labeled here as "Interactive Comic." Yet, the vast majority of published comics are only interactive in terms of the community functions that the platform offers.

THE WAITING ROOM

Another work by Sarah Glidden, *The Waiting Room* (2011), shall serve to compare both platforms. The work stems from the same trip to Syria as her later Book *Rolling Blackouts* (2016a), in which its creation is briefly mentioned as well as Glidden's "first piece of comics journalism" (2016a, p. 297). Besides the paratextual elements already described above, the piece features a short additional text, which introduces the piece:

> Syria is home to the world's largest urban refugee population; hundreds of thousands of Iraqis have poured in since the 2003 invasion. Barred from joining the Syrian workforce, they attempt to navigate bureaucratic hurdles and find a new place to call home. Sarah Glidden, with contributing reporting from the Common Language Project, gives us a window into their lives [2011].

"The Waiting Room" could, thus, be described as an early ultra-condensed version of the 300 pages long *Rolling Blackouts*. Both works tell the stories of Iraqi refugees in the then stable Syria, using their example to make more general statements about refugees. "The Waiting Room" is told through a frame story of an 18-year-old Iraqi girl waiting in line for food in the waiting room of the United Nations refugee center in Douma, Syria. Several Iraqi refugees are introduced with their occupational backgrounds as examples that counter stereotypes evoked by the term "refugee," as well as aid and charity works that also appear in the book. Besides the personal stories, Glidden includes several maps and statistics that add background information. While the information portrayed in this comic is dated regarding the situation of the particular people portrayed, Glidden seeks to make a more general point about the nature of being a refugee, which is arguably an enduring aspect of human history. The drawing style in this early piece of hers is more abstract than in her later work, which makes the characters encountered less specific and leaves the potential for readerly projection.

Additionally, the promise of interaction is, to an extent, fulfilled in this case, as Glidden answers a reader's question about her work routine in the comment section. The comments, though, were all posted throughout the year 2011, which may serve as indicator of the attention span that the work received. Interestingly, Glidden posted the comic on her personal website as well a year later. Here, she published it all vertically on one page. While the canvas in this case is not exactly infinite, as one can clearly see the borders of the individual images, the reading experience is more continuous and less contained to single hyperframe units.

Platforms Between Activism
and Professionalism

Both publishing platforms clearly seek to establish themselves as media alternatives to the mainstream, but also emphasize professionalism in their works and generate a form of income through merchandise or licensing or are part of a larger business. As such, they differ considerably from the underground comix, which harnessed an explicit anti-establishment DIY-aesthetic. Nonetheless, they share the approach to publish comics aside the mainstream, only less anarchic and more oriented towards presenting credible sources of information for particular audiences. The claim to be journalistic outlets can be understood as an effort to authenticate their works and to substantiate their will to be taken as legitimate alternatives. At the same time, their reach is limited, and the medium of comics appears more suited to complement and challenge conventional reportage than to replace it. This is also mirrored in their mottos: challenging the existence of absolute truth as means of authentication or ironic comments on the world being doomed present both platforms clearly as anti-establishment efforts. As such, political activism appears to be central driving force behind documentary webcomics platforms.

Project-based Documentary Webcomics

While documentary comics platforms indeed publish the vast majority of content, another form should also not be overlooked, which I shall call "project-based." These comics generally involve a fixed team of creators in a likely temporarily limited project and are often transmedial. Accordingly, far less individual works are created in this category, although they may reach larger and possibly altogether different readerships. While both of these forms similarly publish comics online to address real events and encounters, they make use of the affordances of their digital environments differently, address other target readerships, and are framed through their specific environments. These projects all entail cooperation with conventional news media and thus comprise a transitory phenomenon between alternative and mainstream. As such, they make use of digital affordance differently in order to cater to other readerships. In the following pages, the website Positive Negatives (positivenegatives.org), as well as the online article "The Road to Germany: \$2400" (Malek, van Agtmael & Neufeld, 2016) by the magazine *Foreign Policy* (foreignpolicy.com), which includes a comic sub-section by Josh Neufeld entitled "The Wanderings," will be described in more detail.

Positive Negatives

Positive Negatives is a nonprofit organization that in their own words "produce[s] literary comics, animations and podcasts about contemporary social and human rights issues. We combine ethnographic research with illustration and photography, adapting personal testimonies into art, education and advocacy materials" (Positive Negatives, 2012). Working with a staff of seven artists, they have produced 13 comics since 2012. While the project is transmedial, it has a clear focus on comics, which is also the medium directly available in its navigation bar. In the comics section, the reader is presented with a text field headlining the actual comics, which reads:

> Comic books are a familiar medium throughout the world. Telling stories principally through pictures, they are instantly comprehensible and usually associated with humorous stories for children. However, comics have a repertoire of expression equal to cinema and there is an expanding genre of comic-book literature, autobiography and journalism intended for adult readership [Positive Negatives, 2012].

This gentle introduction to the medium of comics appears to be aimed at readerships unfamiliar with graphic narrative—providing a stark contrast to The Nib's statement.

Their most recent publication is the trilogy *A Perilous Journey* (Positive Negatives, 2015), which is comprised of three individual stories by Syrian refugees—Hasko, Khalid, and Mohammad—and was also published by the British *The Guardian* and Norwegian *Aftenposten*, as well as exhibited by the Nobel Peace Center. The website lists 21 sponsors and collaborators in total. Besides the three comics, *A Perilous Journey*, like other *PositiveNegatives.org* publications, includes animations for each story, as well as translations of the stories, and a "Resourses"-section (Positive Negatives, 2015) where several links to articles, media outlets, and NGOs are listed that provide further background information relevant to the stories. The animations are video clips that are around 30 seconds long and feature either animated effects on the comics images or Ken Burns–style panning and zooming within these. Importantly, they are underscored with naturalistic soundscapes that add an effect of realism to the drawn images. The content by Positive Negatives is framed only by the navigation menu on top, which includes social media functions. The comics then are presented in simulated page-segments that contain panels in a white rectangular on the black backgrounds. Thus, units analogous to the hyperframe of the print page are created, yet the reader can scroll through these pages seamlessly. The graphic style is once again adherent to print comics and each story features a photograph at its end. The stories, on the one hand, identify the protagonists only by the first name and thus protect their identity and also leave the potential to read them as a stand-in for refugees in general. The photographs, on the other hand, call to mind that these stories belong to actual people. Still, only in one case does the photograph show the face of the person. One refugee, Mohammad, is shown as a headless upper body with his hands folded in a pleading motion with the caption underneath telling us that he is still waiting for the decision whether he'd be granted asylum.

Together with the comics that elaborate the stories, these photographs thus serve to authenticate but also to drive home the moral immediacy through the affective potential of photography (Schmid, 2016). Interestingly, the same stories as they are posted on the website of *The Guardian* (2015) are presented somewhat differently. Here, most of the non-diegetic text is adapted to the *Guardian* house font and the panels are presented as uninterrupted infinite canvas, similar to the regular *TheGuardian.co.uk* articles. Likewise, the comics are framed by page-like other articles, as well.

While the decision to alter the comics that way may have to do with the website structure, it appears likely that it may ease the transition to graphic narrative for those readers unfamiliar with comics. Thus, it can be stated that in the case of Positive Negatives, the documentary webcomics are aimed to tell stories that may not be able to tell visually in other media—primarily for the fear of reprisal that these refugees may face—but also to aim them at audiences that are not avid comics readers. It is significant that they include other media such as animation and photographs, albeit the latter being also a standard element in print comics (Schmid, 2016). Digital affordances are primarily employed here to provide an archive of information resources to educate readers but also to receive donations towards their educational charity "Why Comics?" that seeks to provide free comics materials to teachers and students (Positive Negatives, 2012). One exception, in this case, are the short webcomics that introduce the Methodology of the project. To describe the routines and procedures of the work involved, the comics uses single panels that, via clicking, circulate from right to left on the screen to the next panel. The last panel reads, "Then we start all over again" and the comic starts over again with the first panel creating a loop, thus adding a performative meta-element to the story (Positive Negatives, 2012).

The Road to Germany: $2400

Project-based documentary webcomics may also be singular endeavors. Josh Neufeld's contribution to "The Road to Germany: $2400" (Malek, van Agtmael & Neufeld, 2016) was published as a transmedial project of narrative journalism on the website of the magazine *Foreign Policy* (foreignpolicy.com) and the January/February issue of the print magazine as part of a reportage by writer Alia Malik and Magnum-photographer Peter van Agtmael. The article traces the journey of a group of Syrian refugees identified by their first name towards Germany during the height of the 2015 refugee crisis, which Malik and van Agtmael encountered in Greece. One subchapter of this article, labeled "The Wanderings," is then presented as comics and shows the part of the journey beginning with a boat voyage from Greece and ending with the group arriving in Frankfurt. As Neufeld and Malik explain in an interview podcast (Bricker, 2016) on the creation of the piece, Malik did not accompany the group through this part of the journey and their experiences were later told to her. She then retold the story to Neufeld, who subsequently created the comic. As the comic is framed by written accounts and the reader is familiar with the characters and setting, it starts in medias res. Neufeld claims that the comics enhance the potential for identification that the reader holds towards the characters in a story, and Malik states that she believes comics may generate renewed interest in the topic that readers are already well-informed about (Bricker, 2016). The comic itself contains units similar to print pages, but at the same time integrates photographs and animated GIFs within its panels. In this regard, the online version thus integrates further modes than the print article. The animated GIFs that show short loops constitute a very interesting example as they add a time-based element to the otherwise conventional comics layout—at the same time though they do not present a change of state inherently as they show only one short moment. Thus, their primary function seems to integrate more realistic moving images that serve to point out the nonfiction status without altering the process of comics storytelling. As interviewer Mindy Kay Bricker (2016) remarks, the photographs serve "to ground the reader, to remind the reader, this is, this is real" (14:49–14:53). Besides the aforementioned qualities of documentary comics, such as the potential for readerly identification and protection of the protagonists' identities, Malik explains that the actual persons whose experiences were portrayed are not literate in English and thus could not read the text, but were able to understand the comics (Bricker, 2016).

"The Road to Germany: $2400" exhibits webcomics' potential to become part of established journalistic publications. Accordingly, Rosler's (2004) above-cited suggestion that documentary photography may be reused in journalism, can be transferred to documentary webcomics or even documentary media in general, it appears. But it is certainly no coincidence that, akin to photographs, the comics here complement the written article rather than stand on its own. In addition, the comic makes use of webcomics' means by introducing GIFs as time-based elements, which appears to be a strategy to make the text more engaging and not necessarily to convey additional information.

Project-Based Documentary Webcomics as Bridge to Media Institutions

While documentary webcomics platforms are clearly aimed at readers familiar with comics, project-based documentary webcomics seek to reach audiences beyond comics enthusiasts, which also might explain the integration of and proximity to other media that serve to authenticate the documentary status of the comics. Finally, the collaboration with established media institutions shows that here it appears not to build an alternative media platform but rather to harness the educational potential of comics to raise awareness within a network of well-established media organizations and NGOs. To these organizations, comics may serve as a way to provide a different angle on and engage audiences with already reported topics. The aim of generating readerly engagement with challenging topics may also explain the integration of further modes such as animations, photographs, and moving images.

Often, these projects include further materials; for instance, the above-mentioned *Madaya Mom*-website provides a discussion plan for teachers including a behind the scenes-video clip (ABC News, 2016). Thus, clearly in this category of webcomics the educational potential of comics is highlighted.

Conclusion

As was shown throughout the essay, most documentary webcomics are close to the mediality of print comics and only occasionally make use of elements exclusive to digital media, such as animated GIFs. Rather, they embrace digital affordances that their online publications contexts facilitate: the rapid spread of the individual comics, participatory functions such as communication between readers and author or within communities of readers, and the possibility to hyperlink to other resources of information. The two categories presented in this essay—platform-based and project-based documentary webcomics—differ considerably in their focus among these functions. Platforms emphasize the spread of comics or the building of a community and appear to attest cultural capital to a form of comics close to print that is therefore hardly altered by digital possibilities. As such, platforms present themselves as alternative media that use comics as a channel that challenges conventional reporting and lays claim to being a legitimate alternate source of information. Documentary webcomics may indeed present a form of alternative media activism that is able to reach the public aside established medial power structures. However, the medium of comics poses natural limits to its reach and, also, it should not be overlooked that this format demands access to the Internet and digital reading devices (Dittmar, 2012). Documentary webcomics projects at the same time do not appear to involve contesting the power of established media but rather employ comics to raise awareness for specific issues and to cooperate with media houses. Here, especially the educational potential of comics, its novelty value and role as a gateway to further information are central.

Documentary webcomics, in general, exhibit a mediality that is not inherently interactive or nonlinear and thus differ from so-called interactive documentaries. Instead, comics decidedly appears to be employed as a counterpart to other digital imagery, while the use of digital affordances is mostly relegated to its medial contexts. Both for platforms and projects the very subjectivity of comics poses another challenge for their documentary effort. While the platforms seem to harness defiant confidence in the medium and embrace comics' subjectivity as means to generate multifaceted discourse, project-based documentary webcomics rely on other, more conventional documentary media for authentication as a safeguard.

As an outlook, a rise in the integration of interactive elements appears likely, especially for project-based documentary webcomics, while at the same time the format as it is established now ideally serves the purpose of the platforms to become alternative media targeting a media-conscious readership. While documentary webcomics, in general, cannot fulfill the function of news journalism and are far from being accepted as a vessel for reportage, it serves to challenge and interrogate conventional media practices and its power structures. It will be interesting to see how the further development of comics as a necessarily subjective medium will align with further sociopolitical developments with regard to Truth and commonly accepted facts. As it is, a slogan like "There is more than one truth" (VJ Movement, 2010) may fit well with the anti-establishment attitude of alternative media documentaries, yet it sounds strikingly similar to the phrase "alternative facts," expressed by U.S. Counselor to the President, Kellyanne Conway (cf. Blake, 2017). This showcases that in the post-truth era, similar logic may be used to challenge as well as to consolidate power and while deconstructive claims about truth and factuality, which are arguably inherent to comics, may serve to empower critical voices they may also be used to silence them. As comics will become more established as sources of information, discussions of how to balance objectivity and subjectivity, especially in the digital sphere with its immeasurable recontextualization processes, as well as strategies to facilitate transparency can only become more relevant. Documentary webcomics have the potential to address and reflect these dynamics and thus hold a mirror to the digitalized media landscape.

REFERENCES

ABC News (2016, Oct. 3). A teacher's guide for discussing "Madaya Mom" with students. Retrieved from http://abcnews.go.com/Politics/teachers-guide-discussing-madaya-mom-students/story?id=42419439.

Archer, D. (2011, Jun 20). The Nisoor Square shootings. *Cartoon Movement*. Retrieved from https://www.cartoonmovement.com/icomic/11.

Archer, D. (2015, Sep 29). Ferguson firsthand. *Archcomix*. Retrieved from http://www.archcomix.com/portfolio/ferguson-firsthand/.

Atton, C. (2006). *Alternative media*. London: Sage.

Bateman, J., Wildfeuer, J., & Hippala, T. (2017). *Multimodality: Foundations, research and analysis. A problem-oriented introduction*. Berlin: DeGruyter.

Blake, A. (2017, 22 Jan) Kellyanne Conway says Donald Trump's team has "alternative facts." Which pretty much says it all. *Washington Post*. Retrieved from https://www.washingtonpost.com/news/the-fix/wp/2017/01/22/kellyanne-conway-says-donald-trumps-team-has-alternate-facts-which-pretty-much-says-it-all/.

Bourdieu, P. (1990). *Photography: A middlebrow art*. Cambridge: Polity.

Bricker, M.K. (2016, Jan 29). The power of narrative comics [Audio podcast]. Retrieved from http://foreignpolicy.com/2016/01/29/the-power-of-narrative-comics/.

Bruzzi, S. (2006). *New documentary: A critical introduction*. (2nd Edition). London & New York: Routledge.

Cavna, M. (2016, Sep 16). Meet the man who is creating a space for longform journalism—In graphic novel form. *Washington Post*. Retrieved from https://www.washingtonpost.com/news/comic-riffs/wp/2016/09/16/meet-the-man-whos-creating-a-space-for-longform-journalism-in-graphic-novel-form/.

Chute, H. (2016). *Disaster drawn: Visual witness, comics, and documentary form*. Cambridge: Harvard University Press.

Curran, J. (2013). Global journalism: A case study of the Internet. In N. Couldry & J. Curran (Eds.), *Contesting media power: Institutions, politics, and culture* (pp. 227–42). Lanham, MD: Rowman & Littlefield.

Delisle, G. (2007). *Pyongyang: A journey in North Korea*. Montreal: Drawn & Quarterly.

Delisle, G. (2017). *Hostage*. London: Jonathan Cape.

Dittmar, J.F. (2012). Digital comics. *Scandinavian Journal of Comics Art 1*(2), 83–91.

Duncan, R., & Smith, M.J. (2009). *The power of comics: History, form and culture*. New York: Continuum.

The Economist. (2016, Sep 10). Art of the lie: Post-truth politics. Retrieved from https://www.economist.com/news/leaders/21706525-politicians-have-always-lied-does-it-matter-if-they-leave-truth-behind-entirely-art.

El Refaie, E. (2012). *Autobiographical comics*. Jackson: University Press of Mississippi.

Fenty, S., Houp, R., & Taylor, L. (2004). Webcomics: The influence and continuation of the comix revolution. *ImageTexT 1*(2). Retrieved from http://www.english.ufl.edu/imagetext/archives/v1_2/group/index.shtml.

First Look Media (n.d.). *The Nib*. Retrieved from https://thenib.com/about.

First Look Media (2013). *Field of vision*. Retrieved from https://firstlook.media/.

Gaudenzi, S. (2014). Interactive documentary. In M.L. Ryan, L. Emerson, & B.J. Robertson (Eds.), *The Johns Hopkins guide to digital media* (pp. 282–283). Baltimore: Johns Hopkins University Press.

Genette, G. (1997) *Paratexts: Thresholds of interpretation*. (J.E. Lewin, Transl.). Cambridge: Cambridge University Press.

Glidden, S. (2011, Apr. 13). The waiting room. *Cartoon movement*. Retrieved from https://www.cartoonmovement.com/comic/10.

Glidden, S. (2016a). *Rolling blackouts: Dispatches from Turkey, Syria, and Iraq*. Montreal: Drawn & Quarterly.

Glidden, S. (2016b, Aug 8). Spoiler: On the campaign trail with Jill Stein. *The Nib*. Retrieved from https://thenib.com/jill-stein-spoiler.

Groensteen, T. (2007). *System of comics*. Jackson: University Press of Mississippi.

Groensteen, T. (2013). *Comics and narration*. Jackson: University Press of Mississippi.

The Guardian (11 Nov. 2015). A perilous journey: Khalid's flight to Europe from Syria—An illustrated account. Retrieved from https://www.theguardian.com/world/ng-interactive/2015/nov/11/a-perilous-journey-khalids-story-syrian-refugee.

Hatfield, C. (2005). *Alternative comics: An emerging literature*. Jackson: University Press of Mississippi.

Hickethier, K. (2010). *Einführung in die medienwissenschaft*. Stuttgart & Weimar: Metzler.

The Intercept (n.d.). About the intercept. Retrieved from https://theintercept.com/about/.

Keyes, R. (2004). *The post-truth era: Dishonesty and deception in contemporary life*. New York: St. Martin's.

Kirchoff, J.S.J. (2013). It's just not the same as print (and it shouldn't be): Rethinking the possibilities of digital comics. *Technoculture 3*(1). Retrieved from http://tcjournal.org/drupal/print/vol3/kirchoff.

Kress, G., & T. van Leeuwen (2006). *Reading images: The grammar of visual design* (2d ed.). London: Routledge.

Kukkonen, K. (2014). Web comics. In M.L. Ryan, L. Emerson, & B.J. Robertson (Eds.), *The Johns Hopkins guide to digital media* (pp. 521–523). Baltimore: Johns Hopkins University Press.

Malek, A., P. van Agtmael & J. Neufeld (2016, Jan 29). The Road to Germany: $2400. *Foreign Policy*. Retrieved from http://foreignpolicy.com/2016/01/29/the-road-to-germany-2400-refugee-syria-migrant-germany-nonfiction-comic/.

Mattoni, A. (2016). Alternative media. In K. Fahlenbrach, M. Klimke, & J. Scharloth (Eds.), *Protest cultures: A companion* (pp. 221–227). New York: Berghahn.

McCloud, S. (2000). *Reinventing comics: The evolution of an art form*. New York: Morrow.

McIntyre, L.C. (2018). *Post-truth*. Cambridge: MIT Press.

Mickwitz, N. (2016). *Documentary comics. Graphic truth-telling in a skeptical age*. Basingstoke: Palgrave Macmillan.

Neufeld, J. (2010). *A.D.: New Orleans after the deluge*. New York: Pantheon.

Nichols, B. (2001). *Introduction to documentary*. Bloomington: Indiana University Press.

O'Neill, X., & R. Momtaz (2016). Madaya Mom: The story of one mother's unimaginable struggle for survival. Retrieved from http://abcnews.go.com/International/deepdive/madaya-mom-mother-struggle-survival-syria-civil-war-42362213.

Positive Negatives (2012). *Positive negatives*. Retrieved from http://positivenegatives.org/.

Positive Negatives (2015). A perilous journey. Retrieved from http://positivenegatives.org/comics/a-perilous-journey/a-perilous-journey-comics/.

Ricciardelli, L. (2015). *American documentary filmmaking in the digital age: Depictions of war in Burns, Moore, and Morris*. New York: Routledge.

Ritchin, F. (2010). *After photography*. New York: W.W. Norton & Co.

Ritchin, F. (2013). *Bending the frame. Photojournalism, documentary, and the citizen*. New York: Aperture.

Rosler, M. (2004). Post-documentary, post-photography? In M. Rosler (Ed.) *Decoys and disruptions: Selected writings, 1975–2001* (pp. 207–244). Cambridge: MIT Press.

Sacco, J. (2012). Preface: A manifesto anyone? In J. Sacco, *Journalism* (pp. xi–xiv). New York: Metropolitan.

Schlichting, L. (2016). Interactive graphic journalism. *VIEW: Journal of European Television History and Culture* 5(10). DOI: 10.18146/2213–0969.2016.jethc110.

Schmid, J.C.P. (2016). *Shooting pictures, drawing blood: The photographic image in the graphic war memoir.* Berlin: Bachmann.

Sontag S. (1977). *On photography.* New York: Farrar, Straus & Giroux.

Sturken M., & L. Cartwright (2001). *Practices of looking. An introduction to visual culture.* Oxford: Oxford University Press.

Tagg, J. (1988). *The burden of representation. Essays on photographies and histories.* Minneapolis: University of Minnesota Press.

Vanderbeke, D. (2010). In the art of the beholder: Comics as political journalism. In M. Berninger et al. (Eds.), *Comics as a nexus of cultures. Essays on the interplay of media, disciplines and international perspectives* (pp. 70–81). Jefferson, NC: McFarland.

VJ Movement (2010). Cartoon movement. Retrieved from https://www.cartoonmovement. com/.

Weber, W., & Rall, H.M. (2017). Authenticity in comics journalism. Visual strategies for reporting facts. *Journal of Comics and Graphic Novels.* DOI: 10.1080/21504857.2017. 1299020.

Woo, B. (2010). Reconsidering comics journalism: Information and experience in Joe Sacco's *Palestine.* In J. Goggin, & D. Hassler-Forest (Eds.), *The rise and reason of comics and graphic literature: Critical essays on the form* (pp. 166–77). Jefferson, NC: McFarland.

It Came from the Woods (Most Strange Things Do)

Emily Carroll's Through the Woods *and Interactive Internet Reading*

EDEN LEE LACKNER

Emily Carroll, Canadian artist and writer, has a penchant for taking her readers by the hand and leading them to the lip of dark forests, where she then pushes them beyond the trees to find their way through the nightmares that populate her woods. Carroll's texts reach back to the thematics found in the cruel fables collected by the Brothers Grimm, opting for chilling visions and bleak outcomes rather than the more comforting fairy tales found in works such as those by Hans Christian Andersen. Many of her narratives concern solitary journeys in the dark of night, sometimes voluntary, sometimes necessary, and always with horror right on the main character's heels.

A major component of this unsettling atmosphere is the way in which Carroll bends and shapes the reading experience to create a physical journey for her audience. The reader must visually traverse the path of the story even as he or she reads about Carroll's characters finding their way through their own pathways. Carroll invites the reader to become invested in these wanderings, as the visual act of textual consumption mimics the winding routes embedded in her narratives. She uses the trappings of the comic strip form in her favor, exploring ways in which bleeds, panel layouts and the page itself can be reimagined in digital form in order to reshape traditional conceptions of space and time in sequential art. Indeed, as Jerneja Petrič (2009) noted, comics require a visual literacy from their audiences, as they pair the written word with

> non-verbal language. Not just the right typeface and the size and the shape of the let-
> tering matter in a comic book or a graphic novel but also the panel shape and border
> ranging from straight to wavy edged to scalloped to jagged to no frame at all—each
> of the above used to convey sound, emotion of a character or the general atmosphere
> of the panel [p. 72].

Not only do Carroll's texts expect her readers to be adept in these visual, non-verbal languages, but they require readers to apply these techniques alongside active reading strategies that allow for a thorough immersion in her narratives via her words, illustrations, and formatting.

In this manner, Carroll's recent collection of illustrated stories, *Through the Woods* (2014), explores the boundaries of format and panel placement in order to expand her settings beyond the strictures of the page. Dialogue spills from panel to panel in order to draw the reader seamlessly from scene to scene, and fully black pages serve as the night against which characters dig holes and climb down into them, the resultant tunnels existing as small, narrow, solitary illustrations against a wash of black. Carroll's website (emcarroll.com) takes this play with format one step further, as the looser structure of an internet page and expansive possibilities of scrolling and linking give her the space to create stories that are even more interactive and free-form, where the reader must decide what path to follow or physically shift the entire text, mimicking ascending and descending, walking and running alongside her protagonists.

The Page and Beyond

Despite the lack of boundaries imposed by print mediums—including the practicalities of page and book size, and the restrictions of a visual-only format that come with traditional paper printing—many web comics still adhere to the familiar layouts associated with printed comics. For many, this arrangement remains in step with newspaper strips, in which a series of panels sit side-by-side in one long row with little to no overlap between each one; for others, the larger length and breadth of a rectangular graphic novel page dictates the boundaries of each installment. For instance, Kate Beaton preserves this side-by-side, discrete panel arrangement in most of her *Hark! A Vagrant* strips (2006 to present), as did Emily Horne and Joey Comeau in *A Softer World* throughout the one thousand, two hundred and forty-eight comics that made up its run (2003–2015). Ryan Sohmer and Lar DeSouza's *Looking for Group* (2006 to present), and Angela Melick's *Wasted Talent* (2004–2016), however, adhere to the larger graphic novel page format, mixing side-by-side panels with splash pages, background bleeds, and gutter work. As Thierry Groensteen (2013) has noted,

Comics is an art of space and an art of time: these dimensions are indissociable. To the intrinsic tabularity of the images it adds, by a process of construction, both a linearity and a more encompassing tabularity, that of the page [p. 12].

Newspaper strip layouts are entirely a function of the boundaries of the page: they are beholden to the economy of space in stricter ways than the graphic novel or illustrated text. Scott McCloud contextualizes these strips in *Reinventing Comics* (2000), as they began as "a marriage of convenience with 20th century newspapers. Newspaper comics weren't so much an industry of their own as a craft within the industry—and not a very respected one at that, despite their high popularity" (p. 65). Although they grew more popular over time, they began as afterthoughts to the larger business of reporting newsworthy events, existing in a grudgingly ceded space, not permitted to spill over or move beyond their regimented page allotment.

Essentially, the newspaper strip began as a format subject to strictures that continue to affect the practicalities of page layout and printing format today, as "[t]he choice of a particular mode of composition may be imposed upon the artist, in conformity with a publisher's house style, for example, to ensure compatibility with other work in the same magazine or series" (Chavanne, 2015, pp. 120–121). Therefore, the panels must be self-contained in order to facilitate shifts in basic layout—whether from horizontal to vertical, or from a long, singular row of panels to multiple shorter rows—leading to a more equal relationship between form and content than the looser boundaries of fully illustrated pages or websites. Yet the economy of the newspaper strip paired with the traditional form of the joke—from the story framing through the process of telling to the punch line—also affords a familiar structure within which the web comic can operate. The compact, regular panel layout combined with an enjoyably predictable narrative structure thus appeals to an audience familiar with printed comics, shifting the printed page directly into a digitized format.

For those web-based artists whose work encompasses ongoing and extensive narratives, however, the graphic novel format offers a more expansive canvas. It is within the covers of an individual comic issue or graphic novel collection that an artist can vary panel size and number; deliberately choose horizontal, vertical, and diagonal panel layouts; play with borders and borderless images; overlap images; allow for text and illustration to bleed into the gutter; and take over full or half-pages with one panel. Indeed,

One of the most marked tendencies in recent comics production is the increased frequency of full-width panels, which could also be called "landscape panels," panels that extend across the whole page and so coincide with the strip. The next size up, the panel that occupies half a page, is also much in evidence. And there are numerous [French hard-cover] albums in which, every three or four pages, an oversized panel breaks up the rhythm of the layout, creating a small visual surprise, obviously intended to give extra pleasure to the reader [Groensteen, 2013, p. 45].

Modern graphic novels have increasingly moved away from what Groensteen (2013) termed "the orthogonal grid known as the *waffle-iron*" (p. 44), embracing instead a more organic and visually striking mixture of bordered and borderless panels. For many web artists, their websites become sites of digitalized graphic novels, porting over this play with form on virtual pages.

While the graphic novel form affords more of a chance for panels to be of a variety of sizes and shapes, to overlap and bleed one into the other, and otherwise move beyond a rigid set of standardized boxes, it is still bound by the dimensions of the page. This rigid adherence to the dimensions which exist in print by web-based artists speaks to the strong influence and importance of traditional publishing as the foundation of these visual media. Yet the internet affords a freedom from the stricture of the page, with the potential for illustrative stories to burst out from the confines of the panel to spread in all directions on a *web* page whose boundaries are limited only by scroll bars and computer resource-use. Scott McCloud, in *Reinventing Comics: The Evolution of an Art Form* (2000), articulated this progressive dissolution of paginated boundaries when he explained that

> the monitor which so often acts as a page—may also act as a window.... The page is an artifact of print, no more intrinsic to comics than staples or india ink. Once released from that box, some will take the shape of the box with them—but gradually, comics creators will stretch their limbs and start to explore the design opportunities of an infinite canvas [p. 222].

The "infinite canvas" exists as an outgrowth of previous size and space-regulated forms, allowing web artists to recreate or discard the page as best suits their texts.

Margot's Room

It is onto this expansive field that Carroll steps. Her web comics do not just push at the boundaries of the traditional page format; they go beyond pagination and explore panel layout and illustration by bending static two-dimensional space into a moving, active format that encourages personal investment by her readers. When readers click on the entry thumbnail on Carroll's website for *Margot's Room* (emcarroll.com), a horror story about the loss of a child and the end of a marriage, they are immediately taken to a black index page sporting a centered illustration of a bedroom spattered with blood and in major disarray. The edges of this solitary image are indistinct, and the blackness of the rest of the page pushes inward on the bedroom, as if the larger darkness of the web page stands in for the darkness looming just outside of what faint light illuminates the room. Rather than being bound by sharp panel borders, this image is instead framed by an ominous stanza, which reads,

> first he gave me flowers
> & second I made her a doll
>   But third he'd be gone for hours
> & fourth we hit a wall.
> LASTLY THERE WAS BLOOD, (rich & raw in the light of the moon)
>   I can't forget
>   I will always regret
>   what happened in
> MARGOT'S ROOM [Carroll, 2011]

While this poem hints at the larger narrative, Carroll does not provide any other instruction on how to go about reading the full piece. Unless the reader begins to move his or her cursor over the image, self-directing his or her exploration of the bedroom, he or she will not be aware that there is anything more to the story than the image and the poem. The active reader, however, is rewarded when the cursor changes to indicate the presence of links, and thus other pages. Still, *Margot's Room* is not structured as a linear tale. The poem provides the means through which the reader can decode a chronological order of events, but he or she must look for the referenced items in the image—such as "first he gave me flowers" requires that the reader find and click on the bouquet of roses hanging above the bed—in order to follow that "proper" progression. Given that Carroll provides links to all five of the events that make up the poem in this initial image, the reader is not bound by this order; in fact, for the first-time reader, it is even more probable that he or she will experience the events in random order, and thus experience the narrative in a more disorienting, visceral way. This disorientation feeds off of the digital format, as works that involve hypertextual engagement include a measure of self-direction. When explaining this intersection of hypertext and viewer, Daniel Merlin Goodbrey (2013) noted that these works

> are ergodic in nature, meaning that the reader's experience of the work will often be locally unique based on the specific pathway taken and choices made in navigating the comic. This process of navigation requires a non-trivial effort on behalf of the reader. Rather than simply turn the page to progress through the story, progression comes about as a consequence of intention, deliberate choice or inadvertent action on behalf of the reader [p. 2].

Indeed, by approaching *Margot's Room* out of traditional narrative order—in which the reader does not move through the events from the beginning, to the middle, and then on to the end—he or she experiences the story in a far more fragmentary manner. Events that occur towards the middle and the

first he gave me flowers
& second I made her a doll
But third he'd be gone for hours
& fourth we hit a wall.
LASTLY THERE WAS BLOOD, (rich & raw
in the light of the moon)
I can't forget
I will always regret

what happened in

MARGOT'S ROOM

end of the tale, such as the slow disintegration of the narrator's marriage and the death of her husband, may be experienced first, before the reader encounters the causes of these events. Carroll's writing takes advantage of the potential for disorganization within the narrative, as each section only obliquely refers to the events of the other parts. As a result, the reader traverses the narrative backwards, or out-of-order, if he or she does not use the poem on the index page as a guide. By creating a narrative with the potential for backtracking and disorganized reading, Carroll facilitates an experience which requires active decoding and reorganizing events by the reader, which is at once interactive and a mirror of the chaotic and jumbled ways in which the audience encounters other people's lives and narratives outside of fiction.

When read in the order the poem prescribes, however, *Margot's Room* not only takes advantage of the seemingly borderless layout afforded by the internet, but as the narrator explores the tragic circumstances of her marriage, Carroll pushes her layouts for each successive part further and further. "Part I: Flowers" begins with the narrator speaking to her future husband for the first time ever during her father's funeral. The two of them spend time talking of her father's long illness (which will later echo in their daughter's own illness), their own ideal funerals, and the flowers he wants any girls mourning his passing to wear in their hair. Here, however, *Margot's Room* picks up on the floral detail and the narrator closes out "Part I: Flowers" with, "But I wore flowers in my hair on our wedding day instead. And he promised he'd live forever. with me. he promised" (Carroll, 2011). In addition to the inversion inherent in the narrator wearing flowers during their wedding, rather than at his funeral, these last lines invoke the first strains of dread that will pervade the full narrative. The color palette also shifts quickly into russet oranges and red tones, already signaling the outcome of the story, but it is the long thin stretch of panels down the center of the webpage that pull the reader slowly down into the tale. Additionally, two thirds down the page is a panel that already hints at the ways in which the overall layout will begin to bleed and shift. Blurry around the edges, this red and white panel is streaked with ink which not only interrupts the background and obscures her husband's face, but creates a channel through which the seemingly endless blackness of the page's background floods past the panel's boundaries. While the characters remain fairly static—standing, sitting or embracing while leaning against a tree—the panels and color bleed take the place of motion and movement, pushing the reader quickly onwards through the narrative.

Each section of *Margot's Room* ends not with a link to the next chronological page, but with a link that simply reads, "return home." Clicking takes readers right back to the first page of the work, positioning them, once again,

Opposite: Figure 1: Margot's Room (Carroll, 2011).

on the index page, effectively returning them to the narrator's home and the scene of the crime-to-come. Carroll uses this simple click-and-return format to keep readers physically tethered to this singular moment in time even as they dart forward into the dark to read the next part of the narrative.

"Part II: Doll" frames the loss of the couple's daughter, Margot, to illness with visuals of the doll the narrator makes for her child. Where Part I draws readers *down* into the story, Part II stretches the long string of side-by-side panels familiar to newspaper comic readers into a shallow stairway that requires viewers to actively shift their physical reading strategies by forcing them to scroll sideways, then down, then sideways again. The short step down accompanies the narrator's musings on her suitability as a mother:

> Everyone used to say that Margot and I were so alike. our hair, our faces, (though she had her father's blue eyes). But I never thought so. If we were so alike, so similar, then why didn't I know how to be a mother to her? Why hadn't I been able to save her? [Carroll, 2011].

These questions occur one after another in a long panel that ushers in a second sub-level of panels. The act of reading downward visually steps the audience down from the compliments heaped upon Margot's mother to the doubts, fears and overwhelming grief and guilt that engulf her once Margot has passed. This physical movement therefore indicates that the narrative is shifting inwards into the narrator's thoughts and fears. The first two panels chronicle and respond to external commentary on Margot's resemblance to her mother, yet as soon as the narrator rejects their physical similarities, the third panel lengthens and descends as she descends into her doubts and memories. This shift in placement invites readers to journey with the narrator into these thoughts and feelings, informing the audience how to interact with and understand the progression of the narrator's grief. Towards the end of this sequence the memories collapse in on themselves in a set of three panels that decrease in size only to telescope back out again into the present, depositing the readers right back into Margot's room. The physical shifts in panel size continue the work begun by the larger panel layout. As the narrator descends into her memories, not only does the reader need to follow the panels downward, but the panel borders shrink. These visual cues physically represent the process of looking inwards, into memory, and then expanding one's scope outward to once again take in present events.

"Part III: Gone," in which the narrator's husband retreats from their marriage before stumbling upon the creatures who will ultimately change him, returns to the same long, thin stretch that characterizes Part I. At this point, Carroll divides the narrative into two: the point of view of the narrator, and her husband's point of view. The narrator's recollections of her husband's increasing emotional distance are tied to square and rectangular panels with reasonably straight, but not entirely perfect, edges. With the exception of the dark shape of the edge of her home at the end of this part, these edges are minimally interrupted, only very slightly bending, primarily around low-impact edges such as the flat ground or the wall of a room. Although these edges are not perfect, as Carroll uses them to suggest a larger landscape existing in the darkness that lies beyond them, they still create regular boundaries with very little encroachment from these dark shapes and shadows. Indeed, Carroll's color choices inform a particular reading of the narrator's story, as her panels showcase warm reds, oranges, and pinks. Even though the interior of the narrator's home is white with spots of shadow, the window continually frames a landscape of warmth. Carroll layers these colors in wide horizontal bands that meld into each other. The narrator waits for her husband's return against sunrise and sunset, both times of transition and suspension, as day turns to night and to day once again. The landscape effectively parallels her positioning within the story, suspended between her husband's comings and goings.

By virtue of existing within regular panels with defined boundaries and bright colors, Carroll's narrator offers up a point of view which is more solid and believable than that of her husband. Carroll presents the husband's point of view as a *story* told to the narrator, however, undercutting the reliability of his account both through words and illustrations. His story of his time in the woods exists within panels where these edges become fuzzier and dissolve as he becomes lost. The darkness of the webpage bleeds into the panels, allowing the forest to spread both inward, towards the center of the panels, and outward, into the unknown. The husband is therefore not simply lost in a small wood, but lost in an ever-expanding, boundary-less forest in the depths of night. Carroll effectively uses not only the panels and the gutters between them, but also the expansion of the webpage to represent the fear and disorientation that accompanies confronting the unfamiliar. Just as the panel sizes shrink and expand in Part II, Carroll again changes panel size to reflect a shift in a character's attention. These panels shrink to small ragged ovals of illumination which conjure up the claustrophobia of night before expanding back outward into something approaching regular rectangles. The smallest of the ovals is also the first of a pair: within it is simply the tiny white silhouette of the husband as he becomes lost, emphasizing how small one human is in the face of the wider natural world. The second oval is far larger, although not occupying the same space as the larger of the rectangular panels, and acts as a frame for the unfamiliar path the husband follows. It becomes a tunnel, centering the new path and drawing the reader's attention through it, bringing he or she along on the husband's journey even as it mimics the shape of the trees lining the path within the illustrations themselves. The narrative returns to rectangular panels once the husband makes the decision to follow the path, restoring a sense of order to his actions, and the narrative as a whole. Additionally, just as the narrator's panels in this part are color-coded, so too are the husband's. The husband's story unfurls in cool blues, blacks, and purples. His panels evoke the coldness of a forest long after the sun has gone down and reflect his own increasing coolness towards his wife. The depth of these colors work to conceal the creatures that hunt him, and it is only when his encounter in the woods is over and a new day has begun that the shadows give way to a brighter, more complete color palette. Once he returns to his home, the narrator's point of view becomes the primary one once again, and the illustrations return to reds, oranges, and pinks.

"Part IV: Wall," where the narrator waits for her husband to finally come home, returns to the horizontal slide of panels across the page, culminating in a last panel that ever so slightly steps the reader down once again. By keeping all but the last panel on the same horizontal plane, there is no sense of forward motion for the narrator. Time progresses from panel to panel, but the narrator remains trapped in the same space and thought process throughout. The three oval panels that begin Part IV help to fix the narrator in this unchanging space, as they represent a static mirror hanging on a wall. In the first panel, the narrator sits with her back to the reader, staring at the door behind her, and over the course of three panels, slowly turns to face the reader. By situating the readers behind the reflective glass of the mirror, the panel acts as a window separating the audience from narrative action, but also connects them to the story in a more active way. This technique builds upon Carroll's larger project of drawing her readers into her stories and inviting active reading strategies, as the reader is no longer completely separate from the text, but rather becomes part of the landscape of *Margot's Room*.

It is in "Part V: Blood," however, where the freedom of the web format truly shines. "Part V: Blood" requires readers to not only change the way in which they interact with the text by scrolling up or down, but it also merges orientations so that the audience must actively switch the direction of reading five separate times. In this part, the narrator is surprised by a lurking creature, much like those her husband encountered in the woods, and finds herself fighting for her life. As she fights back, she begins to realize that the creature is, in fact, her husband transformed, yet even in the midst of that realization, she is unable to stop violently attacking him until he has fully transformed back into his human form. As each narrative turn unfolds, the text requires readers to shift back and forth between scrolling sideways and downwards, over and over again (Carroll, 2011). Once he returns to the man she loved, the one who promised to live with her forever, both the narrator and readers are returned to that ever-present image—this time included directly at the end of tale—of Margot's room. Instead of a "return home" link, the entire image of the room is hyperlinked back to that original index page, and it is here that we realize that for all the expansive narrative time and physical movement involved in reading this story, the narrator—and by extension, the audience—is trapped in this singular murderous moment, unable to move beyond Margot's room.

Timelessness and the Bleed

Margot's Room is a study in the bleed; Carroll presents her viewers with a room, the very definition of a bordered space, yet never draws the terminal lines and edges of the walls. Her room slides into darkness on all sides, and the subsequent narrative parts bleed both figuratively and literally all over the almost endless, timeless blackness that spools out around them. Scott McCloud (1994) has asserted that

> When "bleeds" are used—i.e. when a panel runs off the edge of the *page*—[the effect of timelessness] is *compounded*. Time is no longer contained by the familiar icon of the *closed panel*, but instead *hemorrhages* and escapes into *timeless space* [p. 103].

For McCloud, a bleed expands both the boundaries of the comic and that of time, uncoupling from Groensteen's waffle-iron grid and the concept of sequential art as necessarily *sequential*. The bleed is a conduit through which the comic form can shrug off the one characteristic that separates it from the illustrated text.

This notion of the timeless bleed, however, is in direct contrast to Groensteen's (2013) explanation of the anchoring purpose of the consecutive nature of the comic. He explained that if we recognize sequential panels

> as being typical of comics, then its conventional configuration, possessed of its own potency, will invite a linear decoding, that is to say a reading, even if it is immediately obvious that the images, in this instance, do not represent, and consequently do not recount, anything. The apparatus invites the reader to look at the images one after another; contiguous images are perceived as consecutive, and this ordering constitutes a discourse, the discourse that vectorizes the visual field of a comics page. Instead of being viewed together, the images are caught in an oscillation between a global apprehension and a fragmented, one-after-another apprehension. It is under this condition that, while still not defined as a narrative, the drawn or painted surface ceases to be simply a tabular surface and becomes a comics page [p. 13].

The association with time is, for Groensteen, a defining characteristic of the comic page, anchored to panel presentation, but not wholly indivisible from the boundaried image. Where McCloud sees firm lines as a declaration of time and a lack of lines as timelessness, Groensteen sees time as a basic function of the comic page. By virtue of presenting a selection of related images, the comic artist invites the audience to associate the images with each other in consecutive order. Bordered or borderless, these panels are connected through the progress of time.

Yet just as *Margot's Room* expresses timelessness through Carroll's use of the bleed, it is also firmly rooted in time. Time, however, is not merely a function of sequence in this text, but rather an important part of Carroll's narrative. Practically, there is always an element of time associated with the act of reading, as it is impossible to experience a full narrative simultaneously. Beyond that, however, the poem which begins the piece lays out the order of events within the narrative, and each part, while virtually without panel borders, leads the reader through a chronology of tragedy; and each part brings the reader back to Margot's room. Narratively, each recounted event circles around to the room; it is the central hub adorned by touchstones which allow the reader to actively choose his or her next path. Each choice results in the reader traveling through another part of the chronology before returning to the same frozen moment in the room. Each instance in which the reader returns to the room, however, he or she has experienced more of the narrative, and therefore is more knowledgeable than he or she was previously. There is no requirement that the reader traverse the narrative in order from beginning to end, allowing him or her to engage with the narrative in multiple ways. Although the index page does not change from visit to visit, the reader's increased knowledge of the story as he or she goes through each part facilitates an individualized experience of narrative chronology, dictated entirely by the reader's choices. It is in that active reading process, where the reader must find clickable objects in the room, journey through each part and return to the room, that Carroll deftly fuses time and timelessness. Instead of aligning her story with the chronology embedded in consecutive panels, or the formless, timeless expanse embedded in the bleed, Carroll melds the two states together.

Just as *Margot's Room* is a study in the bleed, it is also a study in frozen time. No matter which narrative thread the reader follows, each one leads only one place: back to the room itself, suspended in the moments after the death of the narrator's husband. Carroll literalizes the metaphor of the web; while there are story strands to follow, there is no escaping the narrative's central hub. *Margot's Room* thus transcends two of the basic units of comic structure by presenting a scenario of time-out-of-time. The room and her tale are unable to progress past the moment of the husband's death, preserving in a state of timelessness, this particular point in time.

His Face All Red

While *Margot's Room* is one of the strongest examples of Carroll's ability to stretch beyond the boundaries of the printed page, *His Face All Red*

(Carroll, 2010) demonstrates her proficiency in translating the boundary-pushing layouts of her web comics to a traditionally printed medium. *His Face All Red* traces the downward spiral of a man who is deeply jealous of his brother, coveting every advantage or goodness his brother displays. The narrative itself begins by laying out the full extent of the events to come:

> This man is not my brother. My brother has a cottage with a hawthorne tree and a lilac bush. And a plump young wife with starry eyes. My brother has a fine coat, a vest the colour of moss, And a way with people that makes them trust him. This man has all these things 4(and my brother's face) (his handsome face) But just last week…. I killed my brother [Carroll, 2010].

As with *Margot's Room*, the web version of *His Face All Red* relies on long stretches of panels pulling the reader down the page even as it follows a more linear pattern. The audience follows the jealous brother as he covets all his own brother has, then agrees to accompany his brother into the woods in order to help hunt down a creature who is killing villagers' livestock. Once they are in the woods and confronted by the beast, the jealous brother gives into cowardice, runs and hides, while his brother stands his ground and kills it. After a journey in which the jealous brother fears everything that might be strange or hidden in the woods, the same journey in which his brother offers rational reassurances for each new fright, the terrorizing beast turns out to be nothing more than an ordinary wolf. Angered by the idea that once again his brother will be praised, the narrator kills his brother and dumps his body in a deep hole they stumbled upon in the woods. Unsurprisingly to anyone who has even the most glancing relationship to horror, three days later, his "brother" returns to the village, seemingly unharmed and happy to support the jealous brother's version of events. At the end of the tale, after increasingly unsettling evidence that this man is not the narrator's brother, the jealous brother returns to the woods to find out what has truly happened to the body of his brother. In order to do so, he must climb down into the very hole in which he dumped the body (Carroll, 2010). In this moment, Carroll once again pushes against the boundaries of the traditional page, taking full advantage of her web format to coax the reader into descending into the hole with the narrator. As the viewers scroll downward, they mimic the trip down the rope and down the hole, the narrow walls of which constitute the boundaries of the panel. The shape of the hole thus becomes the shape of the page, with the black background once again existing as an all-encompassing blackness that oppressively pushes inward even as it extends outward endlessly in all directions. The narrow images of the descent into the hole are nearly dwarfed by the blackness that takes up the rest of the browser window, which, by virtue of variations in screen resolution and size, widens and narrows depending on the settings of each audience member's electronic device. Finally, Carroll uses the last two panels to shrink the expansiveness of the web format down to two very similar images, one after the other, which round out the tale with an ambiguous ending that is truly full of dread (Carroll, 2010).

The print version of *His Face All Red* (Carroll, 2014b), as represented in *Through the Woods*, is nearly identical to the web version. The narrative progresses in the same chronological form, yet because it is limited by the boundaries of the printed page, Carroll makes some small but effective changes to preserve that sense of movement and expansiveness that is so much a part of her web-based work. Where the web version of this story punctuates the jealous brother's confession in its opening moments with a very small square panel showing merely a part of a slaughtered sheep's head—hinting at his brother's eventual fate—the print version splashes blood across one full page, positioning the sheep's head in the bottom right-hand corner so that the blood can spread freely across the rest of the page (Carroll, 2014b). This page thus replaces the physical act of scrolling through the story with an image that invites the viewer's eyes to slide across the pool of blood and on into the black background, coaxing the reader to anticipate the way in which that blood will continue to pool and spread. Similarly, the journey down the hole remains intact in the print version, but Carroll cuts it in two, splitting it where the color palette begins to change, so that the reader must at least turn a page and travel down to the bottom of the hole, replacing the fuller physicality of scrolling with at least one simple movement. *His Face All Red*, as one of Carroll's earliest digital offerings, is far more of a transitional comic than later texts such as *Margot's Room*. It shifts easily between the boundaries of the page and the expansiveness of the internet precisely because it more entrenched in the traditions of the printed page than Carroll's later works, where she experiments with format more extensively. Regardless, even though *His Face All Red* is beholden to the printed form, it stands as testament to Carroll's abilities to adapt traditional sequential layouts to fit a digital landscape, and reverse that process with minimal narrative disruption.

Beyond Panel Placement

While traditional sequential art is the starting point for many digital comic artists, experimenting with layout expands available options for storytelling. Despite the prevalence of criticism which prioritizes panel placement as integral to narrative decoding, Neil Cohn (2014) has maintained that linear readings of panels are not the sole method of deciphering meaning in visual media. Cohn explained that although viewers do indeed follow changes in narratives from panel to panel, this strategy does not account for comprehensive connections which require more decoding than the transition

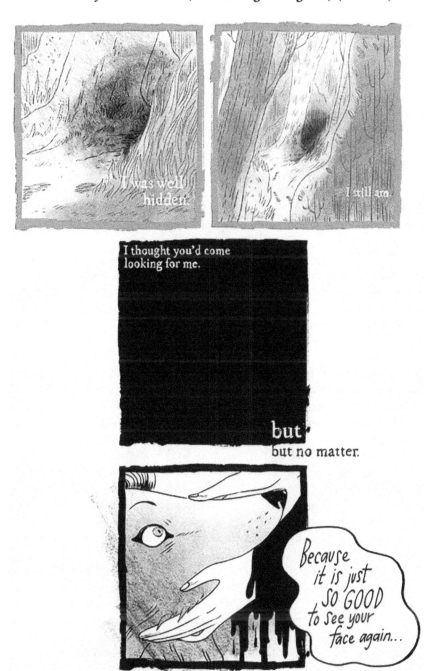

Figure 2: The Hole the Fox Did Make (Carroll, 2014a).

between side-by-side illustrations can provide, as "non-adjacent panels sometimes necessitate long-distance connections in a sequence and panels often form meaningful groupings beyond linear relationships" (p. 2). Further, viewers not only habitually make those long-distance connections, but there is also a high degree of agreement between individuals on where narrative arcs and episodes begin and end. As a result, Cohn suggested that another existing approach better encapsulates the reading and viewing strategies that allow for appropriate narrative decoding, prioritizing point of view, character, or chronological changes. This alternative reading strategy highlights the importance of such hierarchical organizational strategies, which can explain otherwise ambiguous panel relationships. Further, Cohn found that "[t]hese basic groupings eventually gave way to observations that panels play functional roles in a sequence, similar to—yet somewhat different from—traditional narrative categories" (p. 2).

Here, Cohn shifted the focus from proximity to context, complicating the importance of sequence to the comic form. Rather than relying solely on layout to guide the eye and direct the narrative, contextual clues create connections between events that require the reader to engage actively with the story. Just as Carroll's texts push against rigid sequential layouts and take advantage of the expansiveness of the bleed, she also relies on the content of her tales and the minds of her readers to create meaning inside, outside, and between her images. The digital format, where the page does not conform to fixed, immutable dimensions, is a perfect canvas upon which Carroll exercises her craft. Even *The Hole the Fox Did Make*, Carroll's (2014a) story of dreams and drowning, presented in regular four panel pages, breaks away from the waffle-iron grid. Two-thirds through the tale, Carroll expands the four panels into a larger orthogonal grid of five rows, and begins to employ the bleed. Five of those twenty panels exist without borders, melding into the whitespace of the webpage, intensifying the ominous presence of supernatural forces and long-buried memories. She then discards the grid entirely, as she places seven more panels at the bottom of the five rows, two side-by-side, and the rest spooling out in one long line. Of these final seven panels, two are blocks of color, swallowing up their own borders as solid planks of red and black adorned by nothing but white text, and one is completely borderless and larger than the rest of the regularized images. The latter panel fits into that same otherworldly framework as the previous five borderless panels, as all six reference events that exist in the realm of memory and dream. They are part of an expansive field specifically because they cannot be bound by physical space. In fact, the borders of the final two panels—including the solid black rectangle—begin to break down as their text runs off the edges into the surrounding whitespace. Reality mingles with fantasy as Carroll leads the reader into the unknown.

Navigating the (Web)Page

As with the transition between digital and print copies of *His Face All Red*, Carroll manipulates the traditional panel layout throughout her print collection, *Through the Woods*. Although her texts must now conform to the boundaries of the page, Carroll continues to push against its edges, echoing her digital work. As Aaron Kashtan (2015) noted, "[i]n order to compete with electronic literature, the printed book has to emulate electronic literature, adopting its properties of visuality and interactivity" (pp. 420–421). In an increasingly digitized world, physical objects, such as books, must provide an experience that transcends the corporeal, as material items are far less portable and accessible than the immateriality and ubiquity of an easily available and transportable file or website. Given that Carroll is at home within the digital realm, it is no surprise that she is adept in adapting digital techniques to the printed page. As the texts on her website demonstrate again and again, comics are exceptionally adaptable to both print and digital form because sequential art is a medium of fragmentation. Side-by-side panels require an audience to make logical leaps between illustrations in order to comprehend action and narration, much as the hypertextual nature of the webpage require viewers to make connections between clicks and links. *Margot's Room* relies on a fragmentary reading, and Carroll expands this technique to the works within *Through the Woods*.

In *My Friend Janna* (Carroll, 2014d), a print-only piece, as two girls learn the consequences of pretending to be mediums, Carroll inserts disturbing sketchbook pages to interrupt the expected graphic novel form. A two-page spread, these journal pages upend proper alignment, as Janna, the narrator's friend, writes nonsense in all directions. Her sentences are accompanied by strange sketches and smudges, all of which visually mimic the feeling of disorientation that builds over the course of the tale. Similarly, in *The Nesting Place*, Carroll (2014e) uses the bleed to full effect, as a young woman finds out the full nature of the woman her brother has married when the things living inside her brother's wife skitter across the page and expand outward to all edges. It is in *A Lady's Hands Are Cold* (Carroll, 2014c), in which a young bride very literally unearths the dismembered pieces of her new husband's previous wife, that Carroll most viscerally reminds her readers of the journey she invites them to take, as she uses disorienting angles, and unspooling and curving dialogue to invoke movement and pathways that would otherwise remain static on a printed page. Each time the dismembered wife speaks to the new bride, all panels and borders are disrupted. The dead wife's words float out as white text on a curving red ribbon, twining around the live woman, waking her from sleep, spilling over the gutters and echoing her twisting, curving journey from her previous home to her husband's lonely mansion. At all times, Carroll treats her audience as what McCloud (1994) called "a willing and conscious *collaborator* [where] closure is the agent of *change, time* and *motion*" (p. 65). This assertion is the core of Carroll's narratives, and it is in full force in *Our Neighbor's House*.

In *Our Neighbor's House*, (Carroll, 2014f) Beth's father leaves his three daughters home alone while he goes hunting. He instructs the girls to go to their neighbor's house should he not return home in three days, but instead of heeding his words, the girls remain in their house, waiting, once the three days have elapsed. Seeing a blood-red moon in the sky, Beth knows that her father has died, and over the course of the next few days, her two sisters report the visits of a strange man in a wide-brimmed hat, each vanishing the night after their individual encounters. There are no explanations in *Our Neighbor's House*, as Carroll never reveals who the man is, nor what is happening to the sisters, preferring instead to linger on Beth's feelings of certainty regarding her father's death, the strange man, and her sisters' disappearances in the face of no tangible proof. Carroll allows her narrative to sink into ambiguity, shifting the focus to the pervasive atmosphere of doom which builds even as the mystery deepens. While Beth is convinced that she is following the correct plan of action when she finally leaves for the neighbor's house, the reader does not have the same confidence. Instead, the story's images encourage the viewer to inhabit the gutters between panels and actively reach for closure, connecting each still image together into one continuous narrative. Once Beth decides to leave her now-empty home and journey to her neighbor's home, Carroll opens up the panel layout into a full, textless page depicting Beth's preparations. She puts on her red hooded cape—invoking images of Red Riding Hood before her encounters with the wolf—over the course of three small, descending panels. These panels lay overtop a full-page illustration of Beth walking across the snow, her footsteps visible behind her, tracing her path through the shadow of the house and leading towards the distant woods. Just as on the night of her father's death, there is a blood red moon in the sky, wisps of white clouds skittering across its face. With no text to guide the reader, the page projects an all-encompassing silence. The whiteness which extends between the sky and ground is at once the blank page, offering no words, and the snowy night, dampening all sound.

McCloud (1994) framed the process of closure in comics as "foster[ing] an intimacy surpassed only by the *written word*, a *silent, secret contract* between *creator* and *audience*" (p. 69). Yet just as Carroll sidesteps time and timelessness in her use of panels and the bleed, she also uses comic-based closure to reach beyond the written word into a profound intimacy between her readers and the narrative. *Our Neighbor's House* does not offer its readers the certainty of textual meaning, nor the regularity of the orthogonal grid. Instead, it asks readers to look into the gutters and follow the bleeds in order to experience the certainty of narrative uncertainty. In these silences and frozen moments Carroll lodges ambiguity of meaning alongside the timelessness that marks supernatural tales, fairy stores, and horror. Her stories are not prescriptive; rather, they require an active transaction between artist and viewer.

Despite its ties to the printed page, *Our Neighbor's House* (and the rest of *Through the Woods*) stands as testament to Carroll's expertise in exploiting the expansiveness of the digital format. In interacting with traditional, paper-based publishing in similar ways to newer media, Carroll brings the transformative properties of a page without edges to her book. Much as Kashtan (2015) contextualized "the physical form of the book [as serving] to concretize the abstract object that constitutes the literary text" (p. 423) when discussing Chris Ware's *Building Stories*, Carroll's play with digital and printed formats prioritizes the marriage of content with form, as "'[t]exts' are abstract, free-floating entities that can be instantiated in many ways; the e-book leaves these entities in their natural disembodied state, while the printed book gives these entities a local habitation and a name" (p. 423). Thus, Carroll pairs her stories with the format that will best serve her narratives.

Yet the division between print and digital is not as sharp as Kashtan suggested. Indeed, "[p]rint books are valuable precisely by virtue of the qualities that make them inconvenient—their weight and size, their tactile materiality—because these qualities make the reading of a printed book a materially rich experience" (p. 425). Carroll's *Through the Woods*, in hardcover form, is large and heavy, with thick, glossy pages that slide underneath the reader's fingertips as he or she turns pages. Pauses and breaks in narration happen across pages, requiring parallel pauses as the reader physically turns over a new leaf. This tactile experience, however, is not exclusive to her printed works. Her website is rife with rich, active experiences as each viewer must scroll, shift, and physically follow panels as they spill past the initial browser spaces. Carroll's texts are neither wholly disembodied in digital form, nor completely corporeal in print, as she asks readers of both website and book to engage with her texts in remarkably similar ways.

Even in print, Carroll remains a digital artist, one for whom the boundaries of time and format exist only to be tested. Truly, Carroll uses the more fluid and flexible nature of the internet to create an immersive journey for her readers, and she continues to test the boundaries of printed text in order to preserve and replicate a similar experience. Given her roots as a web-based artist, her texts are excellent examples of the ways in which illustrated narratives continue to shift and change as more and more published texts begin as web-based works. While *Through the Woods* demonstrates her ability to manipulate a rigid format, her web-based texts, such as *The Hole the Fox Did Make, His Face All Red*, and especially *Margot's Room* allow Carroll's understanding of the structures of comic construction to shine. Within these narratives, Carroll upholds time and space as dimensions indivisible from visual art even as she rejects any linear decoding of these properties. For Carroll, the page is a malleable entity, bursting with promise and not bound by chronology nor dimensions. Both her website and *Through the Woods* blend horror and fairy tale into narratives that require readers who are not simply engaging intellectually, but also quite literally physically involving themselves in the reading process. Her page is a portal to a darkened, mysterious pathway, a rewriting of sequential art as a journey through the viewer's mind rather than simply the tracing of a gaze over a page. These tales are not merely images standing in solidarity, but exist to provoke a closure that is more visceral and ambiguous than that of the purely written word.

REFERENCES

Carroll, E. (2010). *His face all red.* Retrieved from http://emcarroll.com/comics/faceallred/01.html.

Carroll, E. (2011). *Margot's room.* Retrieved from http://emcarroll.com/comics/margot/index.html.

Carroll, E. (2014a). *The hole the fox did make.* Retrieved from http://www.emcarroll.com/comics/fox/one.html.

Carroll, E. (2014b). His face all red. *Through the woods.* New York: Margaret K. McElderry Books.

Carroll, E. (2014c). A lady's hands are cold. *Through the woods.* New York: Margaret K. McElderry Books.

Carroll, E. (2014d). My friend Janna. *Through the woods.* New York: Margaret K. McElderry Books.

Carroll, E. (2014e). The nesting place. *Through the woods.* New York: Margaret K. McElderry Books.

Carroll, E. (2014f). Our neighbor's house. *Through the woods.* New York: Margaret K. McElderry Books.

Chavanne, R. (2015). The composition of comics. *European Comic Art, 8*(1), 111–144.

Cohn, N. (2014). The architecture of visual narrative comprehension: The interaction of narrative structure and page layout in understanding comics. *Frontiers in Psychology, 5*(680), 1–9.

Goodbrey, D. (2013). From comic to hypercomic. In J.C. Evans & T. Giddens (Eds.), *Cultural Excavation and Formal Expression in the Graphic Novel* (pp. 291–302). Oxford: Inter-Disciplinary Press.

Groensteen, T. (2013). *Comics and narration* (Ann Miller, Trans.). Jackson: University Press of Mississippi (Original work published 2011).

Kashtan, A. (2015). "And it had *everything* in it": Building stories, comics, and the book of the future. *Studies in the Novel, 47*(3), 420–447.

McCloud, S. (1994). *Understanding comics: The invisible art.* New York: HarperCollins.

McCloud, S. (2000). *Reinventing comics: How imagination and technology are revolutionizing an art form.* New York: HarperCollins.

Petrič, Je. (2009). Comic strip as literature: Art Spiegelman's *MAUS* in Slovenian. *Acta Neophilologica, 42*(1–2), 69–81.

Death's "Friend Hug"

Analyzing the Personification of Death in Three Webcomics

KARIS JONES

> One short sleep past, we wake eternally
> And death shall be no more; Death, thou shalt die.
> —John Donne, *Sonnet X*, 1633

Though Death itself as a force may never change, society has an ever-fluctuating perspective toward it. Take, for example, John Donne's (1633) famous poem. On the one hand, he acknowledges that some are afraid of Death and see it as all-powerful, while he himself takes a stand against Death, listing all the forces that control it—most of all, God's promise of eternity. He personifies Death to belittle it, to minimize its power, and even to threaten it. Modern webcomics, on the other hand, paint a very different picture of Death. In the webcomic *Cyanide and Happiness*, Death is a squat practical joker who wears sunglasses and philosophizes about tag. The webcomic *Life & Death* portrays Death as your average new hire in a big company. Additionally, the webcomic *Mary Death* lovingly depicts Death as half of a Calvin & Hobbes–esque duo. These three current webcomics take the liberty to use Death as either their protagonist or the punchline of multiple jokes, making Death into something unconventional, funny and strange all at the same time. What do these personifications say about how our present society views Death?

Scholars often look to literature to reveal trends in cultural perspectives over time. According to Ariès (2008), the prominent French scholar who studied Western attitudes toward death, historical documents or works of art that are accepted and appreciated by contemporaries must necessarily conform in some respects to general societal understandings. Thus, scholars of death often draw on established historical texts to discuss society's changing perspective. By that same logic, one would expect that products of popular culture like webcomics would also reflect society's general attitudes, though few scholars have analyzed webcomics to understand feelings toward death. It stands to reason that if we want to understand attitudes toward death in this digital age, we may want to examine the works of popular internet artists. I argue that since we can find several popular webcomics entirely devoted to Death's personification, webcomics are fertile ground for the analysis of modern attitudes toward death.

Progression of Western Attitudes Toward Death

It is important to understand the historical progression of Western attitudes toward death to see the modern attitudes in context. I draw primarily on two Western scholars of death: Hoffman (1964) and Ariès (2008, 2010).

Synthesis of Ariès and Hoffman

Ariès (2008, 2010) looked at the overarching evolution of attitudes toward death in the Western world by examining themes relating to burial and funerary customs revealed by historical structures (churches, cemeteries, tombs, etc.) and texts (wills, literary and artistic works, religious documents, etc.) from the Middle Ages to the latter half of the twentieth century. Hoffman (1964) analyzed a selection of major Western authors and poets in the beginning of the twentieth century (such as Juenger, Dostoevsky, Dreiser, Kafka, Stevens, Eliot, Joyce, Lawrence, and Proust, to name a few) to pinpoint how literature reveals shifts in attitudes toward death over time. Synthesizing their perspectives, one sees the following progression: Ariès (2008, 2010) argued that in the Middle Ages, the underlying belief in God led to a general acceptance of death. This changed by the twelfth century as people began recognizing the importance of the self due to the ecclesiastical emphasis on individualized judgment of the soul. By the eighteenth century and into the nineteenth, he claimed that the focus shifted to the death of the other, with emphasis on memory and the pain of loss, leading to the romanticizing of death and the "cult" of tombs and cemeteries. In the twentieth century, Hoffman (1964) examined how individuals struggle to define the self in light of the loss of assurance in eternity: "one may say that the violent destruction of the possibilities of grace has forced upon the self the responsibility of adjustment to death" (p. 4). Taking a slightly different angle, Ariès (2008, 2010) argued that modern society (mid–twentieth century) moved toward an erasure of death through the sterility of hospitalization. He claimed that though the impulse behind minimizing death is to affirm the happiness of life, it instead led to suffering in silence.

STUDYING DEATH OVER TIME

Ariès (2008) insisted that these slowly changing attitudes needed to be viewed across a span of at least a thousand years to recognize the continuation of themes across the centuries. Thus, it seems productive to compare current attitudes toward death with the twentieth century attitudes described by Hoffman and Ariès. Despite these warnings that attitudes toward death change slowly, I find that twenty-first century depictions of Death in webcomics seem to stand in stark contrast with twentieth century portrayals of the self struggling against death or the individual family mourning alone.

STUDYING DEATH IN COMICS AND WEBCOMICS

As said before, Ariès (2008) studied historical sites and documents relating to funerals and burials to trace changing attitudes toward death, and Hoffman (1964) examined literature and poetry to see what evolution of visual metaphors said about the cultural phenomena of death. I specifically analyze graphically visual mediums like comics and webcomics to see how creators personify Death as a character. As Walsh (2006) says, stories are tools for humans to make sense of reality, and the process of storytelling is inherently anthropomorphic: "not because stories are about people (though they usually are), but because they are by people: their frame of reference is human experientiality" (p. 861). Thus, the way an author or artist chooses to represent Death embodies certain attitudes they hold toward death in society. This is a productive site for analysis because graphic personifications of Death abound, appearing in comics across the world. As I have previously argued, looking at Death as personified in an American graphic novel, a French bande-desinée, and a Japanese manga, one sees a different take on the phenomenon of Death than those described by Ariès and Hoffman in different textual mediums (Jones, publishing as Schneider, 2013).

To expand on these findings, this essay asks specifically about the portrayal of Death in webcomics: how are authors using the medium of the webcomic to explore philosophical facets of Death? Some may think that webcomics (or as they are defined here, digitally-created self-published online serial comics) are not as complex as professionally-published print or digital graphic novels and dismiss these portrayals by claiming that Death is being used in these comics for cheap laughs. However, I argue that by viewing these webcomics not only in light of features related to print comics but also digital features only available to webcomics, one sees a clear shift in twenty-first century attitudes toward Death in contrast to twentieth century attitudes described by Hoffman and Ariès.

Framework for Analysis

Kogel (2013) defines a webcomic as "a screen-based medium sharing many common principles with [print] comics but expanding upon those principles using the systems of the Web" (p. 10). This means that to analyze a webcomic, one must look both at features of the print comic medium as well as the webcomic's unique Web 2.0 affordances (Hicks, 2009). In order to construct a framework for analyzing content in this medium, I will both attend to print features and web features, including how these web features structure genre and afford reader participation.

Features of Print Comics

First, one cannot make sense of a webcomic without examining the "comic-ness" of its content. The influential Scott McCloud (1993) defines comics as "juxtaposed pictorial and other images in deliberate sequence, intended to convey information and/or an aesthetic response in the viewer" (p. 9). Thus, one needs to attend to the sequencing of images and their effect. Round (2007) suggests there are the three primary elements for print comic analysis: time-as-space, open narrative, and hyperreality. Time-as-space is the way the layout of panels shapes the pacing of the narrative. A reader must interpret both the physical space a frame takes up and the conventional pacing of action within that frame to interpret the way time progresses in and across the panels. For instance, while a large zoomed-out frame depicting two small people walking down a road may represent an hour of strolling, a large frame representing part of an action sequence in a fight may take a mere instant of story-time. The reader needs to interpret how time plays out in the context of the dialogue, pictures, and panel boundaries.

Another comic element, open narrative, relates to how readers must act as contributing authors to fill in the gutters. A gutter is the physical gap between panel boundaries, representing narrative omissions that the reader must fill to understand the story. For instance, if one panel shows a child at home and another panel shows the child sitting at a school desk, the reader must imagine what happened in the interim: possibly a walk to school or a ride on the bus. This means that no two readings of a comic are the same: "The reader works alongside the creators as a kind of contributory author, both by interpreting the panel content, and by filling in the gaps" (Round, 2007, p. 317).

Finally, hyperreality is the effect created by blurring what is real and what is an ultra-stylized representation through the constantly shifting perspective and the abstraction of the comic aesthetic. Round (2007) specifically examines how comics can create hyperreal shifts in perspectives by dynamically positioning the reader in different ways, both pictorially and narratively. She argues that these perspective shifts blur the boundaries between creator and reader and highlights the postmodern possibilities for telling stories from multiple points of view.

Features of Webcomics

Next, one needs tools to examine the "web-ness" of the webcomic. First, the analysis of individual webcomic pages themselves include more features than print pages. As Kogel (2013) states: "webcomics need to be understood as comics on a surface level, but also as image files on a coded level" (p. 3). He explains that this means webcomics include features like alternative text and hyperlinks. Alternative text, also known as alt text or hover text, allows webcomic creators to hide text in their comics that only appears when a reader hovers their mouse over the image. This text often serves as a source of additional information, commentary, or a punchline. Another feature, hyperlinking or tagging, is used for organizing content for quick access by readers. For instance, some webcomic creators will tag comics with words or phrases that, when clicked, automatically organize the content by that theme, functioning similarly to a hashtag.

INFINITE CANVAS

The Web 2.0 environment does not just add new features to the webcomic, but it also influences its overall genre. First, time as space can be expanded when a comic is imagined within potentially limitless computer windows instead of print pages, known as Infinite Canvas comics, a term coined by Scott McCloud (Kogel, 2013). This type of comic goes beyond needing panel boundaries to represent time; instead, the distance between panels and the reader's movement through that space influences the way the reader experiences time within the story, which Kogel (2013) argues is useful to create certain effects: "It emphasizes spatiality, movement and flow and can make complex use of scrolling to build suspense" (p. 66). Though most of the webcomics studied in this essay generally use traditional panel boundaries, the concept of an Infinite Canvas will be important for studying how scrolling influences the perception of time.

MICROSERIALIZATION

Second, many webcomics (and more importantly, all the webcomics analyzed in this essay) update in short installments over time in a process of microserialization (Romaguera, 2010). These "webcomic strips" (Kogel, 2013) are often originally posted as part of an overarching narrative, but they can also be decontextualized as individual strips that are linked or shared across platforms. This means that webcomic strips must both "be significant enough to be a standalone text while still be cohesive with the previous and following texts that can be found in the ever growing documents of the ongoing work" (Romaguerra, 2010, p. 98). This constraint causes webcomic updates to have a "certain repetitive rhythm, one where each page has to provide closure through punchlines or use cliffhangers to keep readers coming back" (Kogel, 2013, p. 57). Both Kogel (2013) and Romaguera (2010) argue that webcomics are unique in that, through this process of microserialization, the work as a whole evolves as the creators update over time, which can lead to interesting alterations in style and direction.

Romaguera (2010) argues that microserialization affects the webcomic medium in another way, in that it "foregrounds the narrative construction of webcomics, which allows for the continuous study of authorial intention and the influences of a highly participatory reading community on the work" (p. 1). Since readers can interact with the webcomic creator as part of the update process, he highlights the webcomic as a platform for unique author-text-reader relationships, arguing that webcomic readers ought to be studied as "a community actively engaging with each other and with the author" (Romaguera, 2017, p. 157). For example, he explores a case where webcomic fans added "(un)official" background information to the main text of the webcomic by asking questions of the author through web channels (like social media, forum posts, or live drawing streams) and then publicly posting this information for "the rest of the interpretive community" (Romaguera, 2017, p. 188). This then allowed for readers, interacting beyond the text, to influence the community's interpretation of the text itself: "These reception performances of archiving the author's words serve to expand the facts surrounding the text" (Romaguera, 2017, p. 188). In this case, Romaguera described how extratextual information expanded the official webcomic text. Relatedly, I argue that reader comments recalling author content on individual webcomic pages can structure other readers' experiences of the text, especially as web templates that place comments in close visual proximity to original texts "shrink both time and space between writer and audience" (Gallagher, 2015, p. 397).

In this essay, not all print or web features will reveal something salient about the personification of Death. Therefore, each analysis will focus on the combination of print and web features that are relevant to understand what the webcomic is specifically saying about Death (in relation to rhetorical moves of perspective and the portrayal of time). Specifically, *Cyanide & Happiness* will be analyzed in terms of how the work as a whole evolves over time through microserialization; *Life and Death* will be analyzed in terms of reader expansion of the text via comments; and *Mary Death* will be analyzed in light of features of alt text and scrolling.

Twentieth Century Themes for Analysis

To see if twenty-first century webcomics orient toward death differently than twentieth century literature, we must first identify the important themes described across the twentieth century by Hoffman and Ariès. First, we see the connection between death and personal identity. Hoffman (1964) focused on the importance of the individual's response to death: he said that one of the most important decisions the modern person makes is how to define themselves, especially in relation to death and what one believes about death. Ariès (2010), on the other hand, focused not on how the individual alone responds to death but how we as a society respond to it. He argued that modern society feels ashamed of death and wishes to avoid the strong negative emotions associated with it. As the traditional idea of community is further dismantled, he argued that the presence of death is no longer tolerated in public spaces, forming a new isolation for the mourning family. In other words, because society wishes to focus on the happiness of life, death must be sterilized and contained.

Rhetorical Orientation

How can authors substantiate their claims about death through literature? Hoffman (1964) argued that literature inherently reflects the way a culture orients toward death through its images and metaphors. However, he also described how twentieth century authors use rhetorical moves to portray individual orientations toward death. For instance, he showed how authors focus on "the spatial qualities of life" (p. 4) instead of the actual death itself, using a blunt rhetorical style when describing death to portray "the exposition of reality without either ceremonial or philosophical mitigation" (p. 361). He argued that this shows how there is no longer time for the beauty of reflection; instead, authors can only describe the stark self-consciousness of the moment of death through focusing on the objects and place where the death occurs. They limit their words in a futile attempt to represent the unrepresentable. Another rhetorical technique he described is how some authors, like Proust, approximate eternity by extending moments of consciousness. He said the more a moment is considered and extended and intensified, the more the self is defined as "real." Experience becomes the antithesis of death and the crux of identity. Thus, Hoffman noted, modern existentialism is always positioned in respect to death and how one accepts it and yet still sustains life at the same time. The way authors use rhetoric to present death is essential for understanding their positioning toward death.

In order to make claims about how twenty-first century webcomic creators take up twentieth century themes, one must look at how they use the rhetorical moves of the webcomic medium in respect to Death. I will look specifically at how authors use print comic elements such as time-as-space, open narrative, and hyperreality to portray individual or societal reactions toward the personifications of Death, as well as rhetorical effects related to digital environment like alt text and scrolling. This will show how webcomic creators make rhetorical shifts of perspective through such features, purposely positioning the readers in certain (sometimes conflicting) ways in relation to Death. These rhetorical positionings will reveal key aspects of these creators' orientations toward Death.

Orientation Toward Time

Time is another important concept for modern authors representing death. Hoffman (1964) posited that the way authors view time is dependent on their understanding of eternity. He explained how, when one believes in God, each moment is to be savored based on how it exposes something about eternity: "The moment is itself within time; it is the only 'actually real' substance of a life. But it is also, in terms of its being realized, a physical actualization, a 'moment,' of eternity" (p. 342). Each moment connects the past, present, and future, as these constructs make sense in a framework supported by the assurance of eternity. However, without God's guarantee that eternity exists, time has to be reconceptualized: "there is no past and no guaranteed future; there is only a present instant, which is itself uncertain" (p. 342). One can therefore look for hints of author's beliefs about eternity through the way they represent time in the literary medium. As Hoffman said:

> One of the most astonishing characteristics of modern literature is the imaginative extension of temporal limits. Since man lives in time, and eternity is a debatable and unproved hypothesis, the discrete circumstance, the image of boundaries, dominates the literary sense [p. 381].

He then argued that twentieth century authors either (a) accept that time inevitably leads toward death, (b) explore how the self experiences time in limited temporal moments by intensifying the experiment, or (c) struggle to see the self as both in time and also understand how time relates to eternity.

To examine the webcomics' orientation toward time with respect to Death, I will consider how the webcomic creators use time-as-space as well as computer windows and page delivery. As said before, Round (2007) argues that space in comics (both dialogic space defined and pictorial space defined by panel boundaries) represents time, and Kogel (2013) argues that time in webcomics is influenced both by use of space in digital windows and reader navigation using digital tools. The combination of these elements allows creators to make meaningful statements about Death and time through the way the reader experiences time while navigating webcomic spaces.

In the following sections, I will introduce three individual comics from three different webcomics. I will then examine the personification of Death in each instance in relation to identity and time, drawing upon features established in the frameworks discussed above. This will allow me to make claims about how these twenty-first century webcomic creators conceptualize modern attitudes toward Death.

Death in *Cyanide & Happiness*

The webcomic *Cyanide & Happiness*, visited by over one million readers every day, is full of minimally-drawn stick figures who are often dying grotesquely or making horribly distasteful puns; the webcomic itself is well-known for its "unusual, graphic, and insensitive" jokes (Medina-Tayac, 2012, para. 2). As one of the four current authors described in an interview with *Yale Daily News*, this webcomic's humor plays off the "darker side of humanity." The author went on to state, "My inspiration comes from people and how horribly they treat each other.... I don't think of it in terms of what's okay and what goes too far—just in terms of what's funny and what's not" (Medina-Tayac, 2012, para. 3). The comic, which has been running since 2005, now has more than four thousand pages and is still currently updating.

Romaguera (2010) argued that webcomic creators need to have cohesion between updates in order to make a narrative whole: "Because it is a microserialized work as well as an ongoing narrative, webcomics are in constant textual fluidity" (p. 91). However, for this sprawling webcomic with several content contributors, the reader's experience may be more disjointed than not. In fact, as one of the creators said, they purposely do not intend for readers to look for a cohesive narrative:

> [Our use of stick figures] makes the characters seem very transient, as if they only exist for a given comic. "Cyanide and Happiness" prides itself on having no characters or themes. If we ever bring up a character, we usually retire it after its share of original jokes has run out [Johnson, 2006, para. 12].

Since the creators are intentionally not creating main characters, many of the stick figures look the same, with the only difference being the color of their shirts. Even characters who look exactly the same may not be the same character. For instance, similar-looking characters may die multiple times in different ways, and sometimes the same character will even have different names in different comics.

Though it may be difficult to see how *Cyanide & Happiness* creates a sense of a cohesive whole through the narrative plotline, there is still a "sense of [textual] fluidity" (Romaguera, 2010, p. 91) through the use of recurring jokes and punchlines. For instance, the webcomic in its early years had a string of jokes where the punchline was men squeezing women's breasts at inappropriate times (e.g., Melvin, 2005a). This punchline was developed in a later page when a woman instead squeezed a man's breast at an inappropriate time (Melvin, 2005b). The punchline was developed yet again when a man, faced with Death, inexplicably reaches over to squeeze Death itself (Jo, 2005). Though one could possibly find the absurdity of the situation funny even out of context, the action makes more sense with how it fits with the other punchlines that came before it. Thus, when analyzing an individual update of this webcomic, one must consider its context in the narrative development of particular situations or punchlines.

As Death's personified presence is often a key part of recurring punchlines, *Cyanide & Happiness*'s depiction of Death is different from most other characters. Unlike the majority of characters, Death surfaces again and again across the years with completely different designs, as different creators envision it in evolving ways. In 2005, Death is shown as a black tube with a hood, a sleeve and a scythe (Melvin, 2005c), the bare minimum to signify a grim reaper. Literally five days later, Death is drawn by a different artist as an amorphous grey and black shape with a green scythe (Jo, 2005). In 2012, Death is designed by yet another artist as a more detailed chibi-style hooded figure with skeletal hands, speaking in a black and red gothic scrawl (Wilson, 2012a). In 2014, Death is reimagined once more as a slightly taller figure in a simple hood (McElfatrick, 2014a, McElfatrick, 2014b). Finally, in 2016, Death (though drawn by the same creator) suddenly has a visible and detailed skeletal face and hands (McElfatrick, 2016). Despite this character's many faces, it continues to be a recognizable personification of Death, and there appears to be some cohesion across the personifications. Both the transient identity of the recurring stick characters and the cohesive identity of Death become salient in *Cyanide & Happiness* "Comic 3691" (McElfatrick, 2014a; see Figure 1).

In this comic, Death encounters Orangeshirt, a recurring stick-man with an orange shirt. In the majority of comics, Orangeshirt has no name; interestingly enough, in this comic, he gains a temporary identity when Death talks to him in the first panel: "I'm here for you, Ted." Ted is (understandably) alarmed by Death's words. However, in the next panel Death assures Ted that his visit does not mean Ted is about to die. Death explains, "What I mean is I'm here for you as a friend," offering Ted a "friend hug." In the next panel,

Figure 1: Cyanide & Happiness "Comic 3691" (creator owned; Explosm.net).

the man is shown unmistakably (and comically) dead, lying on his side with his eyes Xed out, while Death brags, "Gets em every time."

The joke is set up very similarly to a previous *Cyanide & Happiness* comic, in which Death comes to call on a distressed "Mr. Smith." During their conversation, the man realizes Death is actually looking for his brother Bill and explains the mix-up (Melvin, 2005c). For this comic, Death as a personification is important for the context of the joke but not as important for the punchline. Instead, the joke rests on Mr. Smith's reaction, as stated very aptly by a commenter, "Never seen someone so glad to hear their brother is going to die" (PSES reborn, 2017). As "Comic 3691" also begins by giving a name to a generally unnamed character, one might think that the punchline will (like the previous comic) depend on Ted's name and his escape from Death. However, this comic subverts those expectations—the focus instead is on the way that Ted dies. I argue that a close reading of this webcomic strip in context of several surrounding punchlines related to Death reveals some interesting implications about the modern perceptions of Death.

At first, this webcomic page portrays Ted resisting Death. The portrayal of the self fighting for autonomy in response to Death corresponds with Hoffman's (1964) representation of the modern individual stance toward Death. He argues that self-definition is the crux of the portrayal of death in modern literature: "the self is in this view of it the beginning, the source, and the responsible center of all revaluations of life and of the death that superintends and haunts it" (p. 493). From this first panel, one expects that the newly christened Ted will get the chance for a confrontation with Death: an argument, a trick, maybe even a chess game. However, a key assumption underlying the traditional friction between the self and death is that the characters are aware that they are going to die: "The choice of dying, of being aware that one is dying, is closely linked to the psychological problem of willing the persistence of self-identity in time" (Hoffman, 1964, p. 317). The awareness is key. It is not death itself that haunts twentieth century authors—it is the knowledge of it, the inevitability of struggling to shape one's identity when death will make that struggle meaningless.

However, Ted is robbed of his awareness. As he is tricked into complacency, he loses the chance to choose a position with respect to Death. The significance of Ted's death is relegated to the gutter (the panel boundary) between the third and fourth panel. As Round (2007) says, drawing on Scott McCloud:

> Each reader fills in the gutter in his/her own way—although similar, no two interpretations can ever be identical. This process applies to all comics and the gutter is often the site of major events. The reader works alongside the creators as a kind of contributory author, both by interpreting the panel content, and by filling in the gaps [p. 317].

In this comic, the actual "friend hug" itself is not shown in panel—instead, the comic jumps directly from the offer of a hug to the dead body. There is no information about how the moment of death plays out. What exactly is the look on Ted's face as he dies? What is the last thing he sees? Does he die immediately or have a moment of realization? What is Death's response to his last moments? All of these questions would shape the final interpretation of Ted's self-awareness and identity: is his death a moment of betrayal, ignorant bliss, or acceptance? However, the author does not engage with any of them. By tricking Ted, Death completely hijacks Ted's specially-bestowed identity; the creator raised him from obscurity only to immediately take that identity away. He becomes just another dead body punchline.

The authorial choice to leave these questions for the gutter signals that this webcomic portrays a different attitude toward Death than those described by Hoffman. Ted does not have a struggle with Death that shows his resilience—instead, we see his gullibility. Though modern authors may reject the concept of the religious ascension to eternity, "that awesome pause between the last minute of 'j'existe' and the time of 'je suis mort'" (Hoffman, 1965, p. 320), this webcomic not only rejects God's role in death but also glosses over the moment of death entirely, skipping over the conflict that Hoffman deems most important for modern authors.

This personification of Death is absolute and inescapable, allowing Ted no time to process his identity in light of its absolute finality. On the one hand, we could connect this to Ariès's (2010) arguments that modern society tries to marginalize and hide the dying in order to pretend that "life is always happy or should always seem to be so" (p. 87). Though it is possible that Death has brought Ted the illusion that life is always happy and saved him from fearing Death, this illusion also makes Ted the butt of the joke. His gullibility is not celebrated but ridiculed. Though the creator may hide the moment of death, he certainly does not hide Death himself, who is actually the protagonist of this webcomic page. Instead, in line with the overall tone of the webcomic, it becomes clear that McElfatrick (2014a) is instead purposely disrupting modern sensibilities through this personification of Death. In no other historical era would someone believe that Death just wanted to share a "friend hug"; for centuries, people have accepted (or struggled to accept) that Death comes for everyone. Only in this era of denial (and self-delusion) could people fall for this prank over and over again. It is indeed laughable that this prank, as Death notices, "Gets em every time."

In addition to ridiculing modern society's denial of Death, we see a new attitude toward Death taking shape. Round (2007) claimed that the comic medium allows the author to manipulate perspectives through both switching textual voices and visual perspectives, creating a hyperreal effect for the readers: "The reader is thereby given multiple perspectives and situated both within and without the story" (p. 328). She constructed a framework for categorizing panels based on their textual and visual perspectives, combining first-, second-, and third-person narration with heterodiegetic (the absence of a narrator as a character in the plot) or homodiegetic (the presence of a narrator as a character) labels (as proposed by Gérard Genette in 1980). This effect can be observed in the switch between panel three and four in Figure 1. For the first three panels, the characters are speaking in first-person homodiegetic ("No, **No!** I'm not ready to go yet! **I won't go!**"), but in the fourth panel, Death (turned away from the dead Ted yet still speaking) seems to switch to second-person homodiegetic, addressing the reader directly: "Gets em every time." This change in narration makes us complicit with Death, the primary audience of its joke. This identification with Death is heightened through the style of the comic. Though there is a dead "body" depicted in the comic, the hyperreality—including how Ted's dead body looks almost identical to his alive body, except for the comical Xs on his eyes—distances the readers from the actual physicality of a dead body. This allows readers to focus on the punchline instead of dwelling on the reality of death as a force, seeing Death not as something to fear but as a "smart badass," as one of the webcomic comments describes him (Cyanide & … cyanide, 2015).

Returning to the tone of the webcomic, one can see how the humor is achieved: the distance between the real and the hyperreal allows readers the liberty to feel a sense of schadenfreude at Ted's misfortune. It allows them to dissociate from the human condition, to ignore the fact that Death will eventually come for us all by portraying Death's unilateral power as awesome in a cool way, not a terrifying way.

One might think this analysis is reaching too far, especially as this comic is explicitly committed to cheap laughs and a lack of deep themes. However, note that this idea of Death's cool persona lasts beyond this comic, further developed in the subsequent page, "Comic 3738" (McElfatrick, 2014b). As we see in Figure 1, the same orange-shirted character, now alive again, asks Death, "Death, who touches you when its your turn to die?" Death responds matter-of-factly, "Death **can't** die, but if I had to…." The next panel zooms in to show Death sliding on a pair of sunglasses, bragging: "I'd touch myself." The act of putting on sunglasses to look cool or punctuate a joke is a trope well established in the *Cyanide and Happiness* universe (e.g., Wilson, 2012b; Wilson, 2015) as well as being a popular meme on the internet. However, it is a particularly striking move coming from Death. First, the beginning of the conversation seems somewhat serious because of the orange-shirted character's facial expressions; he appears to be inquiring in earnest. In any other context, a question about someone else's death might be a heart-to-heart conversation. But that feel is completely disrupted in panel 3 as Orangeshirt is completely cut out of the panel. Because of the pictorial shift in perspective, the zooming in on Death's face, the narration again seems to switch to second-person homodiegetic, like Death was planning that joke directly for the readers all along. The sunglasses meme itself is also disruptive; the traditional vibe of a Grim Reaper is more "grim." Besides, this iteration of Death has no face; one does not expect it to put on a pair of sunglasses. The sunglasses are purely for the aesthetic vibe of "cool," adding to the impression that this Death is different from other Grim Reapers; it is not to be feared but to be admired.

In sum, this webcomic rejects the *human* "ego as center of existence" (Hoffman, 1964, p. 490), which distances it from Hoffman's modern existentialism. However, neither does this webcomic align with Ariès's (1981) claim that modern society is embarrassed or ashamed by Death (though it does distance the reader from the reality of the dead body). Instead, from this webcomic, one might claim that modern society instead wants to *be* Death.

It rejects the fragility of the human condition, instead asking us to identify with how "badass" Death is.

Death in Life & Death

Life & Death is a webcomic about the daily grind at the office for the characters Death (Steve) and Life (Bobby), both employed by their boss, God. In this webcomic, Death is generally trying to keep up with his busy schedule of personally and sardonically killing all the people on his daily list. When he is not working, he is usually the middle of some sort of drunken mishap— or possibly trying to sneak a mini-fridge into his office.

First, what can we say about the presence of God in this webcomic? Both Hoffman (1964) and Ariès (2008, 2010) assume that modern individuals and modern society itself are grappling with Death in a world that rejects the possibility of eternity. However, God in this webcomic is consistently present, represented as a short man with a white beard and a beige robe, bossing Death around and keeping him accountable for his quota of deaths. There is no question about God's place in the company; he is the top of the hierarchy, a strict (but benevolent) leader who does not shy from reprimanding Death when he plays hooky or from turning the Devil into a pumpkin after an insult. This portrait of God as unquestionably powerful, though obviously somewhat satirical, still seems oddly traditional, and the potential of an eternity in heaven (or hell) is a given; one might imagine that these factors would lead to a more antiquated representation of Death as well. As Hoffman (1964) says:

> One may say that if eternity is accepted without doubt, it is easier for man to make his peace with temporality. That is, a man expecting and believing in eternity will be less concerned with his temporal experiences, will see them less in depth than as a move toward eternity [p. 4].

However, again, the key here is that humans must believe in God and their assurance of eternity in order to accept Death without a struggle. The individual humans in this webcomic do not: they live in the modern world and seem ignorant of the bureaucratic cosmology, meaning they are unaware of the possibility of a life beyond death. This is shown by their continual dismay when confronted by Death. Within the world of the comic, they have no reason to believe in God or eternity. In this portrayal of heaven, God the boss does not interact with people; he is far too busy managing his cosmic employees. Instead, the dying confront Death alone, and he does not pull any punches easing their passage or promising eternity to assuage their fears (as one would expect from someone God calls a psychopath). Though we the readers know that God exists, the individuals in the webcomic do not.

In fact, there are several ways that the limited perspective of the humans in the webcomic, compared to the more omniscient perspective of the readers, distances them from the human condition of dying. The readers are following the story from the perspective of the higher cosmic forces, not from the perspective of the humans, who are treated simply as tasks to be checked off a busy workload. Similar to *Cyanide & Happiness,* the readers share the joke of each death that Steve carefully orchestrates for his (and their) amusement. A typical example of this omniscience is the webcomic "Monkeying with a toaster" (Oliver, 2007), which shows a man in the foreground fiddling with a screwdriver and a toaster. Death lounges in the background, unbeknownst to the man, casually holding the toaster plug. Though the man is in the dark, both Death and the reader know the punchline—this is yet another clever way to check a death off Steve's list. Note too that the readers are not presented with the moment of death or the dead body itself. In fact, the serial nature of the webcomic medium itself purposely shifts attention away from the individual humans and the physical act of dying. As one clicks through the extensive webcomic, it is impossible to focus on how each unnamed, similarly-drawn (hyperreal) person struggles to make a unique identity in the face of Death, especially as the entirety of the webcomic spans across thousands of comics and more than a decade of updates. Instead, most of these humans blend together in the readers' memories. The experience of clicking through a webcomic, as Kogel (2013) argues, creates an effect on the reader; in this case, it allows them to experience the Sisyphean mundanity of Death's job. One sees how Death's job would be boring for him (and the readers) unless he went out of his way to be sadistic and funny.

This webcomic alternates between short one- or three-panel comics, more-involved consecutive storyline arcs, and returning gags, not dissimilar from comic strips published in newspapers. However, unlike physical serial comics, the webcomic's situation in the Web 2.0 environment allow individual comics to be connected across time and space by extratextual features. Since the construct of time (and how a medium represents time) is very important for understanding the meaning of the portrayal of Death, I will turn to the study of how readers use digital tools to traverse the space-time of the comic as another important layer of analysis. Specifically, I will follow one recurring arc to examine this phenomenon: Death's hunt of the immortal phoenix.

Steve generally very diligently and successfully "takes care" of the people on his list. However—to his great frustration—each time he tries to hunt the phoenix, it manages to escape him. The very first time he tries to catch the phoenix, we see Death stretching across a ravine to reach the phoenix's nest—that is, until the branch he is holding breaks. One year of webcomics later, he tries again: Death tries to sneak up behind the phoenix to catch it while it is napping, but while trying to survive a close encounter with a tiger, Death instead accidentally rescues the phoenix. The phoenix in turn purposely rescues Death. After a brief truce, the phoenix sets the bottom of Death's robes on fire, restarting their chase. Finally, after several more encounters with the phoenix and ten more years of webcomic posts, the most recent phoenix comic titled "Back on the Hunt" depicts Death riding a handglider (Oliver, 2017; see Figure 2). In the first panel, he calls out: "Where are you? You can't hide forever." In the next panel, Death looks up as he hears a loud *WHUMP!* In the last panel, the perspective shifts to show the phoenix looking down on him from the top of the glider. Death pleads, "Ah … look, this thing's rented, so please don't set it on fire. Unlike the majority of the posts in this webcomic, the punchline of this joke is on Death himself: the hunter has become the hunted.

The interpretation of this recurring arc is influenced by how readers connect the microserialized updates across the space-time of the webcomic. Recall that an aspect of microserialization is that webcomic strips can function both in context of a larger narrative and as single, stand-alone texts. Kogel (2013), drawing on Aarseth (1997), describes webcomics as ergodic

Figure 2: Life & Death "Back on the Hunt" (creator owned; The Duck Webcomics).

texts, meaning that the process of traversing a webcomic requires "non-trivial effort" (Aarseth, 1997, p. 1) from the reader. He argues that because the readers have a choice in how they navigate these digital texts, their reading experience is fundamentally different from readers of print comic books (Kogel, 2013, p. 53). Remember that readers are inherently experiencing this phoenix arc in different ways: for readers following this webcomic in real time as it updates, there could be years separating some of these webcomic strips, while newer readers could easily encounter this page out of the context of the whole, as the default home page of the webcomic's site is the most recent webcomic strip.

To understand the reading of an ergodic text, one must attend to the digital tools the reader can use to traverse the text. Most webcomics have several digital tools for navigating webcomics, including archives, "next" buttons, or hyperlinks. One creator-added feature that links this particular arc across time and space is the title. As implied by the title "*Back* on the Hunt" (emphasis added), this phoenix chase strip recalls other strips posted across space and time. However, none of the other phoenix strips have titles that explicitly reference the phoenix or the hunt, so it is difficult to compare the strips directly from searching the archives. The creator also does not use other common features like tags or links to connect related comics from the webcomic strip pages themselves, which would make it easier for readers to collapse and compare this page to other previous pages.

The vacuum of creator-added navigational features is filled by reader participation. Another key aspect of the Web 2.0 environment is the possibility for a "highly participatory reading community" (Romaguera, 2010, p. 1). As said before, the ways in which webcomic readers post information for the interpretive community affects the perception of the original text (Romaguera, 2017). If this is true about information posted on websites that do not host the original content, how much more so can readers posting directly under a webcomic update affect the interpretation of that page? I argue that a key feature of traversing this ergodic text is the presence of navigational reader comments.

For instance, one commenter of "Back on the Hunt" says, "HA, I love the ones with the phoenix, they remind me of the old Looney Tunes episodes with Wile E. Coyote and the Roadrunner," (weeble-wobble (Guest), 2017). This both establishes that the update is not a stand-alone episode and recalls the outcomes of the other phoenix arcs, as well as comparing the cyclic nature of the webcomic with the cyclic nature of TV cartoons. Another commenter also alludes to specific moments in previous webcomic strips, speaking directly to Death:

> Honestly, Steve, I'd have thought you'd have learned by now: Things have a tendency
> to go for the worst when you go after the phoenix: Your parachute gets caught in a

tree, you get attacked by a tiger, you end up physically in the Dreamtime.... Did you really expect a rented glider to survive? [namtap032892, 2017].

Aarseth (1997) argues that readers of ergodic texts have more active control over the narrative than readers of print texts: "The effort and energy demanded by the cybertext of its reader raise the stakes of interpretation to those of intervention" (p. 4). Though the webcomic strip itself represents an isolated episode, those commenting on the webcomic page—and those synthesizing other reader comments with the content of the webcomic strip— are actively connecting the present storyline with past arcs. Even from reading *one* page, readers can draw on the readership's collective memory to collapse the arcs into a continuous cycle, despite not being tangibly linked by creator-provided digital tools.

The way this arc portrays time, then, does not mirror Hoffman's (1964) analysis of how modern authors portray time as disjointed and fleeting. Instead, through reader navigation of this webcomic, they experience how time for Death is linked together—past, present, and future, structured by the certainty that the chase with the phoenix will continue in the same way, no matter what. This corresponds more closely with the way Hoffman describes the view of time in relation to a certain eternity, back when society believed in God. However, here it is not God who gives this certainty but the identity of Death and the phoenix themselves. Their very nature demands that Death can never catch the phoenix, no matter what he tries.

Returning to the reader's identification with Death, one can see that because this comic distances the reader from the humans and instead aligns them with Death, they too can take a different attitude toward time. Time is still limited for the humans portrayed in the comics. But the readers are not limited like the humans in the comics. As Round (2007) argued, the medium of the comic allows for new possibilities of postmodern perspectives. Here, because the medium of the webcomic allows readers to step outside of time, they can experience it from Death's perspective instead of a human perspective. Through their navigation of the ergodic text, the readers can experience time as cyclic, not linear, an effect only afforded by the webcomic medium itself.

Death in Mary Death

The creator of *Mary Death* describes his work as a webcomic "about life, death, and everything in between" (Tarpley 2017). The main characters in the story are Mary, a young scientifically-minded girl and her best friend Death, only visible to her. The creator purposely states that "the personification of Death in this comic may not be considered 'canon'" (Tarpley, 2017) as he subverts and plays with artistic and literary tropes surrounding familiar characters like Death, Life, and other legendary forces personified (Pestilence, the Universe, etc.). Many readers comment on the webcomic's artistic and narrative similarities to *Calvin & Hobbes*, though the author has stated in a comment the similarities are unintentional, despite his having read many *Calvin & Hobbes* comics growing up (marydeath, 2013). The images in this webcomic include digital hyperlinked tags and alt text, features which become pertinent to the analysis of these pages.

This personification of Death is epically cool. Whether imagining himself fighting off a horde of zombies, remembering riding his pet T-Rex named Fido, or literally defeating Cthulhu, Death has a flair for the dramatic. It is clear that he is one of the most powerful forces in the universe. However, despite all the amazing things he could be doing, he chooses to spend most of his time with Mary. Thus, his presence is important in shaping her individual identity as she learns about the world around her and her place in it. Unlike mortals in the other comics, Mary is keenly aware that she will die one day; she spends many nights on the roof looking up at the stars and asking Death questions about the meaning of life and the secrets of the universe. Strangely enough, Death also helps her to navigate the obstacles of growing up, almost like a guardian angel. He takes a personal interest when the undefeated chess captain challenges Mary to a game, enthusiastically providing in-game coaching, and when a bully tries to make her pay to walk down the sidewalk, Death scares him away by flashing his life before his eyes. This teaches Mary to be assertive and brave, as she knows that Death is watching out for her.

Mary struggles with thinking about her own mortality as she navigates her relationship with Death. She goes to great lengths to learn about the rules of the universe, which lands her in sticky situations like almost playing a chess game with Life for her life or nearly avoiding being eaten by a serpent (possibly the original from the Garden of Eden). She discovers that Death guides people into the afterlife but does not actually kill anyone; Life is the one who kills people (in fact, she uncovers that Death and Life are locked in a chess match for every soul). Though still afraid to face what comes after Death, she is comforted to know that she will not have to face it alone. However, Death teaches her that curiosity needs to have some limits: she discovers that Death already knows what her final moments will be, but when he asks, "Is that something you really want to know?," she reflects for a panel and decides, "No, I guess not" (Tarpley, 2014b). Most importantly, Death reminds Mary to live and to appreciate each moment of her life. When she complains, he is quick to remind her that things could always be worse. In one webcomic, his presence sitting next to her (sharpening his scythe) reminds her to stop studying inside and go outside to play. Together, they appreciate the small moments of life, like the leaves changing color on a fall day or the sun setting over a scenic forest view. This personification, oddly enough, resonates with personal attitudes about death described by Hoffman (1964), though with slightly different conclusions. As he says:

> Death turns us toward life and forces us to admire or cherish it (even though we may despair of it as well), to begrudge the passing of time (which is signified by changes occurring in objects) and eventually to despair of conclusions [p. 4].

However, for Mary, she learns to admire life by living with Death, not struggling against him. Though she does not have the certainty of eternity guaranteed by God (in fact, Death pointedly calls religion a fairytale and denies God's existence), her confidence in Death's kindness leads her to acceptance instead of despair.

Despite her friendship with Death (or perhaps because of it), Mary muses about time in a way that is similar to other twentieth century characters. Recall Hoffman's (1964) claim that the portrayal of time represents the self's attitude toward Death; he says that authors such as Proust defeat death through moments of deep consciousness: "The struggle for 'real existence' is actually a struggle to defeat death-in-time; that is, to discover pure meaning in life processes is to achieve an immortality within the limits of consciousness" (p. 384). This is echoed by Mary as she struggles to discover meaning in each comic—and not only does she discover meaning, but that meaning allows her to literally step outside of time. In the webcomic "Chrono," she recognizes the urgency of being mortal while cloud-gazing with Death:

> I wonder what it'd be like to forget time altogether. TO be free from the shackles of urgency … our lifespans demand a structure to base our lives around. A distinct beginning, middle, and end. A constant sense of pressure. I suppose without it, we would fall into chaos. But it would be nice to forget it all, even for a second [Tarpley 2013b].

This is followed by one panel where she sits with Death, watching the clouds go by—the only panel in the comic without borders. Recall Round's (2007) claim that space functions as time, and that readers must determine how much narrative time a panel takes by examining the size of the panel in context of the action. Here, the image of Death and Mary watching the clouds combined with the lack of borders means that the reader is unable to say whether this moment lasts for one second or an eternity. This allows the two characters to momentarily step outside of time. The moment is broken in the next panel when her mother calls, "Mary! Dinner time!" Mary stands up. "Then again…" she says, "We might miss out on the important stuff!" (Tarpley 2013b). With that, she runs off to dinner, leaving Death behind. This perfectly echoes the Proustian portrayal of time as described by Hoffman.

Though Mary's perspectives toward Death and experience of time in conjunction with Death echoes twentieth century attitudes, the webcomic medium allows us to also experience Death's perspectives and experience of time. One would not expect Death to be influenced by his friendship with a mortal; however, oddly enough, we actually see how his character develops because of his relationship with Mary. Near the beginning of the webcomic, Death has a checklist of to-do's, with the last item being to "strike fear in the heart of all mortals" (Tarpley, 2013a). However, looking over his shoulder at Mary playing with some *Doctor Who* action figures, he is moved to cross this to-do off his list, as if he cannot bear to scare Mary like that. In another comic, Mary asks Death if he guides animals to the afterlife and is disappointed when he says no. Based on her reaction, he changes his idea of his role—we later see him guiding a tiger to the afterlife, even allowing it one last run across the savannah before it dies. In another comic, Death questions whether his existence has meaning. Mary reassures him that he is performing a vital task of balancing the universe—and then reminds him that part of the meaning of his existence is to be her friend.

However, his friendship with Mary causes him to struggle when he must choose between their friendship and doing his job. In one comic when he finds out that Mary's grandfather has passed away, he pauses to ruminate on how he feels about his task: "THOUSANDS UPON THOUSANDS PERISH EVERYDAY AND I GREET EVERY SINGLE ONE WITHOUT COMPROMISE. SADLY, ON THIS DAY, THAT VIGILANCE WILL CAUSE GRIEF TO SOMEONE DEAR TO ME./FOR THE FIRST TIME IN EXISTENCE, I DREAD WHAT HAPPENS NEXT" (Tarpley, 2014a). The image shows Death striding through a sea of souls. However, there is an extra layer of meaning added to the image of the file through the use of alt text. Though alt text is intended by web designers to be used to describe images, webcomic creators often use it as an extra source of information for the reader: "Webcomics add a coded level to image and text and challenge readers to fuse these three levels to fully understand a webcomic" (Kogel, 2013, p. 35). When the reader hovers their mouse over this particular image, a text box appears with external narration of the image:

> Who [the souls] are and what they did are of no concern to him. Indifferent to their greatness or treachery, he does what is required of him. He has maintained the balance since the dawn of time and, in a marvelous display of unwavering dedication, will continue to do so for eternity.
> We call him Death [Tarpley, 2014a].

Kogel (2013) describes alt text as playful and personal: "It represents a dialogue between creator and comic, it is a sort of preemptive comment on [their] own work" (p. 35). However, this alt text appears to be magnifying the moment represented by the image with external narration. This allows Round's (2007) framework to operate on a new level: the comic simultaneously narrates as first-person homodiegetic *and* first-person heterodiegetic at the same time, in the same panel. The presence of the heterodiegetic narration emphasizes the gap between what Death ought to be (indifferent, consistent, diligent) and his personal introspection (how tempted he is to protect his friend's feelings).

In one comic describing Death's laws, we realize that it is actually unlawful for him to be friends with Mary—and yet he continues to do it anyway. In another comic, he even saves her life, catching her when she accidentally flips off a bike. Death's care for Mary causes his nemesis Life (an inverted carbon-copy of Death) to specifically target Mary. Because Life begins to purposely put Mary's life in danger, Death is forced to literally pause time to save Mary from being hit by a car. Despite the heterodiegetic narration that so confidently emphasizes Death's omniscience and his future commitment to his job, we see that the character Death is actually concerned with who Mary is and what she does. This gap between Death's actions and the expectations of the narrator is intended to trouble the readers. If part of Death's function is his indifference, his unwavering conviction to doing his job, what happens when he begins to care for a human? In a universe where Death is good and Life is evil, the reader is forced to wonder whether his affection for Mary may have dire consequences. The author purposely does not explain why Death is Mary's constant companion. In *Doctor Who* (a British TV show that the webcomic constantly references), the inhuman Doctor needs a human companion to remind him to have empathy. However, this webcomic asks: despite what people might think they want from Death, is it really good for Death to have empathy? Is it possible that empathy could tip the balance of the universe—tip it the wrong way? A friendly Death may mean a weak Death, a Death that cannot perform its function or maintain the balance between good and evil.

The reader also experiences time in a different way through viewing the world from Death's perspective. One example of this effect is the webcomic "Parallel" (Tarpley, 2015; see Figure 3) which has four panels, stacked vertically. When clicking to open the page, the reader sees only the first panel, which depicts Mary and Death walking through a light snowfall with Mary commenting, "I wonder what my life would be like in a parallel universe." As readers scroll down, they encounter three similar panels, one on top of the other, with Mary asking the same query. Though Mary and Death are walking in the same position for each panel, the following differences register: in the second panel, Mary is dressed as a knight and there are floating islands and dragons in the background; in the third panel, Mary is dressed in a scuba suit and they are walking underwater; and in the fourth panel they are still walking in a light snowfall, except Mary has shorter, bushier hair. In all four panels, Mary is the only element in color.

WWW.MARYDEATHCOMICS.COM

© 2015 MATTHEW TARPLEY

Kogel (2013) describes Scott McCloud's concept of the Infinite Canvas, a format where comics could "abandon the structure of the printed page and instead use the infinitely scrollable browser window as its canvas" (p. 63). He explains that the reader's experience of scrolling influences their perception of time and can build suspense. As "Parallel" does not fit on one screen, it is important to examine how scrolling in the computer window affects the reader's experience of time in this webcomic. Generally in webcomics (and comics in general), one begins with the assumption the succession of panels from left to right represent a linear timeline. However, as one scrolls down "Parallel" and sees each of the three panels portraying the same moment as the first panel, the reader realizes that this comic represents a snapshot of the same moment across four parallel universes. The act of scrolling (instead of seeing the four universes at once, like a print comic would do) creates the effect of *shifting* the reader's perspective from a third-person human viewer (who can only see one timeline) to an omniscient viewer who can see several parallel universes at once, approximating Death's point of view, as he is the only character who is the same in, and possibly aware of, all four parallel universes at the same time. This effect of looking through Death's eyes is heightened by the panel layout and use of color: in each panel, not only is Death always gazing at Mary, but Mary is the only part of the four panels which is in color, making her changing outfits stand out. This draws the reader's gaze to Mary, despite the potentially interesting parallel universes playing out quietly in the background. Only through scrolling, though, does the reader literally experience the hyperreal shift in perspective from first-person homodiegetic to (visually) third-person heterodiegetic.

Because the readers are able to see from Death's eyes in a way that Mary cannot, they are able to experience Death's struggle with his role. In order for Mary to gain security, strength, and bravery from their relationship, Death must suffer insecurity, weakness, and dread. Because of the implications of Death's role, he is more than just an imaginary friend like Hobbes—indeed, his role seems almost Christ-like in that he gives up his self-identity for Mary. Hoffman (1964) argues that modern humans try to replace God with themselves, but here the comic creator both replaces God with Death while simultaneously making the readers into Death themselves.

Conclusions

If Hoffman asks what makes individual lives meaningful in light of death, and if Ariès asks why we as a society want to ignore death, these webcomic

Opposite: Figure 3: Mary Death "Parallel" (creator owned; Tarpley).

creators ask us what it would be like to be Death. In *Cyanide & Happiness*, we reject the idea of the individual struggling against Death; Death instead performs his job like it is a game or a giant joke, and readers are allowed to share in his superiority as they "get" Death's punchlines. *Life & Death* subverts the expectation that Death is infallible, showing how Death performs his job just like anyone else does. Finally, *Mary Death* disrupts the idea that Death is far removed from life, showing how Death's presence makes us appreciate life all the more; we can experience the beauty and the pain of friendship between Death and a mortal, both from the perspective of the mortal and the perspective of Death.

Instead of literature approximating our mortal experience of time, these webcomics approximate Death's experience of eternity. Instead of relying on the existence of God to connect past, present, and future, we rely on the existence of Death. Instead of struggling with the meaninglessness of human experience, we examine Death's experience of us. With respect to Ariès, it does seem like these moves tend to marginalize the imminence of one's own death and distances us from the reality of the physical dead body. However, unlike Ariès, the webcomic creators do not try to remove Death from the picture. By shifting the focus off the tragedy of the individual death, we see the significance of Death for all of humanity. Instead of being isolated by Death, we are all connected by our encounters with Death.

In terms of personification, it remains clear that one of the main purposes of anthropomorphizing Death in comics, regardless of whether the comic is a print comic or a webcomic, is how personification allows Death to be humanized. As I argue in a previous work,

> Through personification, the graphic novel is able to force the reader to face that which modern society fears and marginalizes, and to discover that the modern practice of hiding death away is far more terrifying than looking Death straight in the face [Schneider, 2013 p. 88].

This remains true in webcomics. Instead of enabling the reader to avoid Death, the humor of these webcomics allows readers to interact with it, albeit in a safe, hyperreal form. We as readers experience an anthropomorphized Death—cynical or manipulative or obsessive as it may be. And sometimes, unexpectedly, the reader may discover Death's capacity for kindness or friendship.

An interesting deviation from print comics is that all three of these webcomics choose to represent Death as some sort of traditional Grim Reaper, with a black hooded robe, a sickle, and some sort of skeletal body (notably, even though *Cyanide and Happiness* continually changes its representation of Death, all of these representations are variations of Grim Reapers). This is not a given for graphic representations of Death. As I described in a previous work, graphic authors can (and do) imagine Death as everything from a spiky goth girl to a bird-headed man in a suit to an inflatable tubeman with a cutesy skull mask (Schneider, 2013, p. 6). What accounts for this lack of experimentation? I hypothesize that these representations of Death in webcomics may be fundamentally shaped by the process of microserialization. Because each of these webcomics is made of individual updates, there is always the possibility that a webcomic strip will be decontextualized, either when a reader visits a page for the first time—as the default landing page for all these webcomics' websites are their most recent update—or if the strip is shared across platforms. However, if Death is personified with the common image of the faceless Grim Reaper, the creators can assume that most readers will recognize the cultural allusion (even if the Grim Reaper is drawn in multiple different ways). This artistic reference activates the reader's understanding of historical attitudes toward Death, like those described by Hoffman and Ariès. The visual allusion to the traditional imagery allows the webcomic creators to highlight the ways that they are departing from traditional attitudes toward Death, making any unusual portrayals clear through the juxtaposition of the visuals and the dialogue. As we see, the use of the hyperreal Grim Reaper form allows these webcomic authors to both accept some twentieth century themes, like the marginalizing of the dead body, while rejecting others, like the assurance of happiness in life or the longing for a tame Death.

These faceless cartoon Deaths also serve another purpose. Scott McCloud (1993) argues that the abstract nature of comics makes cartoon characters more universal, which allows readers to project their identities into the characters: "We don't just observe the cartoon, we become it!" (p. 36). In some sense, the abstraction of Death as a cartoon allows us to imagine ourselves in that role—with all the consequences it brings. We can walk in Death's shoes, perform his role, experience his eternity. This allows us to see how the balance of life and death demands that we as individuals meet our demise. Though modern society may have turned away from God's security, it seems we cannot summon the courage to jump into the abyss of postmodern meaninglessness. Instead, we stand in-between, wondering where to turn for comfort. And when we look to ourselves and find that we are lacking, it appears that we may turn to Death itself instead.

REFERENCES

Aarseth, E.J. (1997). *Cybertext: Perspectives on ergodic literature.* Baltimore: Johns Hopkins University Press.

Ariès, P. (2008). *The hour of our death.* (H. Weaver, Trans.). New York: Vintage Books (Original work published in 1981).

Ariès, P. (2010). *Western attitudes toward death: From the Middle Ages to the present.* Baltimore: Johns Hopkins University Press (Original work published in 1974).

Cyanide & ... cyanide. (2015, September). Re: "3691." [Webcomic comment]. Cyanide & Happiness. Retrieved from http://explosm.net/comics/3691/.

Donne, J. (1633). Death be not proud. In R. Booth (Ed.), *The collected poems of John Donne* (pp. 251). Wordsworth Editions: Hertsfordshire.

Gallagher, J.R. (2015). Five strategies internet writers use to "continue the conversation." *Written Communication, 32*(4), 396–425. https://doi.org/10.1177/0741088315601006.

Hicks, M.T. (2009). "Teh Futar": the power of the webcomic and the potential of web 2.0. In R. Scully, & M. Quartly (Eds.), *Drawing the line: Using cartoons as historical evidence* (1 ed., pp. 1–20). Australia: Monash University ePress.

Hoffman, F.J. (1964). *The mortal No: Death and the modern imagination.* Princeton: Princeton University Press.

Jo. (2005). 211. *Cyanide & happiness.* Retrieved from http://explosm.net/comics/211/.

Johnson, P. (2006, April 1). *Student draws explosive web comic.* Retrieved from https://web.archive.org/web/20100224072613/http://www.utdmercury.com/2.7018/stude\nt-draws-explosive-web-comic-1.1001334.

Kogel, D. (2013). Rethinking webcomics: Webcomics as a screen based medium. Unpublished master's thesis. University of Jyväskylä, Jyväskylä, Finland. Retrieved from https://jyx.jyu.fi/dspace/handle/123456789/40712.

McCloud, S. (1993). *Understanding comics: The invisible art.* New York: William Morrow Paperbacks.

McElfatrick, D. (2014a). 3691. *Cyanide & happiness.* Retrieved from http://explosm.net/comics/3691/.

McElfatrick, D. (2014b). 3738. *Cyanide & happiness.* Retrieved from http://explosm.net/comics/3738/.

McElfatrick, D. (2016). 4446. *Cyanide & happiness.* Retrieved from http://explosm.net/comics/4446/.

Medina-Tayac, S. (2012, October 16). *Cyanide and happiness founder talks web humor.* Retrieved from http://yaledailynews.com/blog/2012/10/16/cyanide-and-happiness-founder-talks-web-humor/.

Melvin, M. (2005a). 110. *Cyanide & happiness.* Retrieved from http://explosm.net/comics/110/.

Melvin, M. (2005b). 115. *Cyanide & happiness.* Retrieved from http://explosm.net/comics/115/.

Melvin, M. (2005c). 206. *Cyanide & happiness.* Retrieved from http://explosm.net/comics/206/.

namtap032892. (2017, April 1). Re: "Back on the hunt." [Webcomic comment]. Retrieved from lifeanddeath.smackjeeves.com/comics/2411838/1749-back-on-the-hunt/.

Oliver, J. (2006). Death from above. *Life & death.* Retrieved from http://lifeanddeath.smackjeeves.com/comics/15273/15-death-from-above/.

Oliver, J. (2007). Monkeying with a toaster. *Life & death.* Retrieved from http://lifeanddeath.smackjeeves.com/comics/130906/344-monkeying-with-a-toaster/.

Oliver, J. (2017). Back on the hunt. *Life & death.* Retrieved from lifeanddeath.smackjeeves.com/comics/2411838/1749-back-on-the-hunt/.

PSES reborn. (2017, August). Re: "206." [Webcomic comment]. Retrieved from http://explosm.net/comics/206/.

Romaguera, G.E. (2010). *Piecing the parts: An analysis of narrative strategies and textual elements in microserialized webcomics.* Unpublished master's thesis. University of Puerto Rico, Mayaguez, Puerto Rico. Retrieved from https://search.proquest.com/pqdtglobal/docview/837419788/abstract/ABAC66F8CA384E91PQ/1.

Romaguera, G.E. (2017). *To start, continue, and conclude: Foregrounding narrative production in serial fiction publishing.* Unpublished doctoral dissertation. University of Rhode Island, Kingston. Retrieved from http://proxy.library.nyu.edu/login?url=https://search-proquest-com.proxy.library.nyu.edu/docview/1946176791?accountid=12768.

Round, J. (2007). Visual perspective and narrative voice in comics: Redefining literary terminology. *International Journal of Comic Art, 9*(2), 316.

Schneider, K. (2013). *The personification of death in the graphic novel.* (Unpublished undergraduate thesis). Princeton University.

Tarpley, M. (2013a). Checklist. *Mary Death.* Retrieved from http://marydeathcomics.com/checklist.

Tarpley, M. (2013b). Chrono. *Mary Death*. Retrieved from http://marydeathcomics.com/chrono.

Tarpley, M. (2014a). Dread. *Mary Death*. Retrieved from http://marydeathcomics.com/dread.

Tarpley, M. (2014b). Mortality. *Mary Death*. Retrieved from http://marydeathcomics.com/mortality.

Tarpley, M. (2015). Parallel. *Mary Death*. Retrieved from http://marydeathcomics.com/parallel.

Tarpley, M. (2017). About. Retrieved from http://www.marydeathcomics.com/about-2.

Walsh, R. (2006). The narrative imagination across media. *MFS: Modern Fiction Studies*, *52*(4), 855–868.

weeble-wobble (Guest). (2017, April 6). Re: "Back on the hunt." [Webcomic comment]. Retrieved from lifeanddeath.smackjeeves.com/comics/2411838/1749-back-on-the-hunt/.

Wilson, K. (2012a). 2742. *Cyanide & happiness*. Retrieved from http://explosm.net/comics/2742/.

Wilson, K. (2012b). 2793. *Cyanide & happiness*. Retrieved from http://explosm.net/comics/2793/.

Wilson, K. (2015). 3933. *Cyanide & happiness*. Retrieved from http://explosm.net/comics/3933/.

MAUS (W)HOLES

Reflections on (and in) the Digitization
of Art Spiegelman's MAUS

JOHN LOGIE

Introduction: *The Missing* MAUS *(or The Curious Absence of Art Spiegelman's* MAUS *in eBook Formats)*

Art Spiegelman's *MAUS* is, without question, one of the most significant works of comic art in the history of the medium. Spiegelman's graphic narration of his father Vladek's torturous journey from Poland, to Nazi-occupied Czechoslovakia, to Auschwitz, and, finally, as a Holocaust survivor, to Rego Park, New York earned Art Spiegelman a Pulitzer in 1992. In the 25 years since its release, *MAUS* has become part of the curriculum in thousands of United States high schools and colleges. Boerman-Cornell, Kim, and Manderino (2017) cite *MAUS* as the kind of graphic novel that is "more and more becoming a staple of high school English classrooms" (p. 2) and later describe it as having been used in "countless classrooms" (p. 53). For many students, Spiegelman's work is one of the ways they come to terms with the profound human toll inflicted by the events of the Holocaust. Given the widespread adoption of *MAUS* within United States high schools and the expanding popularity of eBook-friendly digital technologies in high schools, it is more than a little surprising that there are currently no legitimate eBook editions of Art Spiegelman's *MAUS*.

According to Baker (2017) "12.6 million mobile computing devices [were] shipped to primary and secondary schools in 2016." The majority of these were Chromebooks, but to the extent that these machines were touchscreen capable, they also could offer students a tablet-like reading experience via Kindle Cloud Reader or similar apps. This market alone would represent a substantial revenue opportunity for any producer of a *MAUS* ebook edition. And in many ways, *MAUS* is an ideal candidate for presentation on the Kindle, Kobo, and similar eReader platforms. The pages of the *MAUS* print editions are 6.7 by 9.4 inches, able to be displayed on, for example, an iPad or any of the larger Kindle Fires without significant reduction in size. Further, *MAUS* is presented in stark black and white, perfectly suited to the high contrast black e-ink and white background of the Kindle Paperwhite. In terms of its visual look and feel, *MAUS* is an exceptionally strong candidate for representation on contemporary eBook and tablet platforms.

And yet, reflecting on the subject matter (rather than the form) of *MAUS* offers one possible answer as to why this particular work of comic art has not yet been ported into the eBook space. *MAUS* is, among other things, the story of Art Spiegelman's father, Vladek, finding ways to survive Auschwitz. As such, Spiegelman's painstakingly handcrafted work of comic art is at odds with the technological ethos that Katz (1992) rightly argues was foundational to an "Ethic of Expediency" that facilitated the mechanization of murder on a massive scale. Katz writes:

> [T]echnology is the embodiment of pure expediency. Thus, "the spiritual element." The *ethos* of technology, is expediency: rationality, efficiency, speed, productivity, power.... Both science and technology are "a good" not only because they are a rational means for accomplishing a task and/or achieving leisure and thus happiness (the virtues heard most in regard to scientific and technical progress.... Germans under Nazi rule were an efficient people of an industrious nation who totally lost themselves in the *ethos* of technology [p. 266].

Since its publication, Katz's essay has served as a warning to scholars, especially those in scientific and technical communication, about the potentially extreme risks that await us when the attractions of technology—"rationality, efficiency, speed, productivity, power" (p. 268)—encourage us to lose sight of the humanity building, consuming, and subject to a given technology. Thus, when confronted with the absence of an eBook or Kindle edition of *MAUS*, the intuitive answer for this absence is that because Spiegelman's work both documents and indicts this same ethos of technology and all of its profoundly complex and painful ramifications, the work itself resists digitization. Indeed, because the Nazi program of dehumanization specifically involved the reduction of humans to numbers it seems reasonable to withhold this work from a medium that, at root, reduces everything from Munch to Mendelssohn to memes down to numeric binary code. And yet, Art Spiegelman's *MAUS* was, in fact, the subject of a pioneering project to adapt comics to digital spaces. Indeed, *MAUS* plays an especially significant role in the history of digital comics.

In 1994, the Voyager company, a leading producer of literary, artistic, and educational CD-ROMS, released a Macintosh-only CD-ROM edition of Spiegelman's work, supplemented by hours of interviews, transcripts, archival materials, photographs, and other multimedia content. This project, fully titled *The Complete MAUS: A Survivor's Tale,* was praised by *Entertainment Weekly* (!) as "one of the few CD-ROMs to make the nascent technology look something like art" (Burr, 1994, p. 61). Ty Burr's *Entertainment Weekly* article goes on to quote Spiegelman as saying he was "unable to watch it [the CD-ROM] at home because, he says, he does not have a 'ROM Player'" (Burr, 1994, p. 61). Burr's article also makes clear that Voyager approached Spiegelman, and that Spiegelman had only a limited understanding of the capability and limits of the CD-ROM: "My idea was-click-these 35,000 pieces of paper are now going to be on one little disc. I found out that was naive. It's only 5,000" (Burr, 1994, p. 61). Notable here is Spiegelman's sense that an ideal outcome would be presenting *MAUS* within the broader context of *all* of the paper documents Spiegelman had assembled during the project, be they his own sketches, transcripts, or archival documents from his family's journey. And Spiegelman's insistence that readers grapple with the underlying truths of the *MAUS* narrative have, at times, made him uncomfortable with the project being too neatly binned as a "graphic novel."

The Category-Defining "Graphic Novel" That Isn't a Novel

Indeed, the print *MAUS*, composed from 1978 to 1991, resolutely defies categorization, but it is fair to describe the work as, among other things, autobiographical. The bulk of *MAUS* is given over to Art Spiegelman's representations of his father Vladek's memories of the Holocaust, including Vladek's imprisonment at Auschwitz. Spiegelman based *MAUS* on a series of taped interviews with his father and originally published most of the individual chapters serially within the comic magazine *RAW*. In 1986, six completed chapters were collected and published by Pantheon as *MAUS: A Survivor's Tale. I: My Father Bleeds History.* Four additional chapters were published in *RAW* from 1986 to 1991, and then gathered along with a fifth and final chapter for the 1991 publication of *MAUS II: And Here My Troubles Began.*

Spiegelman's selection of the comics medium for this narrative constitutes a direct rejection of the traditional objectivity of the historian or journalist in favor of a more personal, overtly situated subject position. Also, Spiegelman's use of the comics medium for this narrative leaves *MAUS* oscillating between the poles of high and low culture. The stark sharpness of Spiegelman's black-and-white imagery bespeaks an avant-garde sensibility, while the recasting of Nazis and Jews as cartoon cats and mice links Spiegel-man's work to the lurid exploits of Tom and Jerry, Krazy Kat and Ignatz, and, of course, Mickey Mouse. And the difficulty of distinguishing the real from the copy—the natural from the artificial—is foregrounded as well. In one of the brief interview segments included in the Voyager CD-ROM, Spiegelman (1994) discusses how he substituted typing paper for the much larger art boards he normally uses in order to produce *MAUS* on a more intimate and more directly reproducible scale:

> I wanted to keep it close to writing so that what I was making was a manuscript … something made by hand. That's one of the reasons that *MAUS* is drawn at a one-to-one ratio. The book is printed the same size it was drawn. So it's really as close to getting a clear copy of somebody's diary or journal as one could have. In that sense it's more intimate than, say, a book of prose that's set in type because at that point Jacqueline Susanne or James Joyce can both be set in Times Roman, and it's anonymous until you learn how to decode it. The quirks of penmanship that make up comics drawing have a much more immediate bridge to somebody. I mean, even if you can't read it you're already getting incredible amounts of information about the maker and about what's being told, of course [n.p.].

In traditional print texts, readers recognize that, at minimum, the maker's text has been passed on to others who may have laid out the pages, set the type, or, perhaps, edited the composer's words. Comics, by contrast, often *seem* relatively unmediated. In all comics, but especially in those cases where a given work is attributed to a single artist (as opposed to the teams of writers and artists typically responsible for mass-market comic books) ideas seem to travel from the composer's head to the hand to the pen to the page without any of the layers of technological intervention found in traditional print texts. Spiegelman's process for the print *MAUS* was designed to intensify the reader's sense that the cartoon represents the pure, unmediated expression of an author's intentions. One pronounced problem with the CD-ROM is that it is not capable of delivering a parallel "unmediated" reading experience. First, the resolution of the scanned pages is so poor that the reader cannot help but note it. Additionally, the designers of the CD-ROM were left with margins *outside* the pages of the *MAUS* print text, which they opted to fill with a static image, sketched by Spiegelman, of Jews-as-mice in the midst of a round-up, staring as they confront their bleak future. While it arguably makes artistic sense for the presence of these individuals—lost to the machineries of murder that were central to the Holocaust—to loom over the digitized reading experience, this "frame" persistently reminds the reader of how very mediated this "Complete *MAUS*" really is.

The CD-ROM of *MAUS* also devotes considerable space to Spiegelman's own reflections upon his composing processes. *The Complete MAUS* CD-ROM includes interviews in which Art Spiegelman reflects on his process, and indeed on the degree to which his own life has been transformed by his having composed arguably the most celebrated "graphic novel" to date. Though to the extent that the "novel" in "graphic novel" implies "fictional narrative" the term has proven problematic when applied to *MAUS*, in which Spiegelman specifically held technology at a distance in hopes of reinforcing the truth of the *MAUS* narrative. In the digitally archived interviews, Spiegelman's descriptions of his alteration of his artistic practice in favor of a minimally mediated form are emblematic of his sense of the importance of producing a work which was true not merely to his own vision, but to his father's recollections. While Spiegelman acknowledges inevitable distortions of his, or any, artistic process, Spiegelman is nevertheless insistent upon the core reality of *MAUS*.

When, in 1991, *The New York Times* bestseller list initially categorized the print edition of *MAUS II* as "fiction," Spiegelman (1991a) responded with a letter titled "A Problem of Taxonomy" that acknowledged his authorial interventions, but insisted upon the historical accuracy of the *MAUS* narrative:

> If your list was divided into literature and nonliterature I could gracefully accept the compliment as intended, but to the extent that fiction indicates that a work isn't factual, I feel a bit queasy. As an author I believe I might have lopped several years off the thirteen I devoted to my two-volume project if I could only have taken a novelist's license while searching for a novelistic structure. The borderland between fiction and nonfiction has been fertile territory for some of the most potent contemporary writing, and it's not as though my passages on how to build a bunker and repair concentration camp boots got the book onto your "advice, how-to and miscellaneous" list. It's just that I shudder to think how David Duke—if he could read—would respond to seeing a carefully researched work based closely on my father's memory of life in Hitler's Europe and in the death camps, classified as fiction [p. 4].

The *Times* published an Editor's response to Spiegelman's letter announcing that they were immediately moving *MAUS II* to the non-fiction best-seller list, citing Pantheon Book's labeling of *MAUS II* as "history/memoir" and the Library of Congress' entry for *MAUS II*, which the *Times* presents as "also plac[ing] it in the non-fiction category" (Spiegelman, 1991a, 4). As is so often the case with *MAUS*, this brief description points toward a more complicated truth, as the basis for the *Times'* categorization appears to be grounded on the use of "Biography" as a descriptive category.

The Library of Congress (1991) subject headings are also particularly noteworthy for the extent to which they blur the question of *MAUS's* authorship:

> 1. Spiegelman, Vladek—Comic books, strips, etc.; 2. Spiegelman, Art—Comic books, strips, etc.; 3. Holocaust, Jewish (1939–1945)—Poland—Biography—Comic books, strips, etc.; 4. Holocaust survivors—United States—Biography—Comic books, strips,

etc.; 5. Children of Holocaust survivors—United States—Biography—Comic books, strips, etc. [Library of Congress, 1991, LC Subjects].

While *MAUS II* is indexed under "Spiegelman, Art," the first subject heading refers not to Art but to his father. The fourth subject heading suggests that *MAUS II* is Art's biography of his father, which distorts the degree to which the *MAUS* narrative is delivered by Vladek in a Yiddish-inflected syntax which Art meticulously reproduces. For example, Vladek begins his *MAUS* narrative by saying, "It would take many books, my life, and no one wants anyway to hear such stories," (Spiegelman, 1986, p. 12) and it is these old-world rhythms and quirks that characterize the dominant narrative voice within *MAUS* and *MAUS II*. The fifth Library of Congress subject heading inaccurately describes *MAUS* as a "biography" about the offspring of Holocaust survivors. While Art is indeed numbered among "children of Holocaust survivors," *MAUS's* framing narrative, in which Art painstakingly extracts his father's story, the framing narrative about the relationship between Art as the child of a Holocaust survivor is clearly auto-biographical rather than biographical.

The question of *MAUS's* genre was similarly befuddling for the Pulitzer committee, which awarded Spiegelman a "Special Citation in Letters" in order to avoid having to characterize the work within the available Pulitzer categories of fiction, drama, history, biography, poetry and general non-fiction. And indeed, though portions of *MAUS* seem to belong to each of these categories, the whole seems irreducible to anyone. Thus, the paradox of *MAUS* is that traditional understandings of the author as artificer—as the maker of originary, imaginative works—make it difficult to acknowledge Art Spiegelman's tremendous artistry without implicitly challenging the reality of the *MAUS* narrative. Conventional authorial practices such as embellishment, illustration, and editorial discretion are thrown into troubling relief by the power of Vladek's oral recitation of his Holocaust narrative, which is clearly factual—in the most important senses of the word—despite Vladek's lapses in memory, his embellishments, and even his possible willful distortions. And the gaps between what Vladek said and what Art drew are thrown into awkward relief when one digs into the layers of the digital comic as presented within the Voyager CD-ROM.

Spiegelman's complex structure of nested narratives jumbles together elements of fiction, documentary, biography, autobiography, illustration, and even photography (Spiegelman sometimes embeds family photographs within *MAUS*). Within the pages of *MAUS*, Vladek's recitations of his experiences to his son are surrounded (and at times interrupted) by Art's own autobiographical narrative, in which Art details the often excruciating process of goading his father into telling his story. Both narratives invoke conventions drawn from fictional forms ranging from novelistic prose to the fairy tale.

Thus the factuality that Spiegelman properly ascribes to the *MAUS* narrative is intertwined with—and in some cases arguably undercut by—the markers of Spiegelman's artistry. In this light, Spiegelman's authorization of *The Complete MAUS* CD-ROM, in which the two volumes of the print *MAUS* are surrounded and supplemented by a wealth of additional material, seemed specifically designed to foreclose the argument that *MAUS's* fictional elements might in any way compromise its avowedly factual core. The comic is resituated as an artistic statement in the midst of a larger documentary project, involving painstaking research and recovery of materials needed to ensure that elements of the comic were as accurate as they could be. Reading this digital *MAUS* is a qualitatively different experience from reading the print *MAUS*. The print *MAUS* becomes a node in a larger network that is always hovering on the margins of Spiegelman's initial presentation.

Supplementing MAUS *in Order to Complete It*

The Complete MAUS CD-ROM is a remarkably expansive archive. The introduction contains a series of interviews with Spiegelman, as does a later section, "Art on Art." A section of "Appendices" features a catch-all collection of miscellany (including the letter to *The New York Times* mentioned earlier) which situates the print *MAUS* with respect to its antecedents and its critical reception. Also provided in a "Supplements" section are maps of all of the locales featured in the narrative, giving readers a fuller sense of the spatial displacements imposed on the Spiegelman family (the jacket cover for the print *MAUS II* describes this movement as "from the barracks of Auschwitz to the bungalows of the Catskills"). The Spiegelman family tree is also included within the supplemental materials, allowing readers to bear witness to the family's devastating losses during the Holocaust years. And finally, and most importantly, selections from the transcripts of Art's tapes of his father recounting the *MAUS* narrative are included, allowing owners of the CD-ROM literal and figurative windows into Spiegelman's authorial processes.

What the CD-ROM's table of contents does not reveal is the extent to which these materials are also woven into the corpus of *MAUS*. Transcripts of Vladek speaking, for instance, are often available at the click of a mouse button. In the print *MAUS*, the cross-cutting of Art's pursuit of his father's story and Vladek's narrative often reveals a profound tension—Vladek at times demonstrates a willingness to tailor his story to what he perceives to be Art's wishes, even though Art's stated wish is for nothing more than a coherent, factual narrative. At one point, Vladek responds to Art's insistence upon keeping things chronological with a cavalier, "Okay. I'll make it so how you want it" (Spiegelman, 1986, p. 82). Later, and more poignantly, Vladek explains, "All such things of the war, I tried to put out from my mind once for all ... until you rebuild me all this from your questions" (Spiegelman, 1991b, p. 98). The import of Vladek's statement is clear. Art is forcing Vladek to both clarify *and create* the core MAUS narrative, which otherwise will die with Vladek. In effect, Spiegelman is demanding that his father tell his story, forcing the status of author upon his father; however, as Vladek observes, the authorship which Art's questions engender is a shared possession, in which the ultimate authority is diffuse. This is a delicate balancing act. Within the print MAUS, Spiegelman does a remarkable job of helping the reader navigate this awkwardly shared composition, but in the CD-ROM, this balance is thrown off by the hovering presence of visual cues inviting readers to step out of the MAUS narrative and into the documentary corpus in which the transcripts and recordings of Art and Vladek's exchanges sometimes deviate from how Art Spiegelman presented them within MAUS.

When reading the transcripts or listening to the recordings on the CD-ROM, a MAUS reader gets a deeper and more complicated portrait of the relationship between the Spiegelmans, and also the challenges of making art from an incredibly painful family history. At times Vladek clearly derives pleasure and comfort from maintaining his verbal interactions with his son, but the price of these interactions is often Vladek's being forced to revisit his most desperate hours. Vladek often demonstrates an impulse to purge all memories of his own past. At the end of the MAUS narrative, Vladek infuriates Art by disclosing that he has burned the notebooks kept by Art's mother, who committed suicide in 1968. Thus Vladek's collaboration with Art is delivered with hovering notes of anger, ambivalence, and reluctance. Art and Vladek's interview sessions transpire in an environment crackling with Art's barely suppressed rage at having been denied access to his mother's words, and Vladek's guilt over having deprived his son of this opportunity. At the end of MAUS, Vladek explains:

> After Anja died I had to make an order with everything.... These papers had too many memories. So I burned them.... I'm telling you, after the tragedy with mother, I was so **depressed** then, I didn't know if I'm coming or going! [Spiegelman, 1986, p.159, emphasis in original].

Again and again in the digital archive's interviews and transcripts, the contested nature of the give-and-take between son and father is laid bare. Near the beginning of the second volume of the print MAUS, Art depicts his father speculating about the fate of a fellow prisoner named Mandelbaum. As Vladek recounts the story in the comic, his initial telling of the story as fact is undermined by an admission that he does not know exactly what happened: "I don't **know** if this was how it was with Mandelbaum—only that very often they did so" (Spiegelman, 1991b, p. 35, emphasis in original). This admission is followed by Vladek's speculation about a range of possible horrors which may have been visited on Mandelbaum. But when a reader of the CD-ROM reaches this page, that reader has the option of moving the computer's mouse onto the side of the page (which, distractingly, causes a tiny gloved hand icon looking surprisingly like Mickey Mouse's to appear) and then moving this hand onto an image of Vladek-as-mouse ballooning out of a tape recorder, and Vladek and Art's voices can be heard saying the following:

> ART: What happened to the guy who you were protecting a little in the beginning? Was he alive?
>
> VLADEK: No. You see, it was this work, what they send there, it was such, to finish them out. You know what they did? He had a cap. The guy who, who was watching them, took his cap and threw it far. "Run, and take the cap!" He was running to take his cap. And he shoot him.
>
> ART: They were just toying with them at that point
>
> VLADEK: Yes, and then he reported, "He wanted to run away." He shoot him.
>
> ART: Just for, for fun.
>
> VLADEK: Yes. No! He wrote down that this, "This number wanted to run away from work. I shoot him." He didn't like him; he wanted to shoot him.
>
> ART: And do you know that that's what happened to your...
>
> VLADEK: Yes. Now it—no, I don't know. I don't know whether this happened to him. Maybe it happened that they, that they hit him in the head, that they killed him. I don't know, but I am telling you only how it was done there [Spiegelman, 1994, p. 95: Vladek Audio].

The exchange is much more pointed than the rendition in the comic *MAUS* suggests, which begins with Art asking, "So you don't know what happened to Mandelbaum?" The audio, by contrast, begins with reasonably benign questions: "What happened to the guy who you were protecting a little in the beginning? Was he alive?" Vladek's response is to provide a specific and harrowing example of the ways in which Nazi guards tormented their captives:

> You see, it was this work, what they send there, it was such, to finish them out. You know what they did? He had a cap. The guy who was watching them, took his cap and threw it far. "Run, and take the cap!" He was running to take his cap. And he shoot him [Spiegelman, 1994, p. 95: Vladek Audio].

But Art senses that his father's narrative is not quite accurate, first asking whether the guards did this "just for fun?" and ultimately challenging his father by asking Vladek directly, "And do you *know* that that's what happened...?" [Emphasis added]. Vladek initially asserts the truth of his story, but then retreats, and explains that he was telling what happened generally at Auschwitz, and not necessarily what happened to Mandelbaum:

> Yes. Now it—no. I don't know whether this happened to him. Maybe it happened that they, that they hit him in the head, that they killed him. I don't know, but I am telling you only how it was done there [Spiegelman, 1994, p. 95: Vladek Audio].

In the audio, Art appears to catch Vladek in the process of embellishing his narrative. In the print version, Vladek merely seems vague, and perhaps deliberately so. Spiegelman the comic artist has represented one reading of the conversation, but Spiegelman the archivist has presented a second. The two versions are, in part, contradictory, but in the CD-ROM, they share the same space. At other points, the CD-ROM contents function as a further layering of narrative upon the existing comics narrative. In the print edition of *MAUS II*, Spiegelman begins Chapter Two, titled "Auschwitz: Time Flies," by commenting on the popular success of the first (1986) collected volume of *MAUS*. Spiegelman explains that he is increasingly depressed despite the book's popularity and uncomfortable addressing numerous opportunities to market *MAUS*. Spiegelman expresses discomfort at the notion of turning *MAUS* into a television special or movie and subsequently draws a video camera intrusively zeroing in on him as he is questioned by a feline German interviewer, and "pitched" by a capitalist dog, barking "check out this licensing deal" (Spiegelman, 1991b, p. 42). In the CD-ROM, this page is supplemented by a home video (by Spiegelman's wife, Francoise Mouly) of Spiegelman being filmed by a German camera crew for a documentary.

Thus, in this passage, the CD-ROM's contents complement their print predecessors by precisely paralleling the artistic effect Spiegelman arranged in print. Spiegelman interrupted the overall *MAUS* narrative in order to reflect upon the consequences of *MAUS*'s unexpected popular appeal. This popularity, as Spiegelman illustrates, led to interruptive and invasive interactions with electronic media, many of which served to pull Spiegelman away from the drawing board. Mouly's video of the German video shoot mirrors the perspective of Spiegelman's printed panel. And yet, all of this is made possible through the translation of the *MAUS* narrative into binary code, into complex, machine-readable strings of zeros and ones lurking within the mirrored surfaces of the CD-ROM. This *MAUS* of mirrors is superficially appealing, providing layers of reflection and refraction over and above those possible within print.

Which *Survivor's Story?*

In the print *MAUS*, Spiegelman consistently divides and subverts his identity as author. For example, while the covers of all of the print editions of *MAUS* prominently feature Spiegelman's signature, they also all feature the subtitle, "A Survivor's Tale" which must be understood to refer primarily to Vladek. From the outset, then, Spiegelman's print readers are on notice that *MAUS* simultaneously belongs to both Spiegelmans. Spiegelman is claiming a partial and negotiated authorial responsibility for the *MAUS* narrative. But

Figure 1: **A CD-ROM screen capture of a *MAUS* page with the final panel covered by a video of Art Spiegelman reading at Auschwitz (Voyager Company).**

Spiegelman's identification of his father as a sort of collaborator does not reduce his proprietary claim to the final product. Indeed, Spiegelman is demonstrably possessive about the *MAUS* narrative. In fact, the print edition of *MAUS* owes its very existence to Spiegelman's desire to affirm his ownership of *MAUS* (and perhaps more). In an article by Lawrence Wechsler, which is included in the CD-ROM's appendices, Spiegelman acknowledges that the first volume of *MAUS* was rushed into publication as a direct response to Steven Spielberg's production of the animated feature film *An American Tail*, in which—as Spiegelman explains—"a family of Jewish mice living in Russia a hundred years ago named the Mousekawitzes ... were being persecuted by the Katsacks" (Wechsler, 1991, p. 5). Spiegelman describes himself as "appalled, shattered" and "frenzied" in response to what he viewed as Spielberg's appropriation of key elements of *MAUS*. Spiegelman says:

> I mean the similarities were so obvious, right down to the title—their American Tail simply being a more blatant, pandering-to-the-mob version of my Survivor's Tale subtitle. Their lawyers argued that the idea of anthropomorphizing mice wasn't unique to either of us, and they, of course, cited Mickey Mouse and other Disney creations. But no one was denying that—indeed, I'd self-consciously been playing off Disney all the while. If you wanted to get technical about it, the idea of anthropomorphizing animals goes all the way back to Aesop. No, what I was saying was that the specific use of mice to sympathetically portray Jews combined with the concept of cats as anti–Semitic oppressors in a story that compares life in the Old World of Europe with life in America was unique—and it was called MAUS: A Survivor's Tale. I didn't want any money from them—I just wanted them to cease and desist" [Wechsler, 1991, pp. 5–6].

While Spiegelman was not successful in blocking the production and release of *An American Tail*, and an eventual sequel, *An American Tail II: Fievel Goes West*, Spiegelman's sense of ownership of the *MAUS* narrative was so strong that he found even the superficial similarities between *MAUS* and *An American Tail* too close for comfort. And yet, Spiegelman's claims of a proprietary authorial ownership right in the depiction of Eastern-European Jewish mice peaceably co-exist with Spiegelman's expansive acknowledgments of Vladek as the originator of the *MAUS* narrative. For example, earlier in the same article, Spiegelman describes the *MAUS* narrative as "my father's story," but then counterbalances this deferral of authorial ownership by saying, of *MAUS*, "I still don't know how I'm going to end it" (Wechsler, 1991, p. 4). In the latter quote, Spiegelman clearly articulates his creative control over *MAUS*. He is not only transcribing his father's story, but he is also willfully transforming it.

Spiegelman ultimately ends the print *MAUS* by placing his signature beneath a panel showing graves of the parents whose stories he has preserved. In so doing, he has honored Anja Spiegelman's wish (reported by Vladek) that, "my son, when he grows up, will be interested by this" with "this" referring to the narrative in her burned Holocaust notebooks (Spiegelman, 1986, p. 159). And he has insured that, unlike his mother's voice, his father's will be preserved. Thus, Spiegelman's signature is both asserting and deferring his ownership of all that has come before. Spiegelman has marked himself as the product of his parents and of their tragic history.

Seeing the name "Art Spiegelman" at the end of this narrative might serve to remind readers that in German "spiegel" means "mirror." If we momentarily read the *MAUS* composer as "Art, the mirror-man" or "Art-reflecting-man," this, beyond the more obvious resonances, invites us to consider the mirrored surfaces of the digital archives that surround *MAUS* in *The Complete MAUS* CD-ROM. In these digitally facilitated spaces we observe a "Spiegel-man" ensconced in a high-speed, high-tech medium which allows for a more "complete" *MAUS* even as it reduces the whole of Art's reflections to a series of digits.

Looking at the digital version of the narrative's final page, one can see the trade-offs resulting from the digitization of *MAUS*. In the CD-ROM, the left margin also features a series of icons, more than any other page, alerting the reader to the presence of a tape recording/transcript of Vladek being interviewed by Art, a supporting document, a film segment, an interview with Art, and drafts of six of the seven panels on the page. Thus, where the print text is descending into a graveside silence, the CD-ROM is springing to life.

In the interview accompanying the CD-ROM, Spiegelman describes the three endings which he has stacked upon the print page. The first four panels constitute a "stupid satisfying ending that comes with every movie you've ever seen." Spiegelman has embellished his father's formulation, "The rest I don't need to tell you because we were both very happy," (Spiegelman, 1994, p. 271) so as to create a classic "Hollywood" clinch between reunited lovers. But this first ending is immediately countered by the second, in which Vladek mistakenly calls Art by his deceased brother's name. Spiegelman describes this as the point in the narrative where "the crucible of fiction and non-fiction crushing up against each other is made most manifest for me." Spiegelman describes the third ending as the point at which the narrative collapses: "To have the name 'Spiegelman' above my signature was also conscious. So the book just keeps ending. It falls in on itself in order to get out" (Spiegelman, 1994, p. 271). Here Spiegelman has inserted his signature into the body of the *MAUS* text, monumentalizing it. But in so doing, he has lost (to a degree) his title of ownership over the text, and the text's trebled ending collapses into the signature. The CD-ROM diminishes the effect of Spiegelman's conclusion by its positioning of this "final page" within the architecture of the hyperlinked disc spaces offering 11 clickable options competing with the original three layered endings.

The CD-ROM also provides its own version of a "Hollywood ending" in the form of an extensive credits "screen" listing over 40 producers, designers, production assistants, and other contributors. When contrasted with Spiegelman's powerful invocation of the signature as marker, as link, and as tomb, these names hang dully, carrying little of the possessory power we might associate with similar lists of credits at the end of a film or the beginning of a magazine. And indeed, these credits have been hidden away, within a menu which is typically invisible to the readers of the CD-ROM.

The presence of the parade of "producers" found in the CD-ROM's listing of credits illustrates the degree to which, in moving from print to screen, *MAUS* has been mediated, and thereby lost much of the "hand-made" intimacy so readily apparent in the print editions of Spiegelman's work. *MAUS* depends upon the reader's sense of proximity to each of the narrative's authors. Spiegelman is nothing if not conscious of the politics of textual ownership, and the *MAUS* narrative is repeatedly marked as a property which is initially possessed only by the elder Spiegelmans. Anja preserved her Holocaust notebooks for her son, but Vladek destroyed them, forcing Art to undertake the process of extracting the *MAUS* narrative from his father. As he interviews Vladek, Art consciously shapes his father's memories into a work of art, in which two men who have shared little in their lives enter into a process of joint authorship. Ultimately *MAUS* reflects the authorship of Art, Vladek, and indeed Anja, whose lost notebooks inspired the collaboration. But while the *MAUS* narrative is jointly produced and jointly owned by the Spiegelman family, the print *MAUS*'s final page marks the story as specifically Art's inheritance, and for this reason, *MAUS* resists its relocation into the more diffuse networks of authorship and ownership found within digital media.

The signature features of digital media raise troubling questions whenever computers are called upon to house Holocaust materials, but these questions are especially pronounced in the case of *MAUS*. The Voyager CD-ROM edition of *MAUS* is the product of the breaking down of the *MAUS* narrative into a series of numbers—numbers which are subsumed within a larger mechanized system. The *MAUS* narrative itself testifies to the cruelty of a parallel reduction in which, as Vladek recalls, "They registered us in … they took from us our names. And here they put me my number" (Spiegelman, 1991b, p. 26). While the motivations underpinning the digitization of *MAUS* were noble, they nevertheless resonate uncomfortably with the sinister machinations of the Nazi program, in which individual names and identities were numerically effaced in order to streamline the extermination process. Shortly after Vladek details his dehumanizing entry into Auschwitz, he tells of a moment in which a fellow prisoner, a priest, re-marks the tattooed number as a sign of Vladek's individuality, by pointing out that the numerals add up to 18, which he describes as "'Chai' the Hebrew number of life" (Spiegelman, 1991b, p. 28). Vladek recalls this moment as one which helped carry him through his worst times at Auschwitz. Here, *MAUS* suggests that Vladek's covert maintenance of his identity both as a Jew and as an individual is part of what saved him. With the priest's assistance, Vladek jams the system and rewrites a code which might otherwise have enumerated his fate. But the relocation of the Spiegelman-authored *MAUS* from print into binary code also re-situates the *MAUS* narrative within an ecology in which "processing speed" is understood as a cardinal virtue. While Spiegelman envisioned *MAUS* as a deeply personal artifact, "as close to getting a clear copy of somebody's diary or journal as one could have," (Spiegelman, 1994) the CD-ROM of *MAUS* occupies a technologized composing space which is haunted by the darkest applications of the brutally efficient Nazi war machinery.

The Complete *MAUS* as *Gesamtkunstwerk?*

Max Horkheimer and Theodor Adorno's 1944 essay, "The Culture Industry: Enlightenment as Mass Deception," one of the first essays in their collected *Dialectic of Enlightenment* (1972), speaks to the duo's deep suspicion of the technologically advanced corporate art of the time. Adorno and Horkheimer—then recent refugees from Nazi Germany—see a parallel between the American culture industry (then best exemplified by studio system Hollywood) and the Nazi propaganda machinery which they had escaped. And they envision a future in which the technologies of expression are even more powerful:

> [B]y tomorrow the thinly veiled identity of all industrial culture products can come triumphantly out into the open, derisively fulfilling the Wagnerian dream of the Gesamtkunstwerk—the fusion of all the arts in one work. The alliance of word, image and music is all the more perfect ... because the sensuous elements which all approvingly reflect the surface of social reality are in principle embodied in the same technical process, the unity of which becomes its distinctive content. The process integrates all elements of production, from the novel (shaped with an eye to the film) to the last sound effect [p. 33].

This brings us to the uncomfortable question of whether the CD-ROM of *MAUS* ought to be understood as a Gesamtkunstwerk—fusions of all arts in one, approvingly reflecting the surface of social reality. Clearly, Spiegelman's work fuses many arts, but his reflection of the realities his family experienced is anything but approving. Of course, this expression of personal horror depends, in part, upon Spiegelman's establishment of himself as, to some extent, a reliable author, narrator, interlocutor, and historian. To the extent that the print *MAUS* forces readers to focus on Art's pursuit of Vladek, it intensifies Spiegelman's presence, and thereby the power of this personal expression. The CD-ROM, by contrast, has the effect of depersonalizing the MAUS narrative. While the title *The Complete MAUS* and *MetaMaus* point towards the expansiveness of the Gesamtkunstwerk, the CD-ROM has the effect of overwhelming the balance of the print artefact at their core.

Michael Rothberg (1994) critiques the expansiveness of the *MAUS* CD-ROM archive in terms that almost certainly would have galled Spiegelman:

> The practice of revealing the creation of *MAUS* has achieved new heights (or depths) with the production of a CD-ROM version entitled *The Complete MAUS*... Although it is a valuable resource, especially with the inclusion of Vladek's original testimony, I remain doubtful whether "*MAUS* in cyberspace" (as I am tempted to call it) represents a qualitative artistic advance. Rather, it seems to me another step on the road to the Spielbergization of the Holocaust, something Spiegelman generally resists [p. 674].

Rothberg's implicit critique of Spielberg's 1993 film *Schindler's List* is further evidence of the difficulty of housing the Holocaust within electronic media. Here, even the relatively rudimentary technology of film is seen as inappropriate for the task of testifying to the Holocaust. But what makes these media inappropriate is their tendency to provide *too much* information, to overwhelm the "original" and the "artistic" with a calculated, mass-targeted product. For this reason, Rothberg suggests, the CD-ROM is perhaps best understood as a supplement to the print edition. And indeed, *The Complete MAUS* CD-ROM simultaneously adds and subtracts from the print editions of *MAUS*. Spiegelman's agreement to the production of the 1994 CD-ROM appears to have been motivated by two competing impulses: the desire to demonstrate the rigor of his own creative process, and the need to verify *MAUS*'s factual center. At times these impulses are closely intertwined, as when the CD-ROM provides a documentary photograph of a type of tool which Vladek used while imprisoned, and then shows Spiegelman's commitment to numerous drafts in order to depict the object accurately. But often these supplemental materials tell too much, and place the CD-ROM at odds with Spiegelman's own self-assignment.

In the 1988 film *Comic Book Confidential*, Spiegelman describes his distancing device of depicting Jews as mice, Germans as cats, Poles as pigs and Americans as dogs as a "metaphor [which] is meant to be shucked like a snakeskin" (Mann, et al, 1989). Too often, digital supplements intrude upon Spiegelman's artificed reality, interjecting documentary clarity which is at odds with the artificed, but nevertheless "real" spaces of Vladek and Art's nested narratives. The metaphors which Spiegelman encouraged readers to shuck are thrown into relief by the familiar documentary tone of the supplements. This is not the fusion envisioned by Horkheimer and Adorno. Rather, it is a distracting duel between print and digital media.

In January of 1997, shortly after the release of *The Complete MAUS* CD-ROM, Pantheon released a combined print edition of *MAUS I* and *MAUS II* alone, with no supplementary material whatsoever—no foreword, no introduction, no archival documents—and described it, on the inside jacket, as "the definitive edition ... now appearing as it was originally envisioned by its author" (Spiegelman, 1996, front flap). The title of this book? *The Complete*

MAUS—the same title that had been applied to the CD-ROM. The re-marking of this print *MAUS* as "complete" constitutes a belated acknowledgment of how well Spiegelman accomplished his initial task: the production of a superficially unmediated, print-based illustrated record of his father's story, and of his own struggle to elicit, compose, and complete this record. While digital spaces offer tremendous opportunities as sites from which to revisit and revise traditional understandings of authorship and artistic practice, they do not constitute the only spaces in which richly sophisticated interrogations of these understandings are possible. By providing window after window into Art Spiegelman's creative process, the CD-ROM inadvertently alerts us to the satisfactions of print's silences. They remind us of the pleasure of momentarily giving ourselves over to a creator who struggles first to possess a story, and then to possess our attention.

"Complete" and "Meta"

The degree to which the print *MAUS* is now to be understood as "complete" is underscored by the more recent release of a *second* digital disc edition, a 2011 DVD-ROM titled *MetaMaus*. *MetaMaus* builds on the digital foundation of *The Complete MAUS* CD-ROM edition by including additional archival materials. Indeed, the look and feel of the DVD-ROM is precisely that of the Voyager edition, so the digital *MetaMaus* is perhaps best understood as something like an "Extended Director's Cut" of the Voyager edition.

In keeping with the title, the *MetaMaus* package also includes a 300-page hardback book which offers print versions of some of the materials within the original CD-ROM. And in *MetaMaus* we see, perhaps, a recognition that this work, probably unlike most works of comic art, resists digitization. The handmade quality of the print *MAUS*, combined with the degree to which *both* Spiegelmans succeeded in telling their stories, means that what lies beyond the print pages of *MAUS* is indeed "meta" and not the completion of something that was missing. Schools introduce students to the Holocaust by way of *The Complete MAUS* in print, because it feels complete, and because Spiegelman rightly pursued a minimally mediated approach to telling his family's story.

The degree to which the digital has moved from the core to the periphery of *MAUS* is underscored in various ways in the editions addressed in this article. The 1994 CD-ROM, *The Complete MAUS*, features a portrait of Vladek and Anja (as mice) standing with expressions of worry before a swastika with a sinister feline Hitler at its center. The 1996 collected print edition repurposes the same artwork, effectively re-marking the combined print *MAUS I* and *MAUS II* as "complete." This cover underscores the degree to which *MAUS* is the story of Art Spiegelman's parents, and also repositions the digital archive that surrounded the comic's text as something beyond the complete *MAUS* narrative. The 2011 DVD-ROM expands this archive in dramatic ways, with both a significantly larger digital archive, and a print book that *does not* include the original comic at all, but instead includes a treasure trove of *MAUS*-related material. Within *MetaMaus*, the low-quality scan at the heart of the Voyager edition is repeatedly referred to as a reference copy of the *MAUS* comics, tacitly acknowledging the degree to which *The Complete MAUS* CD-ROM was a compromised edition of *MAUS*. The *MetaMaus* cover notably substitutes an image of Art Spiegelman (as a mouse) with the Hitler swastika image visible in his eye. *MetaMaus* embeds the DVD-ROM in the interior cover, and this arrangement allows us to look through the center of the DVD-ROM and see into Spiegelman's eye. The cover acknowledges that *MetaMaus* is really about Art Spiegelman's need to not only tell his parents' story, but document it in ways that fall outside the artistic accomplishment of the *MAUS* comics.

We are now fortunate to have numerous examples of rich and evocative compositions that wholly depend upon the potentialities of digital media, and which are not reducible to print. We also have benefited from the work of scholars who have leveraged digital spaces to provide expansive annotated editions of works that benefit from their situation in digital spaces. But in this case, both the nature of *MAUS* and the specific relationship of this text to digital Century technologies require us to pause and consider how best to experience Spiegelman's words, experiences, and ideas. In this specific case,

Figure 2: The covers move from Anja and Vladek to Art Spiegelman's eye (from left to right: Voyager, Pantheon, and Pantheon).

despite the layers of information offered to readers through digitization, it is preferable for readers to turn to print when they are prepared to complete *MAUS.*

ACKNOWLEDGMENTS

Elements of this article are drawn from an unpublished chapter of my dissertation, and I remain grateful to Don Bialostosky, Andrea Lunsford, Jack Selzer, and Jeffrey Walker for their comments at that stage in the development of this article.

The editors of this volume have my deep thanks for their suggestions and insight throughout the development of this substantially revised, updated, and expanded argument.

Willy Lee has my profound thanks for first *not* throwing out, and second, making available to me the vintage "Blue and White" Macintosh G3 that was needed to run the 1994 *Complete MAUS* CD-ROM.

REFERENCES

Baker, P. (2017, March 08). Apple may have already lost the battle to Google for a new generation of students. Retrieved April 8, 2018, from https://www.recode.net/2017/3/8/14858162/chromebooks-surpass-apple-ipad-school-students-education.

Boerman-Cornell, W., Kim, J., & Manderino, M. (2017). *Graphic novels in high school and middle school classrooms: A disciplinary literacies approach.* Lanham, MD: Rowman & Littlefield.

Burr, T. (1994, April 22). Tail spin: Art Spiegelman's *MAUS* on CD-ROM. *Entertainment Weekly* (219), 61. Retrieved October 06, 2017, from http://ew.com/article/1994/04/22/art-spiegelmans-maus-cd-rom/.

Horkheimer, M., & Adorno, T.W. (1972). *Dialectic of enlightenment: Max Horkheimer and Theodor W. Adorno.* New York: Seabury Press.

Katz, S.B. (1992). The Ethic of expediency: Classical rhetoric, technology, and the Holocaust. *College English, 54*(3), 255. doi:10.2307/378062.

Library of Congress (1991). Book—*MAUS II*: A survivor's tale: And here my troubles began. Retrieved April 22, 2018, from https://catalog.loc.gov/vwebv/search?searchCode=LCCN&searchArg=91052739&searchType=1&permalink=y.

Mann, R., Haig, D., Harbury, M., Lippincott, C., Kennedy, R., Elliot, K., ... Sphinx Productions (Firm). (1989). *Comic book confidential.* New York: Cinecom Pictures.

Rothberg, M. (Winter, 1994) "We were talking Jewish": Art Spiegelman's *MAUS* as "Holocaust" production. *Contemporary Literature, 35*(4), 661–687.

Spiegelman, A. (1986). *MAUS. A survivor's tale: My father bleeds history.* New York: Pantheon.

Spiegelman, A. (1991a, Dec 29). A problem of taxonomy. *New York Times Book Review,* 4. Retrieved April 22, 2018 from https://timesmachine.nytimes.com/timesmachine/1991/12/29/37092.html?action=click&contentCollection=Archives&module=LedeAsset&region=ArchiveBody&pgtype=article&pageNumber=51.

Spiegelman, A. (1991b). *MAUS II. A survivor's tale: And here my troubles began.* New York: Pantheon Books.

Spiegelman, A. (1994). *The complete MAUS: A survivors tale.* New York: Voyager [Computer software].

Spiegelman, A. (1996). *The complete MAUS.* New York, Penguin Random House.

Spiegelman, A. (2011). *MetaMaus.* New York: Pantheon Books.

Wechsler, L. (1991). "Art's father, Vladek's son." in A. Spiegelman (1994). *The complete MAUS: A survivor's tale.* New York: Voyager [Computer software].

When Funding Is *the* Issue That Prevents an Issue

Are Digital Comics the Logical Platform of Production in a South African Context?

RAY WHITCHER

Introduction

The comic industry in South Africa could best be described as fledgling—the majority of output focuses on corporate-sponsored farragoes of theme, content and oddly-chosen product-placement, wrapped under the dulled veneer of a sports-theme and spouted out in a weekly cartoon strip format, followed by a printed monthly issue. To expand, while demonstrating a long history of cartooning, especially in the editorial sense, South African comics, as can be traditionally understood in the typical Marvel/DC-esque format, only started to appear in the late 1990's. The books, admittedly, are wildly successful—with one particular title, Strika Entertainment's *Supa Strikas*, even generating a popular Disney XD animated series.

The issue that then arises is that this small victory is rather overshadowed by the struggle of other content producers. With no publishers accessible locally and very little support for content outside of the "mainstream" sports comics, most artists opt for independent production and sales, mostly at small conventions and the occasional comic store. Mass-printing is generally not an option for independents due to the exorbitant start-up costs of lithographic production, doubly mired by the lack of guarantee of an audience to purchase the books afterwards. While comics (read: Western Comics, with Manga and Manhwa to a lesser extent) are enthusiastically consumed by readers, locally produced work tends to be ignored due to many factors, ranging from lack of exposure to perceptions that South African comics are not of the same standard as their Western familiars.

With these factors in mind, a group of creators assembled to experiment with a new idea for compiling comics that can get exposure and earn money simultaneously, as well as afford several artists a chance to be part of the project. It was thus proposed that a collaboration be held between four countries: South Africa, Zimbabwe, Australia and New Zealand, the Southern Hemisphere nations sharing ties via expats and comic forums. The book, *Velocity: Darker Forces* was divided in 32 pages, with each page being illustrated by a different artist—16 from Africa, 16 from Australia and New Zealand and boasting names like Sean Izaakse (*Deadpool, The Avengers*) and Ben Byrne (*Killaroo*) as well as various independents (including myself).

The production's main intent was to be hosted on ComiXology (see https://tinyurl.com/m9roh9j for a preview of the title) to allow access of the content to as many people as possible, with printing to be funded by sales of the comic online—the digital format being especially poignant in the sphere of the African side of the production, as the consumer base is significantly smaller than that of the Australian and New Zealanders. The factors around this vary, but it mainly lies in access to and the expense of printed comics in general, with an average monthly title like DC's *Batman* retailing for around the equivalent of USD7 versus the global standard of USD2.99. Online content, however, is actually more easily accessible and consumed as South Africa has a significantly high ratio of internet-enabled mobile devices to population (as I discuss later). The overall intention for this essay is to discuss the production process of the title, the results that followed and why the digital format was highly beneficial to the fabrication and exposure of the book, possibly positing the conclusion that, at least in an African Context, digital comics are the way forward for producing content and reaching a larger audience.

The essay will detail the problems faced by South African artists, with a core focus on funding and consumer support. A close analysis of the *Velocity* project will follow, informed by interviews with founders Moray Rhoda and Neville Howard, and will detail the benefit that the digital comic model has afforded creators, especially in light of the advent of digital comic websites like Tapas (formerly known as Tapastic) and The Spaceman Project, the latter being a platform solely dedicated to crowdfunding of comic production and, in my opinion, a truly viable way for South African creators to deliver content. We must begin, however, by understanding South Africa's history of comics in order to best understand where we need to proceed next.

South Africa and Comics

South Africa as a country is most likely best-known as the home of the great Nelson Mandela—a paragon of hope, tolerance and struggle—whilst equally infamous for Apartheid, a shameful blight in the nation's history. What South Africa probably isn't known for is its comics, despite having a long history with them, especially in the editorial format. Satire and parody have almost become second languages to the citizenry in various forms of entertainment, from traditional literature to television content, and, of course, comics. A nation that's had more than its fair share of troubles often tends to learn to laugh at itself rather quickly, after all. Coupled with a unique and immensely powerful constitution, freedom of speech has allowed some interesting (and rather invective) content to be produced by top cartoonists, from denigrating and insulting depictions of the nation's president through to divisive and provocative social commentary via brand parody and down to the traditional "funnies" found in a newspaper, cartoons have especially found a resounding home with their audience.

According to *Africa Cartoons* (2017), an internet-based encyclopedia of cartoons from Africa, the traditional editorial cartoon format in South Africa can be traced back to the early 19th century, with the first, an engraving by George Cruikshank in 1819, mocking colonization. According to Andy Mason (2012), in his authoritative book *What's So Funny? Under the Skin of South African Cartoons,* Cruikshank holds a special place in the history of South African cartooning because of his two 1820 settler cartoons, published by T. Tegg of Cheapside, London on 8 September 1819. The first engraving served as an invective jab at the people volunteering to venture to the Cape of Good Hope (now Cape Town) and the second served as a prediction of sorts regarding the violent savagery of the (presumed) cannibalistic *hottentots* (now known as the Khoisan).

While not created within the boundaries of South Africa, this cartoon was certainly very telling of a time of great fear and uncertainty—the British Government allowing poverty to become rife, quashing uprisings with violent and deadly force, but insidiously promising a better life to the 5000 people that were unwillingly "transported" to the Cape of Good Hope. The "cannibal cliché," as Mason (2012) terms it, became a repeated theme of many comic strips (and animated films) to come, all sporting the reviled *Sambo* caricature appearance of coal-black skin, large, inflated lips and monkey-like ears. Contemporary South African artists, like Brett Murray, respond to this with satire, and in his 2000 painting *Crisis of Identity* revisits the Sambo-esque "cannibals" faced by a white man adorned in typical British colonial attire, carrying a large suitcase (of emotional baggage), but sporting a biting caption reading: "*If another white artist brings me a portfolio of guilt, crisis of identity and memory.... I'm going to throw up*" (p. 17).

Murray's modern critique echoes a sentiment propagated by South Africa's emancipation from fascism and colonization in its democratic era (post 1994) in which many artists greeted the change with wanton guilt, saccharine apologies and a tendency to "forget" the still fresh wounds of the past. There was, however, an extensive period of bitingly honest content as South Africa began a new, transitional era after its initial cross-colonization by the Dutch, French and British.

Cartoons progressed and evolved over time to represent South Africa's rapidly changing political climate, from the early wars between the British colonists and Zulus in the late 1800's to the Anglo-Boer War (later termed the South African war) which would soon see the country shift away from the Queen's control and become a republic. Interestingly, several of these cartoons were illustrated by French artists in the French tabloid *Le Petit Journal* because of visits from Transvaal (the former Northern region of South African, predominantly held by the Boer faction) President Paul Kruger to Paris. Humor through satire and parody soon became a norm, with cartoonists leading the way in scathing and derisive commentary. After the First and Second World Wars, in which South African soldiers were co-opted to fight by the British Government, South Africa's darkest period dawned in the form of Apartheid, but despite the newly-formed dictatorship, cartoonists still continued to tear away at the leadership in acts of illustrated bravery (it wasn't beyond the Apartheid Government to imprison journalists and cartoonists that dared to show them in a poor light). For brevity's sake, however, and to keep this essay on topic, it is best to move forward to the late 1980's and the early 1990's, the originator years of the South African comic.

New Country, New Comics

From the early 1990's, beloved comic strip characters like Stephen Francis and Rico's *Madam & Eve* (detailing the misadventures of an affluent older suburban woman and her sassy domestic worker Eve) and Tim Mostert's *Speedy* (a minibus taxi passenger and avid soccer fan) have held continued success. Both comic strips have even spawned televised adaptations (the former a live action series and the latter an animation) and a plethora of collected anthologies of the various volumes of content. The characters have become an indentured part of South African culture, bearing witness to the demise of a cruel regime and the country's journey into a new and fledgling democracy. As is always the power of comics, these characters have laughed and cried with a nation, have made us laugh at ourselves and have provided a platform to voice the opinions of our citizens.

Collected anthologies of popular comic strips have enjoyed great financial success over the years, combining the inherent nostalgia of the characters that the country has grown up with as a democracy with the indentured exposure of national serialization through their appearances in various regional and national newspapers and magazines. South Africa is still a print-loving nation, especially because access to affordable publications (the most read national newspaper sells for the equivalent of U.S.$0.20) has traditionally been far greater than that of digital content. As a caveat, though, this is beginning to change rapidly.

Comics, in their more traditional form, were an inevitable progression from the newspaper "funnies," and ever more young artists were starting to dabble in the medium by the late 1990's. This soon lead to the creation of Igubu Comics (later becoming the catalyst for Clockworx), as well as Strika Entertainment and Mamba Media. Igubu, founded in the year 2000, was hailed as South Africa's first true comic collective, and was followed by the corporate mandated Strika and Mamba. The latter two companies, also appearing in the years 2000 and 2001 respectively, focused their efforts on the sports-themed comics *Supa Strikas* and *Soccer Warrior* and the former paved the way for more conventional themes, especially focused in the speculative fiction arena. Igubu, featuring the debut of titles like Karl Stephen's *Sparko* (later published by SLG) and Daniël Hugo's *When Traveling* was minimally funded by private enterprises and produced several titles, mostly centered around life in Cape Town, until the organization folded.

Supa Strikas proved so popular that it eventually spawned its own animated series on Disney XD in 2008, and is still producing new episodes at the time of writing this essay. It is in the success of *Supa Strikas* that a reader could assume that South African comics must obviously be well-received, especially in the light of the generation of ancillary content like animated television series, but this title is an exception to the norm, rather than a constant. As mentioned earlier, the country's comic audience tend to gravitate more towards tangible, printed titles, and *Supa Strikas* set the benchmark by being made freely available in many newspapers, both in the form of a weekly strip, as well as a monthly standalone printed comic. This meant that not only was the title's exposure vast, but because it was free, it was voraciously and readily consumed by a large audience who weren't deterred by any form of financial implication. It is human nature to be averse to something unknown, even when in a familiar format like comics, and one would generally opt for the free title (which is funded by large corporate sponsors, again adding that element of familiarity through a brand's stamp of approval), rather than one sold by an independent artist on a very small scale.

Precluding the formation of Igubu and the generation of local content, South Africa has actually been fortunate enough to not be left wonting in terms of comic content, mostly influenced by the original British Colonial powers that brought many Western cultural artefacts with them. Whether through British and French titles like *Beano* or Goscinny and Uderzo's *Asterix*, or the perennial favorites of the American publishers, we, as a nation, have had relatively good access to international comics. This, of course, has grown exponentially over the years, with specialist comic stores appearing countrywide and stocking titles from a milieu of sources, including local producers, but local creators still suffer from lack of consumer interest and exposure. In terms of numbers, it can be roughly estimated that there are about 40 consistently practicing comic makers in the country (by consistent, I mean with at least a quarterly output), supported by about ten specialist comic stores nationally, as well as several online retailers. Independent artists sell their products mostly at conventions, with only Loyiso Mkhize's title *Kwezi* (2014–present) attaining national distribution in a major book retail chain. The average retail price of a standard 18–22 page printed title varies between an equated $7 to $11, depending on production costs, convention stand prices and even formatting of comics. An average DC or Marvel comic, priced at $3.99 in the U.S., will sell in South Africa for around $7, mostly because of expensive import prices and high profit margins of the specialist stores. Problematically, printed comics in South Africa have no consistent formatting, and is often compiled at the whim of the person making the book. This means that an A5 (5.83" × 8.27") size comic can be sold at the same price as an A4 (letter, or standard U.S. comic size equivalent), or even a single-page A3 (tabloid equivalent) print. This inconsistency becomes immeasurably dubious for both maker and consumer, as the perceived value of a full-length, full-sized comic should ideally be higher than any of the others, but this is not the case.

In an interview with one of Igubu's founders, Moray Rhoda revealed that Igubu pioneered a significant journey for the face of South African comics, and included renowned Graffiti artist Faith47, DC and Marvel Comics artist Jason Masters and Image Comics' Joe Daly, amongst many others (M. Rhoda, personal communication, August 20, 2016). These artists have come to be sources of immense inspiration for the community at large, showing local artists that they can achieve global success with enough passion and hard work. Soon, the now-defunct Clockworx, which began in 2001, forum arose (followed by Comicworx in 2004 and then, finally, LegionInk in 2008), leading the way for artists to collaborate and learn together as a community, rather than in isolation. Arguably, a significant amount of South Africa's first digital comic output began to be generated by these online forums, mostly through collaboration, but also through artists beginning to find new ways of sharing content, as well as receiving and giving hints and tips to and from the community as a whole. This new movement in online community-based comic-making could be seen as a renaissance of sorts for the country's comic industry, as the enthusiasm and passion of the various artists inspired a significant momentum in comic output.

New titles began to appear during this forum era, mostly beginning around the 2007 mark with the advent of news conglomerate Media 24's *Mshana* Magazine (which featured comics by Beat Comics, another studio founded by Rhoda). The stories were laden with locally-relevant content, ranging from humorous tales of an average day at a township car wash to crime thrillers and even a fantasy title. The short-form, anthology-style comics proved to be easier to generate by the team, allowing for greater output than was previously realized by even Igubu. Unfortunately, News 24 pulled funding for the magazine two years after its inception, creating a set-back for, but not deterring the founding members, who were always ready with new ideas. Whilst *Mshana* was a commercial title that again fell under the print domain, the majority of independent comics that were being produced simultaneously were often only consumed by other comic makers, rather than commercial consumers at the behest of not being able to physically produce work at the scale and quantity of titles like *Supa Strikas*. This was arguably the initial catalyst of digital comics in South Africa, with many artists deciding to host their work on ComiXology or self-made websites in an effort to get their work noticed, and selling printed versions on demand or at small conventions.

The Struggling Artist

Jarred Cramer, a prolific creator of both short-format web-comics and full length comics was interviewed about his contributions to the comic scene in South Africa for the past eight years. Whilst also mentioning the spirit of community he shares with his fellow artists, he cites one of the most common weaknesses for comic making being a "…lack of advertising with certain events, lack of commitment" (J. Cramer, personal communication, July 29, 2016). Cramer refers to commitment from the perspective of comic output—most young artists put together a single title over the space of months and tend to abandon their titles afterwards due to the highly demanding nature of the work at hand. Some don't even have the capacity to complete their work, simply because of the demands of other factors in their lives.

N. Hoosen (personal communication, August 20, 2016) offers that a solution to this is to "just make [comics].… And don't try to make it perfect. The key to making anything—music, comics, movies, whatever—is honesty" (2016). An inherent issue that becomes prevalent within the local scope of work is that aspirant artists tend to want to create high quality, massively detailed work that is the equivalent to its foreign counterparts, but in doing so, often feel frustrated by the time it takes to produce the work without the large creative teams that American comics use (as the majority of artists generally work alone and after work as a hobby, rather than as a sustainable career). The problem isn't a lack of talent, but rather that creators currently don't possess the capacity for those teams. Cramer elaborates on this, as he is the sole creator of all of his work, from writing through to illustration and lettering:

> To be honest I almost had a mental breakdown trying to get Super-Dud #2 finished. It was actually affecting my marriage. I would be upstairs inking and coloring from the minute I'd get home from work till about 3am the next morning. Then still getting up for my day job.... I guess that's what you get for being a one-man comic creator.

This sentiment is telling of the plight of the majority of the independent creators, but Rhoda and Hoosen have adopted a time-honored format and adapted it to a new era of production, hoping to expedite the creation process in a method akin to Japanese Manga. This inspired the creation of *SECTOR*, a title that hearkens back to the classic British title *2000AD*, in which a collection of short-format comics were published in black and white on a weekly basis and included titles like *Judge Dredd* and *ABC Warriors*. The comics were considered as pulp due to their rapid, low-budget output (much like modern manga), but made access to titles that much simpler.

In an interview with Nas Hoosen, a writer and co-collaborator with Rhoda on the new pulp title *SECTOR* (2015–present), the writer attributes this growth, in part, to the rise of the internet:

> The industry ... is looking really healthy right now. I remember just a few years ago how incoherent a lot of it felt and how difficult it was to connect with collaborators or see what everyone was doing. That's changed rapidly in the last few years and I think, like with a lot of scenes across the country, the internet's helped a ton with making things a little easier to follow if you're willing to put in the effort [N. Hoosen, personal communication, August 20, 2016].

In spite of this, though, both Hoosen and Rhoda mention that one of the problems faced by the South African comic community is a lack of set rules or format for the books, with artists often opting for the media that are cheapest or the quickest to print, or even skipping the printing process all together and rather focusing on web comics in order to reach wide audiences. What this does allow for, though, is a vast diversity in style and approach, but this, as Rhoda mentioned in the same discussion, means that it "...is also probably one of [the comic industry's] weaknesses—there is no kind of cohesiveness" (M. Rhoda. personal communication, August 20, 2016). This isn't necessarily problematic for the comics themselves, but a need for unity within the actual formatting of comics becomes quite apparent.

The team's main concern echoes the sentiment made by Hoosen earlier, in which he mentioned that for a South African comic industry to grow and thrive, we need to worry more about content and storytelling than quality of visuals. The reason behind this is that a piece of work can have the most stunning imagery, but fail on a basic level simply because its story is dull or poorly-written. *SECTOR* adopted and modified their output slightly to a quarterly basis, as Rhoda mentions that a weekly output "would need an army and lots of free time to pull that off" (M. Rhoda, personal communication, August 20, 2016), with time being somewhat of a premium when the majority of comic artists complete their work after hours. One of the most important factors to consider in working with a more "lo-fi" approach to work, is that, as Hoosen mentions, it allows room for experimentation—artists can modify and grow their styles with every issue, stories and characters can be tweaked, because they have no history or exposure just yet and audience feedback can immediately be factored into work as it progresses. This isn't to say, however, that the work isn't of a high standard, because *Uncharted Waters*, one of the main-runner and pilot series of the pulp anthology, maintains a high rigor of artistic quality in artist Daniël Hugo's almost flowing, painterly visuals, redolent with detail and emotion. The title is already on ten issues as of 2018, meaning that the format is clearly working for the producers. The production team behind *SECTOR* have also decided to release the comics digitally on DriveThruComics (https://tinyurl.com/yc3wgeax) and ComiXology, retailing at $1.99 for newer issues and $0.50 for the first issue.

The anthology format also allows for a variety of tastes in both storytelling and in visual content—as N. Hoosen (personal conversation, August 20, 2016) mentions, if a reader doesn't enjoy one particular story, they can simply move on to the next and follow that arc, with the title being affordable enough to allow audiences that both holistically and selectively enjoy the books to follow through on the stories contained within.

Most interestingly, *SECTOR* transcends the typical comic narrative of superheroes and rather focuses on storytelling as a whole, offering narratives ranging from piratical adventures off the coast of South Africa through to pop culture-obsessed Mars colonists living out their daily lives in utter isolation from the very things they love. Before *SECTOR*, however, came *The Velocity Anthology*, a project set to change the very landscape of creating comic content by affording artists with a more viable platform of execution. Whilst currently intended for the print platform, the model of *SECTOR* can easily translate to the digital medium, varying in forms from a curated collection of short-stories published under a single title to an actual platform that serves as a digital "pulp" content publisher (a 2000AD.com of sorts).

An Idea, a Platform and a Success Story

As I have discussed, South Africa is not in wont of comic content, but rather in need of a paradigm shift in the way comics are both created and

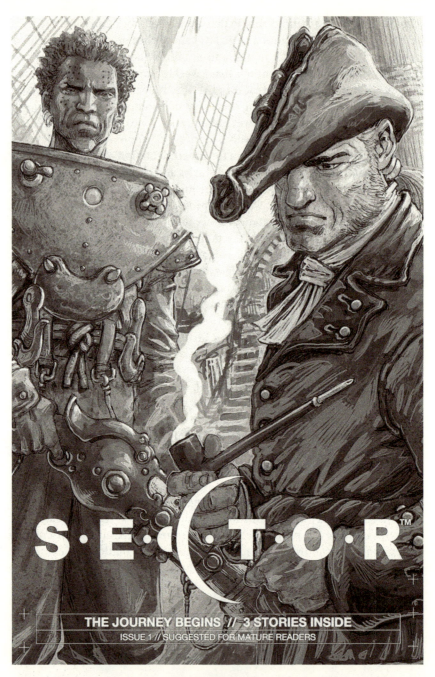

Above and opposite: Figure 1: Daniël Hugo [Cover] and Nas Hoosen [Interior Spread], *SECTOR*, 2015–present (Sector Comics).

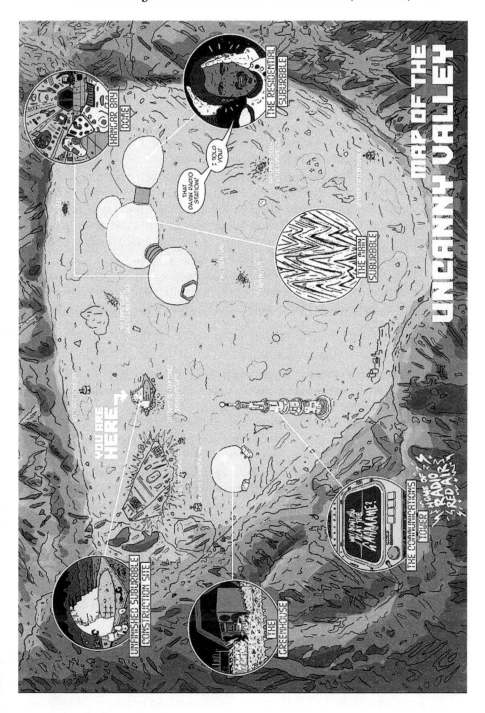

consumed. The country simply cannot afford to follow the American publishing model, nor can it keep up with the prolific output (and readership) of Japanese Manga—factors such as the amount of artists versus available time, the lack of sustainable careers, and the omnipresent issue of funding remain constant obstacles in the way of establishing a fully realized comic industry. It was with these problems in mind that Moray Rhoda and Neville Howard came together with an idea to use digital comics as a better way of reaching audiences, as well as to allow multiple creators to contribute without overt burdens on schedules and other work.

Rhoda, having worked for 18 years in the comic industry, garnered extensive experience after being the originator of the first true South African comic collective Igubu, at the time still following more traditional print outputs. Howard, an Australian-based South African expat, has given 16 years to comics, as well as founding Comicworx, an internet-based forum for South African comic producers, which later became Legionink.

N. Howard (personal communication, August 6, 2017) echoed the earlier sentiments introduced in this essay when, in an interview, he mentioned that some of the main reasons for creating *Velocity* were that he found that creators struggled with:

- Gaining consumer confidence
- Creating a voice for [their] product
- Overcoming the challenges with costs for publication and distribution of creator owned work

Howard approached M. Rhoda in order to address the above issues, as well as potentially exploring "the opportunity of foreign markets and [doubling] the 'reading audience' by combining forces" (personal communication, August 6, 2017). The multinational approach mentioned was an interesting one—previously the two interviewees had only possessed knowledge of a small (local) industry, but Howard's exposure to Australia's far larger and more established community provoked a greater drive to build ties between the two countries for both to benefit. The two soon approached several established artists and began pitching the idea of a collected volume of short comics that would be produced once yearly and allow artists the chance to be published and exposed to greater audiences both locally and across the Indian Ocean.

The decision to launch the title digitally hinged on the notion that online access facilitates greater exposure (and, subsequently, potential for revenue) for a fraction of the cost of traditionally printed titles. This cost-reduction is experienced by both the artist and the consumer—independent artists no longer need to foot the bill for print production, and instead need to focus on on-screen optimization. Additionally, consumers can purchase a title for a dramatically reduced price in comparison to printed comics. This afford-ability potentially grants the consumer agency to purchase more comics more often. The *Velocity* team also specifically reduced the cost of the first issue to $0.50 to further incentivize purchasing in greater volumes (a model echoed currently by *SECTOR*). Contributing artists are given residuals per sale, rather than once-off payments (again due to the lack of financial stability of the comic industry), but the hope is to eventually be able to pay full time creative teams to work on all projects.

This highly experimental idea yielded unexpected results upon the debut of issue one, and upon being asked about the respective receptions of the Australian and South African audiences, N. Howard first mentioned his sur-prise by the volume of sales of the book, especially because he was competing against cheaper, more established American titles in the same venue (personal communication, August 6, 2017). M. Rhoda (personal communication, August 6, 2017) raises a different point: "I think people in South Africa had no idea of the level of local work until they saw [*Velocity* Issue 1]." However, the book at the same time was criticized for "…lacking a relevant local iden-tity." Rhoda expands upon this negative sentiment by explaining: "it is sad that if there is no political or social commentary as part of publications in SA that generally the Art and Media powers that be seldom have positive sentiments about it" (personal communication, August 6, 2017). This obser-vation, whilst seemingly acerbic, resonates back to the earlier section of this essay that discussed South Africa's history in comics—in which generally satire is celebrated and uplifted, whereas more "commercial" titles tend to be forgotten or ignored, at least in a critical manner. An example of this can be found in an interesting sub-genre of South African art called *Bitterkomix*, which is generally regarded by critics as high art. Gallery owner Michael Stevenson, on his personal website, paraphrases a critic's discussion around the medium as "consistently challenging and outrageous, undeniably brilliant, and impossible to ignore" (2006, para 2). Yet in terms of content delivery, *Bitterkomix* follows all the tenets of comic-making, but is laden with horrific representations of race (that echo the original editorial cartoons discussed at the beginning of this essay), wanton pornography, and shocking images of violence, all under the guise of satire. These works are celebrated and sold for large amounts of money at exclusive private galleries, but their commercial equivalents almost always get ignored (with the occasional exception in titles such as Loyiso Mkhize's *Kwezi* or Luke Molver's *Shaka Rising*). This sentiment aside, though, the book's debut still managed a complete selling out of stock, as well as a large upswing in interest concerning the support of and con-tributing towards the newly established title.

The retailing of *Velocity* is where the two creators' opinions and approach differed to an extent. Howard pursued standard channels like selling stock through consignment at local comic stores in Melbourne, with many holding launch events to support the new book. Consignment selling, though, holds the ever-present issue of the upfront financial burden of printing stock in advance, as well as managing stock levels and following up on sales, with minimal profit margins that can get demotivating for small, independent producers. Rhoda followed the same model in South Africa, splitting retail between the two major city centers of Cape Town and Johannesburg as well as selling at larger conventions. They, however, experienced more of the same problems, although perhaps to a slightly larger extent due to higher costs of printing and shipping in the small country, as well as the book being relatively more expensive due to exchange rates. This very rapidly inspired talks between the two creators to move the comic over fully to digital platforms (the digital and print releases were simultaneous, but the latter had more market exposure initially), especially for the South African–based consumers where cost and access were far more problematic factors than they were for the Australian audience.

When questioned on whether he'd do anything differently to better suit the South African market, M. Rhoda answered (personal discussion, August 6, 2017) that he would have opted to rather make *Velocity* available for free access online. His reasoning behind this was that "the aim was never to make a massive profit (or any kind of profit) but to serve as a portfolio of competence for local artists and to set some level of quality. So one could achieve that with just an online version that would by its very nature have a much wider reach." The "portfolio" approach that Rhoda mentions may sound frivolous, but South Africa lies in an odd quagmire of self-critique when it comes to local items, deriving in part from having no choice but to consume locally-produced goods due to the extensive global sanctions imposed upon the country during the Apartheid era. It could be argued that a sense of resentment lingers in this regard, as well as a "foreign is better" attitude, proven by people queuing for hours simply to be the first to buy a Krispy Kreme donut, or Starbucks coffee, or H&M garment whenever one of the global giant brands appear in shopping malls.

Essentially, what Rhoda is suggesting is that, at least within the South African context, there is more of a need of "proof of ability," as it were, rather than to monetize collected works, partly to demonstrate our capability to our own consumers, but also to generate more content more rapidly. This feeling of a need to prove ourselves as artists derives from our audience's lack of belief in that we too can complete compelling, interesting stories resplendent with high-quality art, and that lack of belief is often evoked from an initial lack of visibility of content in the first place. This system has potential, because it affords visibility within a specific medium, as opposed to the more overarching portfolio websites such as Adobe's Béhance or Art Station but at the cost of income for producers, which always falls into the problematic arena of working for "exposure." In my personal opinion, "exposure"-based work is toxic for both an artist and for the comic-creating community as a whole, as expectations of free (high-quality) work then become manifest by consumers; so whilst proving one's worth is important, sacrificing income to do so has severe repercussions that have far more problematic implications. To digress, though, I believe that Rhoda's intentions here are more centered towards the artists, rather than the commercial aspect of comics, because he also posited that this model follow more of a community accord that would allow people to adopt stories and work cooperatively to create them.

The Arrival of the Darker Forces

Thus, after the initial experimentation of *Velocity*, Howard and Rhoda realized that the gap between publications (which was in increments of almost 10 months due to various reasons) was far too great a wait for the book's readers, so they began to investigate ideas for one-off books that could be quick to produce, but still maintain the *Velocity* level of quality and finish. Howard was especially looking to produce a shorter comic once quarterly, which would then lead up to the Annual. This was where the idea for *Darker Forces* was derived—a comic that followed what Howard terms the "comic jam" concept, in which a team of artists is brought together to very rapidly complete a piece of work, but was supplemented by the introduction of a story structure and a final publication goal. This concept, by its very nature, facilitated the need for extensive coordination, especially because it eventually incorporated 32 artists from 4 different countries (South Africa, Zimbabwe, New Zealand and Australia, as mentioned earlier), meaning that the only logical platform for this multi-national endeavor was the internet, and more importantly, the digital comic format.

With the intention of a quarterly release, as well as funding problems looming overhead, Rhoda and Howard decided to host the comic digitally via Amazon's ComiXology website to allow greater overall impact and reach, as well as the ability to generate income through online sales (the book was priced at $1.99 digitally). Despite the price being roughly half of a standard (Western) comic's retail value, ease of access facilitates consumption at higher values, as well as other factors such as not needing storage space for physical books or lack of comic stores (in South Africa's case) inhibiting access advocate heavily for the newer form of the medium. Howard (2017) emphasizes this by stating "[t]he benefit of the digital platform means no printing overheads, no shipping. It's instantly available to the reader, and we can penetrate a worldwide market not accessible to us via the print medium." This becomes

Above and opposite: Figure 2: Emilia Pawlikowska [cover] and Moray Rhoda [writer, art], *Velocity: Darker Forces,* 2013–2014 (creator owned; published by Howard and Rhoda).

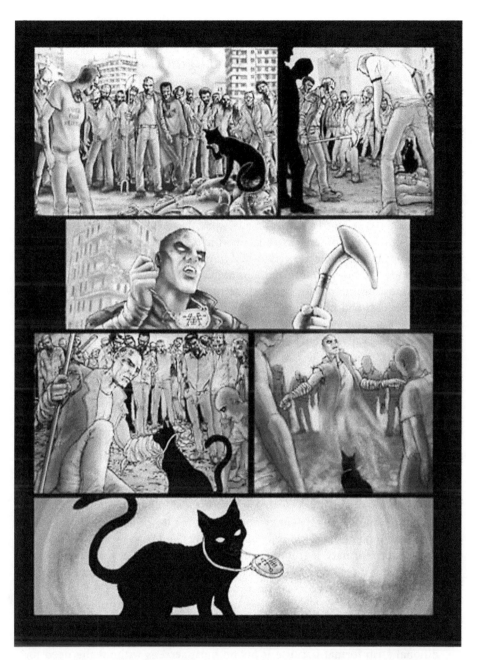

increasingly more poignant if one looks at the current comic market, with hundreds of printed titles being distributed as often as bi-weekly (especially in the case of certain DC titles), resulting in immense saturation by the comic "giants" and a somewhat difficult market to penetrate as a small, relatively unknown upstart.

Conclusion: Comics and the Digital Platform

A paradigm-shift occurs, however, when we look at the realm of both web and web-hosted comics—creators are essentially granted an even playing field; all allowed their own space and the ability to produce content on less demanding schedules and deadlines. When working with such large teams of artists, it becomes increasingly difficult to manage and facilitate content output in more traditional sphere, especially when working with people spread across multiple countries and continents. The digital platform, from aspects as simple as cloud-sharing and VOIP to real-time critiques provide an excellent toolkit to create work, from initial planning through to finishing and content hosting, in which editors now become curators, artist rosters can rotate as needed, and frequency of output can be increased. As a trade-off, however, saturation is arguably far worse in the digital arena, since most online platforms (such as the highly popular Web Toons) are free to access and host work upon, meaning that creators need to conduct extensive marketing and promotion in order to simply get noticed. This also creates a divide between free webcomics and commercial platforms like ComiXology at the simple behest of readers preferring free content, despite the offerings of a professionally curated platform for relatively low prices.

If South African comic creators choose to go digital, they need to also think about what digital format will best suit their needs and goals. Webcomics as a medium are either comic strips or "pages" (generally arranged in a vertical format to allow ease of scrolling on-screen) created strictly to suit the online platform, where scalability and navigability are paramount, dictated by the very vehicle of the internet itself. Digital comics are traditionally formatted comics (with some occasional minor alterations) that are hosted on an online repository and offered for download, where they are then read in the traditional style of left to right and page by page (at least in the Western format). It is important to note that in the case of Webcomics, the format is dictated by the platform, whereas digital comics remain true to standard format, but access is restricted.

McCloud (2006) also discusses how the change from print to screen has raised questions about how comics are read, with the online chapter supplement to this idea explaining how webcomics were early adopters of the traditional strip format because it fits on most screens without the need for scrolling, as well as suiting the reading habits of web users (generally quick, short content with minimal need for time-based dedication). Page-based comics, as McCloud terms them, are more problematic in the online format, with some of the reasons including varying screen sizes, advertising, website navigation bars and scaling often forcing readers to scroll, disrupting what should otherwise be a natural flow of reading, only to have to repeat the process with each subsequent page.

The issues prevalent in page-based digital comics should be a deterrent, but because the formatting already has traditional print in mind, should the creator of the work want to print and distribute the work physically, it is far easier to facilitate than needing to recompose and reformat webcomics to suit print, should the need to do so ever arise. These new options potentially pave the way forward for creating far more expressive and experimental comic media, but can also alienate more traditional readers.

So in this plethora of choice and format, one can ask where digital comics stand and how they actually fit in to an industry that is both deeply rooted in history and at the same time continually striving for new and more pioneering ways of delivering content. This question becomes even more prevalent when one views the potential of comics beyond standard entertainment into more modal and appealing methods of disbursing educational content that can be easily translated, yet still keep context. Admittedly, without a certain degree of localization, not all content is always relevant, but comics, as texts, have a vast potential to reach audiences that other media cannot, especially when used in countries where literacy is problematic.

Essentially, a balance needs to be struck between digital and traditional content output. I've mentioned a few times that the most successful comics in South Africa tend to be print-based for a few reasons: access, tangibility, and establishment. For example, because potential consumers see certain comics, such as *Madam & Eve* or *Supa Strikas,* on a near-daily basis, it becomes easier to have them engage with alternative platforms featuring the same content, simply because the reader is already familiar and comfortable with the characters and stories.

To conclude, South Africa is in a unique position in terms of comics— the industry is still very much at the point of being established, trying to find where exactly it fits and how one can participate within it, but sans the burden of traditional expectations from audiences. Essentially, what the country needs is more localized content, regardless of format, that can reach and be consumed by its citizens. As a developing economy that straddles a tenuous position between first- and third- world, there is a possible base for consumption of printed comics, but that excludes a vast amount of people that live in rural areas and below the breadline, removing any options of purchasing luxuries like comics. However, with recent developments in Government distribution of tablet computers to rural schools through the ICT4RED (Information Communication Technology for Rural Education Development) scheme (Wild, 2015), access to the internet is now becoming more attainable. This means that access to digital comic content can begin to become more plausible within the nation, especially when viewed in conjunction with statistics around smartphone ownership and usage within the country. According to the Pew Research Center (2015), as of the year 2015 upwards of 89 percent of all South Africans own a cellular device and of that, 34 percent own smartphones capable of connecting to the internet. This access is far greater than that to computers, and with such a mobile-centric population, online content consumption is vast.

It can therefore be argued that for a comic industry to truly thrive within the country, the most logical platform lies in digital comics (be it webcomics or page-based) especially when the earlier issues that were addressed by this essay come to light. Rhoda and Howard's experiments with *Velocity* revealed both positive aspects and potentially problematic areas when it comes to creating independent projects, with the majority of problems lying not in creative ability or lack of content, but rather a lack of cohesion, standard formatting and, most decidedly, money. N. Howard (personal communication, August 6, 2017) offers that digital comics are "…a viable alternative to publication, but you need to scale exponentially in effort to recognize the same revenue as you would with hard copies as digital copies you're talking about margins of cents vs. dollars in print medium. The perfect harmony would be BOTH [sic]." Rhoda mentions that good marketing and an extremely strong social media presence are the best way forward for young creators to get their work into the market. South Africa certainly has a ways to go in order to catch up with its global counterparts, but hope lies in the realm of digital comics.

ACKNOWLEDGMENTS

The author would like to thank Moray Rhoda and Neville Howard for being the two true pioneers of South African Comics, never wavering, never giving up no matter what the odds. You two will always be an inspiration to me!

I would also like to sincerely thank Christopher Davies for his instrumental help in editing this essay, as well as my wonderful wife, Chanel, for all of her encouragement and support in making this happen. Finally, to Jeff and his team, for their monumental patience, incredible support and all-round greatness as people, I express my sincerest thanks.

REFERENCES

African Cartoons (2017). *South Africa.* Retrieved from http://africacartoons.com/cartoonists/map/south-africa/.

Howard, N., & Rhoda, M. (2011–2015). *Velocity anthology.* Cape Town: Velocity.

Mason, A. (2012). *What's so funny: Under the skin of South African cartooning.* Cape Town: Taylor & Francis.

Mkhize, L. (2014–present). *Kwezi.* Cape Town: BK Publishing.

Molver, L. (2018). *Shaka rising.* Livermore, CA: Catalyst Press.

McCloud, S. (2006). *Making comics: Storytelling secrets of comics, manga and graphic novels.* New York: HarperCollins.

Pew Research Center (2015, April 15). *Cell phones in Africa: Communication lifeline.* Retrieved from http://www.pewglobal.org/2015/04/15/cell-phones-in-africa-communication-life line/.

Rhoda, M., Hoosen, N., & Diorgo, J. (2015–2017). *SECTOR*. Johannesburg and Cape Town: SECTOR.

Ryba, J. (2001–present). *Soccer Warrior*. Cape Town: Mamba Media.

Stevenson, M. (2006). *Bitterkomix*. Retrieved from: http://archive.stevenson.info/exhibitions/bitterkomix/index.htm.

Strika Entertainment. (2000–2017). *Supa strikas*. Cape Town: Strika Entertainment.

Wild, S. (2015, October 26). Tablets a cure in rural schools. *City Press*. Retrieved from http://city-press.news24.com/Voices/Tablets-a-cure-in-rural-schools-20151023.

Digital Comics
in Francophone Countries

Never Too Late to Be Creative

CHRIS REYNS-CHIKUMA *and*
JEAN SÉBASTIEN

Introduction

While in the U.S. the first prize for digital comics was created in 2005 by the Eisner Awards as "Best Digital Comics," in France, the first "Challenge Digital" prize (a prize that rewards the best e-comics in French or in English) was given at the Festival d'Angoulême in 2015. This lag of 10 years illustrates one of the main realities of French e-comics: Bandes dessinées numériques (hereafter BDN) were behind the American e-comics in their birth, diversity, number, inventiveness and commercialization. We will show, however, that in the last decade BDN has been catching up and very creatively so.

Comics in French speaking countries,[1] known as bandes dessinées (which we will refer to as BD), have blossomed into a highly creative art form. In approaching BDN, creators have in mind those BD works of the past; in this essay, we will show how inventive use of panels and pages in traditional BD has influenced BDN. The reference to the page in presenting BD is of particular importance: in the cultural basin where BD developed, the page, much more so than the strip, has been the main format of publication, and thus has become the expected form of a finished work. As with any constraint, it has become part of the vocabulary of BD, with artists using its creative possibilities.

The particulars of the history of the medium in France, Belgium, Switzerland and Quebec had an overarching influence on the beginnings of the developments in French digital comics. This essay begins by identifying the main factors that have limited the development of BDN. Next, in order to present an overview of the production of the last twenty years, we have decided to choose a few works and to classify them according to formal affinities. The identification of categories in the use of digital technology by comics creators became an issue following Scott McCloud (2000) and has been given greater attention in the recent work of Anthony Rageul (2014).[2]

Understanding the Slow Development of BDN

It is only towards the end of the first decade of the new century that the distribution of BDN appeared on the radar of publishers with any significant importance. Since publishers have started looking into digital publication, the results of their efforts have often been mitigated. Even today, as BDN has become a growing business, it is still fledgling. Yearly reports on the production of comics in francophone Europe make this apparent. It should be noted that most services offering online digital comics in France were founded at that time or just after 2010. Specialized services in digital comics, such as Digibidi, Ave! Comics, Izneo and Delitoon were founded, respectively in 2008, 2009, 2010 and 2011. Two digital bookstores that distribute, among other books, digital comics were founded in the same period: Numilog in 2008 and Youboox in 2011. Accordingly, data on the phenomena was only collected from 2009 and on. We will take a two-pronged approach in our description of the cultural context in which these specialized services came to be. First, we note that France is a country in which the book has kept a strong cultural value and secondly, we highlight how the development of successful and avant-garde telecommunications technology in the 1980s ironically slowed the uptake of the World Wide Web.

The Continued Success of the Hardcover Book

The lively tradition of BD in French speaking Europe might have contributed to a slow beginning for French digital comics. The medium invented by the francophone Swiss Rodolphe Töpffer got off to a somewhat slow start during the rest of the nineteenth century, but from the moment at the end of the 1920's when children's publishers began to show a serious interest, BD developed as a legitimate field of artistic creation. One can think of famous characters like Tintin, Spirou, Astérix and les Schtroumpfs (the Smurfs). In the flow of "la nouvelle vague" (French New Wave) movement in cinema and following the events of May 1968, a place was crafted out for works created within a budding auteur branch of the medium. Thus, in the seventies and eighties, the industry of BD changed. Rather than being centered around characters and series, its center became the author, among them Moebius, Bilal, Tardi, Montellier and many more. And rather than writing stories that children read either in their favorite periodicals or in the standard 48 pages full color hardcover collecting a complete arc, they wrote stories for adult audiences, and these stories were published directly in book form.

Bart Beaty (2007) has shown that the nineties were very productive for alternative publishers like L'Association with authors like Trondheim, David B., and Satrapi and her globally successful graphic novel, *Persepolis* (2000; trans. 2003). Meanwhile in Quebec, Michel Rabagliati's suburban adventures of Paul in Montreal and Guy Delisle's cosmopolitan graphic narratives were very well received in francophone countries and beyond. The field of production of BD had then gained a relative autonomy and a strong symbolic capital through the development of auteur creations, museums and festivals.

The enormous commercial success of the traditional paper-form BD gained in the 1980s, and became even stronger in 1990s; thus, there was not motivation for many creators to explore the nascent digital platform. In effect, BDN developed later than its American or Asian (Japanese, Korean) counterparts. To begin with, and contrary to the American or Japanese publications that are still primarily [pre-]published in periodical formats (magazines, comic books, etc.), after the 1980s in francophone countries, the hardcover book had become the norm. While French comics artists successfully experimented with the book in various artistic ways, the periodical format started to disappear. The number of periodicals dedicated to comics, more than twenty in the seventies, dropped sharply in the mid 80s. As of 2000, one could number eleven such publications in the Franco-Belgian publishing industry (Ratier, 2000). There are innate differences between the book and the periodical and even if both publishers and authors have preferred the book, this has not come without losses. The periodical has characteristics that are in line with the format implied by the Internet: serial publication in short installments works well in developing a strong relationship between readers and author, and the disposable format of the periodical had encouraged innovative practices in the use of paper folding in storytelling as far back as the 1960s. Moreover, contrary to the American comics market that went through a deep crisis in 1995, which pushed American creators to look for other types of venues such as the Internet (Campbell, 2006), the French BD market did not go through a similar crisis until 2010 (Ratier, 2011). Therefore, until 2010, French-speaking authors could still sell their creations in the form of albums and there was no strong economic motivation for them to move to Internet.

The Slow Uptake of the World Wide Web

A market for personal computers, Internet and later mobile phones took more time to develop in Francophone countries than in the U.S. and on Asian markets. When they did start to be available, they were also more expensive. This slowness was partly due to the fact that the French had invented their own network in the 80s, called the Minitel (*Médium interactif par numérisation d'information téléphonique*, or Interactive medium by digitalizing telephone information), small terminals distributed by the national phone operator. In use at a national level as soon as 1982, it became quickly very successful and its widespread use lasted until the early 2000s, dwindling down to its close in 2012. However, contrary to the Internet, it was mostly a top-down and one-way system, distributing useful information (on bus schedule, cultural events, etc.) but not allowing the exchange of data with peers.[3] Hence, Minitel was not a system that would favor the development of creative projects such as comics.

Consequently, because of these various factors, in 2000, only 14 percent of the French population had access to Internet against 44 percent in the U.S. (Baudry, 2016). Hence, what Patrice Flichy described as the "*Imaginaire d'Internet*" (2001; translated as *The Internet Imaginaire* in 2007) in France was first traumatized by the quick decline of French-made Minitel while an Americano-centric Internet rose. The Internet versus the book became a subject of academic and public debates focusing on the symbolic value of the artifact or on the impact on the publishing industry.

This Americano-centrism was felt also through the spread of American webcomics. These webcomics were obviously in English, and even once Internet started in France, they could be appreciated only by the few who could read English. This did not fundamentally change with the advent of the Mosaic browser in 1993, but only made American webcomics more readily accessible to the computing and engineering circles in France. An oddball offer in what could be read in 1993 was *L'idée fixe du Savant Cosinus*, a BD created by Christophe at the end of the nineteenth century that had been uploaded on a website. Over the course of the 1990s, some webcomics were translated. However, the process was slow, possibly because these productions were often heavily rooted in idiosyncratic elements of American culture, and because they were mostly created by and aimed at computer geeks or gamers who were still too few in France. Furthermore, with Internet and webcomics came the theoreticians like Scott McCloud. With *Reinventing Comics* (2000, translated in French only 2 years later, in 2002, and published by Vertige Graphic), he offered a motivating vision of Internet and webcomics that had no counterpart in the francophone cultures. All in all, the 1990s was not a period in which webcomics developed in the francophone world.

On a more general level, a culture of the Internet was scarce in France. For example, there was not an equivalent to the American monthly *Wired* until much later. The main perspective in France in discussing the web was defensive. The United States was seen as having played hardball in the nascent new economic world order. For instance, a history of the Internet published in France summarizes a speech given by Al Gore in 1994 to the International Telecommunications Union as "Democracy = information highways = deregulation" (Flichy 2007, p. 39, our translation.). The academic defense mechanism against what was seen as an American dominance over the Internet took into account the fact that the backbone for the Internet had been put in the hands of industry but was wary that the same should happen to the content available on the web. For example, intense debates took place around the Google books project (Jeanneney, 2010). All in all, privatization of culture loomed much larger in Europe as many of its states have developed important cultural institutions and a tradition of endowment to the arts as a tool in the construction of national identity.

Unsuccessful Early Attempts in Digital Publication

With personal computers becoming common in the early 1990s, especially among graphic artists, BD artists welcomed the savvy of the computer design and programming world and their promises of new digital tools meant to draw. One can think for instance of the 1984 digitally drawn comic "Et dieu naquit la femme" (a pun on "and 'God created woman'") which Philippe Gerbaud and Toffe published in the first issue of *Zoulou*, a short-lived alternative BD periodical (Lafargue, 2010). Before 2000, in France and Belgium, most BDN projects (some two dozen) were developed as CD-Roms. Most of the multimedia of the period were founded on BD books that had a strong following—for instance the science-fiction of Bilal, or the adaptation of a classic 1960's episode of an ongoing series, *Blake and Mortimer*. These CD-Roms basically presented the original works in a panel per panel click-through interface. In the case of the science-fiction works of Bilal, rather than using speech balloons, the dialogues were presented under the panels. Some added content was made available, similar to movies' bonus material on DVDs; for instance, the works of Bilal in BDN gave access to an arborescent document with description of characters and their interrelations. A lone frontrunner in publishing BDN online was the start-up I/O Interactifs with two original works published in 1997 and 1999. However, even after an injection of capital by Dupuis, one of the largest Belgian publishers, I/O Interactifs went into bankruptcy in 2003. From that negative experience, other publishers in the French speaking countries were apprehensive and developed a wait-and-see attitude.

The francophone world has had its early adopters of the web technology. Among these, the interest came from diverse places in the world of BD; some institutions invested money in setting up a portal. On the other end of the spectrum, came individuals who delved in their pockets to set up a small server. However, all have been faced with the issue of monetizing the content that is made available.

Among institutions, examples can be found both in the non-profit and the commercial sector. For instance, *Coconino World*, set up in 1999, counts as one of the early adopters. Their website was launched with a multi-year government grant by a group of students and a professor at the École de l'Image [School of Image] in Angoulême. Initially imagined as a stepping board for young artists, *Coconino World* now specializes in the publication of patrimonial works and artists' sketchbooks which add to the revenue the site gets from different benefactors. In the for-profit world, the lead was taken in 1999 by the satirical periodical *Fluide Glacial*, at the time owned by one of France's large literary publishers, Flammarion. The webzine *@Fluidz* offered original content made for the web. Its demise in 2005 shows the difficulty of monetizing content offered on the web, even if a publisher decided that part of the cost of such publication were to be accounted for as creating value in terms of image branding.

Monetizing a personal website has also risen as an issue; examples of this are Sirkowski's missdynamite.com, a website developed in 1999 which published in French and in English at first, then in English only, and Phiip's lapin.org in 2001, originally developed to publish his comedic BDN using photography as its representational medium. The comparative development of the ventures of these Québécois and French artists proves interesting. In the early stages of the missdynamite website, Sirkowski set up the server as a medium to get his work known as he published both on the web and in comic book form. He has since pursued the website, covering the costs through the advertising revenue for other series of his which are available in English through an American digital erotic/pornographic website, SlipShine. Lapin.org evolved in a different environment. Phiip's success interested other amateur artists who asked if they could hop on the website. The costs of maintaining the availability of such a growing quantity of files grew over the years. Lapin.org saw in the French market's appetite for albums an opportunity to monetize these works and chose to develop as of 2007 a branch that publishes books, many of which being also available online.

Most publishers adopted digital publication when it was mature in the early 2000s and their early forays in e-comics were no success. One of the large French publishers of BD, Média-Participations (a corporation that bought out classic publishers, Dargaud, Dupuis and Le Lombard) developed a website in 2004 that they commercialized under the name Read-box.com.

Designed to promote the publisher's catalogue, the website offered an average of fifteen pages of the books hitting the shelves at the time. The publisher has since developed a new and more dynamic offer to which we will discuss later. However, the concept of Read-box itself shows how timid the publishers have been in moving towards digital publication.

Finding the Right Business Model

The data on the growth of BDN is sparse. One of the most important players in the field of digital comics in France, Izneo, has made some numbers available. This online service, founded by the largest publisher of BD in France, Média-Participations has, over the years, managed to convince many other important publishers to distribute their publications through their platform. Whereas in its initial year in 2010, it sold 10,000 BDN, they declared for 2014 sales of more than 300,000 (Ratier, 2014). More recently the Paris outlet of the worldwide auditing firm KPMG has prepared a yearly study of the digital offerings by French publishers. In a two-year period, as shown by the firm's 2014 and 2016 reports, the percentage of new books published both in paper and digitally grew from 45 percent to around 75 percent, depending on the type of book, with bande dessinée hitting one of the high marks with 80 percent of the new books also offered digitally.[4] In Quebec, publishers have been quite timid. For instance, from the total number of BD published in 2015, only twelve books out of some 200 had a digital version (Viau, 2015).

Another important player in the young BDN market is Ave ! Comics. In 2009, the publisher started to distribute e-comics through a smartphone application. Monthly subscribers to the app would not only get access to the budding collection of comics that Ave ! had bought the rights to, but also find on a daily basis a six-panel page story by star cartoonist Lewis Trondheim. Even if Ave ! Comics is not the most important player in distributing BDN, "this [business] model is the first pay for access BDN after the burst of the Internet bubble" (Baudry, 2016, p. 5, our translation.) and the monthly-subscription model which they initiated is now replacing or, in the least, becoming an alternative to the sales of digital file model that their competitors had chosen.

More recently, between 2013 and 2016, Fabien Vehlmann and others created the monthly webzine, *Professeur Cyclope*, as a freemium. It was offered under a flexible economic system (with different formulas, from free access to some stories, to partial or full subscription) and collaborating with other sponsors like the Franco-German TV channel Arte and the weekly TV and cultural magazine *Telerama*. It is also flexible in its use of formats, emphasizing BDN and using various interfaces with the reader, but also traditional scanned pages of BD.

BDN—An Overview of the Creative Diversity

Some early experiments in BDN might have simply been side effects of fads in the computing or networking world. Even in such cases, the works we have chosen to present have had a historical importance in helping BDN find an audience and making it palatable as a medium. However, we also have identified highly creative uses of the technology. In some cases, works of high value have been the work of artists in mid-career who weren't digital natives. These experienced artists have often tried to use characteristics of new technologies in order to further an aspect of their work published in book form; hyperlinks have been used by creators involved in the invention of a world. An early case of blog-BD became a pressure-free creative space for a high exposure artist; others whose work have questioned the materiality of the sheet of paper have found in moving images a way to further their formal musings. But much of BDN has come from young creators. In the same playful way as successive generations of geeks typed ASCII art, photoshopped pictures or created GIF memes, we will show how artists have used computers and networks in novel ways to tell stories, whether by becoming savvy in the use of a software or by working with the code itself. That artists embrace new technologies is no surprise; working with computers calls for an attention to detail that is not altogether different from the minute movements involved in drawing and painting, and the pleasure such work involves. Theoretician and artist Anthony Rageul's statement that "coding is an activity that makes me feel a kind of jubilation" (2018, p. 1) gives an idea of the extent some creators have given to going fully digital with their work in BDN.

We identify hereafter two families of work, one where an instance within the BDN ordains story elements and another where an instance acts as an arbiter for the reader as s/he engages into gameplay. As any form of storytelling with images, there is a question as to whether there is a narrative instance similar to that of a novel. However, this has been less of an issue in the analysis of BD than it has been for cinema and we will follow the lead of Groensteen (2007) in his use of the concept of arthrology as a means to understand the organization of a story without having to refer to the notion of narrative instance, a notion that only applies if and when a movie or a comic sets up a narrator. For Groensteen, there is an organizing force, an organizing instance, within stories developed in any media. The word arthrology generally refers to the specialty within the study of anatomy centering on articulations. The concept is aptly used as a metaphor considering that in comics, the organizing instance helms a series of articulations (between dialogue and image, between panels, between pages and, if there is a narrator, all of the above with the narration). As is the case for BD, in much of BDN, this function is the main organizing force. Other works of BDN have made a large place to gameplay. This involves coding which takes into account possible uses of the interface by the reader/player, arbitrating if you will, by having certain actions come to a programmed outcome.

The Arthrologic Function in BDN

TRANSMEDIA

Transmedia works are devised in more than one media—for example paper publications, websites, animations or movies, games either within the program or as an IRL (in real life) event—with each media bringing its own history and characteristics. Transmedia works are not specific to the world of comics. If one were to study their history, their development would probably best be followed in the movie industry. In many cases, the use of more than one media has become part of the producers' marketing plan and some of the works created as part of such a plan are conceived to develop a fan base. In some cases, the development of platforms that build on a movie are encouraged by the government grant mechanisms where new media is seen as a plus to a movie project. Surprisingly, Rageul gives very little attention to transmedia and only mentions it when referring to multimedia. This is a surprising choice considering he defines multimedia as works in which "the temporality of the audiovisual becomes a narrative and plastic issue" (2014, p. 102).

In France, the most obvious transmedia project designed to satisfy fans was the website developed for a series called *Donjon* by highly successful artists Joann Sfar and Lewis Trondheim. The website,[5] set up in 2000, built on the series' offbeat take on heroic fantasy. Since those early days in working in transmedia as a marketing tool, others have followed suit. The homepage, the drawing of a room in a castle tower with the title of the series as the only apparent element of text, worked with a simple hover trigger technology: the movement of the cursor over an object made the corresponding menu item pop up. Through the clicking of a series of doors, it also boasted the function of a virtual tour of the castle and included video games that were updated from time to time. Sfar actually was also one of the founders of a small video game company, originally called Pastaga. Similarly, The French video game company, Ankama, which also publishes a magazine with stories featuring some of its characters, has experience with transmedia. In 2011, they developed stories that started in the magazine, continued as a succession of panels with moments of interactive gaming on a website that has now been closed (www.maxi-mini.fr), and concluded in a short animated story broadcasted on television (Karayan, 2011).

A fine example of a transmedia work developed as an effect of the inflexion given to new media by film granting agencies is the work of French producers of Clarke, Costelle & Co. and their Québécois counterpart, Ideacom. As a companion piece to the documentary *Apocalypse: The First World War*, they set up in 2014 *Apocalypse: Dix Destins*, an educational BDN (see http:// www.apocalypse-10destins.com). Ten click-through stories are supplemented by film clips of the war and hyperlinked historical information.

An early example of a transmedia work came in 1995. At the time, most forays in BDN were taking the route of applications made available on CD-Rom. However, with their somewhat steam punk *Obscure Cities*, François Schuiten and Benoît Peeters chose an Internet presence and set up urbi cande.be. Their series, initiated in 1983, counted at the time five albums, and the website they had developed mimed the encyclopedic function most often associated to hypertext, but with facts pertinent only to the fiction (https:// www.altaplana.be/dictionary/urbicande.be). Peeters and Schuiten (1996) have made clear the reason for this conversation between their work in BD and the website as more titles in the series came out and such a website: "the technology of hyperlink navigation offers possibility that stick to the reading activity and are thus more congenial to the development of BD as an art form" (p. 23).

Other interesting transmedia works are native to the Internet. We will give three examples: an early one that worked with different functions of a website and two more recent ones, the first built with different platforms, the second with a storyline built around the use of different web technologies.

In 1997, Bernard Hislaire (or Yslaire) set up the website XXeciel.com [the word "ciel" in French can be translated either by sky or heaven and is used because of its homophony with the word "siècle," century]. The website, which is not online anymore, did not use the design of a combination of panels expected within the BD community. It was presented as the personal notes of a psychoanalyst commenting on drawings sent monthly from an anonymous correspondent. Maaheen Ahmet (2016) has said of this work that it offers a complex reflection on history and story-telling in the age of images. The reflexive nature of the site was made clear by the fact that a section of the website gave summaries of the author's sessions with a psychoanalyst he met in real life. Within the first year of this process, the website had borne the first book of a series, now regrouped as a published book of almost 300 pages. The first two books of the series have been published in English under the title *From Cloud 99* (Humanoids Publishing, 2002).

A more recent work, by writer Simon Kansara and artist Émilie Tarascou, multiplies the platforms where elements of the work are made available. The early episodes of MediaEntity were originally published on the web (http:// www.mediaentity.net) from 2012 to 2014 as a click-through BDN using the turbomedia design (see the next section about this technology). Other than the website, readers could find the clippings of actual news stories, purportedly collected by one of the characters. For this part of their work, the authors simply opened an account under the characters' name on the platform (https://www.scoop.it/t/la-revue-de-presse-de-wilhem-flux). A publisher bought their work and these panels became the first two books of a tetralogy. From the outset, Kansara and Tarascou decided to make their work available under a creative commons license (attribution needed, non-commercial uses permitted, possibility for sharing alike and remixing, generally abbreviated as "by-nc-sa"). Among alternative uses of their characters that came out of this choice, one can find the production of videos (some of which are available as bonus content when a reader buys the second published book) and treasure hunts, one in Paris and one in Geneva, thus treating the story as being linked to real life.

In the case of Quebec publisher, La Pastèque, the decision was taken to encourage artists whom they published to explore different technologies in the production of a BDN. The idea was to publish all through 2017 a serial where each chapter would be produced by a different artist. This became a work titled *Tout Garni* (http://toutgarni.telequebec.tv). The production started with a meeting where the artists were presented with different technologies. The artists set their sights on a technology and brainstormed with the writer possible uses in terms of character interactions. The storyline that came from this process, the tale of a pizza delivery boy going from door to door in an apartment building is, at its best, cute. However, the use of technology in some of the episodes works well. In some cases, the artist has used a very simple technology; for instance, episode 5 works with a simple hover technology, with the cursor seemingly shedding light on parts of a blacked-out drawing. Episode 8 used a more complex apparatus in order to permit IRL gameplay. In order to play this episode to its full extent, one had to go to a specific location in the theater district in Montreal. Passersby could see the projection of a basketball net on the sidewall of a building and use their cell phone as a Wii interface to shoot hoops.

The Gif File

From a technical standpoint, most works in BDN are simply image files, whether scans from paper or drawn with a software. A few artists have combined image files and GIFs; a prime example of this being the work of Vincent Giard. Giard's résumé on his website lists seven such short works using GIFs. The blog function of the site has been eliminated, but most of the works listed can be found using the search engine on the site, aencre.org. His use of GIF is quite versatile and has different functions. Firstly, there are moments where the GIF is meant to produce an effect of verisimilitude, for instance by evoking a continuous motion. For example, a webcomic titled *Le Safari aux Fourmis* [Ant Safari] includes the following: twiddling of thumbs, a character walking down a street or, as two lovers meet, their embrace in a frenetic succession of their heads bending as they kiss and their arms moving across their lover's back. Secondly, he uses GIFs to add expressivity. As Delporte (2009) has noted about *Ant Safari*, the story makes the two individuals' budding love interest apparent to the readers with a panel in which the characters standing in front of each other have GIF heads and, rather than an animated mimic of the face, Giard has chosen a looping sequence of allegorical representations where one would expect the oval of the head (for example a camera objective, a flower, an extended arm and other instances of the representation of desire). In other works he has published, Giard created GIFs with an altogether different function. They are meant to evoke how the characters perceive their body or the environment. For instance, in *Bols* [Bowls], after a character is seen drinking in a few panels, the return home is represented in a series of GIFs in which every element of the image (including the character) moves. Similarly, in *L'Allégorie des Allergies: Un Fort Tonnerre* [The Allergies Allegory: A Loud Thunder], a character on his back in bed has elements of his face moving up to the ceiling in order to evoke how one feels during allergy. The more recent *Brigadière* [Crossing Guard], a series of six GIFs in a first-person point-of-view, makes the reader feel the delight of a couple walking in the street, delight that a crossing guard notes in passing. If the first series of examples stays in line with what we expect of animation or even what we can expect of comics when movement is represented in a single panel by the successive positions of a body connected by motion lines, the other two provide opportunities in storytelling that traditional comics do not.

From Clicking and Strolling to Turbomedia

The bare-boned take on BDN has a charm of its own when one surfs the web. There have been cases in France of artists using the simplest form of click-through slideshow. However, BDN really developed with an even simpler form: scrolling down to read a sequence of panels. In many cases, one would find comics graphically arranged in such a column in blogs, a medium in which the older entries can also be read by scrolling down the page.

If most blogs-BD present a short vertical strip in which the author may seem to jump on the sincerity bandwagon of personal writing, many are subtler. In some cases, bloggers have tackled traditional limits of the comics form. Julien Baudry (2012), the author of a very complete history of BDN, argues that an interest for digital comics grew rapidly in importance with the advent of blogging as a popular cultural phenomenon. In his view, this is partially explained by the fact that it was only in the middle of the first decade of the century that Internet access became common in French speaking

Europe and at that time blogging was the "in-thing"; many artists became fully aware of the Internet through blogs and naturally chose this form to express themselves. Not surprisingly, considering the importance given to the album in French speaking countries (which we have alluded to earlier), there have been from 70 to almost 100 books a year adapting blogs to book form from 2012 to 2016 inclusively (see Ratier, ACBD yearly reports). Explaining this phenomenon would require interviews with participants in the French BD publishing industry, for different players might all have motivations that help in understanding it. The high numbers of books reprinting blogs might be an indication that publishers aspire for a new readership by hopping on the increasing popularity of the geek Internet culture. To this motivation, one could think of another, taking its roots in perceptions given to different modes of publication, BDN gaining in peer recognition and legitimacy within the field when published as a book.

Anchoring our overview of BD published in blog form is *Frantico*. This blog rapidly gathered readership online when it opened in January 2005 at a time when the medium of blogging was still young. It might seem at first glance as a collection of the expected heartfelt confessions, perhaps with a hint of provocation, especially in its dealings with sexual obsessions. The readership of this blog grew rapidly and it became the first blog-BD to be published on paper (Nov. 2005). A further look, however, reveals the work to be more a parody of blogs and their voyeurism. Also, the real name of the author of the blog stayed a mystery for a very long time and actually is still uncertain until today. That mystery also helped in building the hype for this unknown author who seemed, from the entries published, to know and meet every important professional BD artist. Finally, speculations concluded that its author was probably Lewis Trondheim, a star artist to whom we have already referred, which is interesting since he has another "real" blog-BD called *Les Petits Riens* [The Little Nothings].

Many of the successful blogs are auto-fictional. Others are simply tongue-in-cheek. An efficient self-representation uses avatars like an animal or highly simplified representations. Examples of this go from the dressed-up stick figures Allan Barte designed for his *Journal d'un lutin* [An Elf's Journal] (2005–2008; http://laviedulutin.over-blog.com/article-26237084.html) to Maliki's representation of herself in manga-animation style (http://maliki.com/strips/). Most bloggers, however, have used a slightly caricatural representation of themselves in a style more in line with western character design. For instance, highly successful blogger Pénélope Bagieu developed a following through her witty observations of gender issues. In what Baudry (2016) sees as typical of the French blog-BD, she started as an amateur to become a well published author, with one of her books, *Exquisite Corpse*, translated into English. Interestingly, the Internet considerably helped women comics artists to be visible and to publish because of the absence of (male/sexist) gatekeepers in the French Comics world (Reyns-Chikuma, 2016). The French blog phenomenon peaked quickly with the first festiblog [blog festival] in Sept. 2005 and the "Revelation blog prize" of the Angoulême festival in 2008.

Blogging also allowed huge collaborative projects between artists such as with the now 3-year old feuilleton *Les autres gens* [Other People]. The website for *Les autres gens* offers two interfaces to its readers. The first one is the click-through slideshow. If one prefers, one can switch to scrolling, as is commonly found in blogs. Even if *Les autres gens* offers two modes of reading from a technical point of view, we discuss it here with other blogs. The originator of this project, Thomas Cadène, chose a subscription model, which at the time in 2010, was only used by one of the main webcomics platforms. By the end of the project (June 2012), there were over 100 artists participating, each one keeping his/her own and is made up of more than 500 episodes. The work has since been published in book form: 11 volumes of 175 to 250 pages. It was presented to its readers over time as two different seasons, in a logic imported from television. Actually, Cadène presented the work as a BD-novela (a reference to TV novelas). In an analysis of this work, Falgas (2016) noted the intelligence of such choices of wording in opening the medium to potential new readers whose experience frame is television. The telenovala, as a genre, creates the expectation of a story in which the viewer will get to experience the emotional saga of contemporary individuals. Cadène's choice of description for his work announces both the breadth of the work and the emotional tone one is to expect.

Other than navigating a slideshow or scrolling down the story as is most common in blogs, an important development giving a new twist to the slideshow was made by French artists: turbomedia offers the user the possibility of moving from a view of multiple panels (a page or a metapanel to use McCloud's more generic term) to a click-through panel-per-panel view. Quite perceptively, Rageul (2014) notes that the vertical scrolling that is the norm in most blogging formats can be interpreted as the most frequent use of the window metaphor, a creative use of technology to which we will come to in the next subsection; basically, what is meant by window is that if one needs to scroll, either horizontally or vertically, the screen becomes a window giving view onto a larger surface. Atop of this, the artist can choose to have the click stagger elements within a panel, for example making the word balloons appear in sequence as they are spoken. Although created more as an experimental format, turbomedia was exploited by Balak (Yves Bigerel) and Malec (Alexandre Ulmann) in 2009 using multimedia software platform Adobe Flash. It was so successful that 5 years later (in 2014), with other artists and designers he created Turbointeractive.fr. This success impacted the American market and Marvel comics hired Balak in the development of its Infinite

Comics, an online viewing format. This is a rare instance of French influence on American e-comics that shows one of our points about the new impetus in French creativity from about 2010. In an interview, Joe Quesada (2012), Chief Creative Officer at Marvel, said: "What I found so compelling with Yves' [Bigerel] technique is the beautiful simplicity of it. It's essentially an animatic, but what makes it a comic is that the reader controls the timing in the same way that they control the turn of the page." Balak emphasizes simplicity and narrativity over more gadgety BDNs that use animation, sound or panels that let you guess where to click to move forward.

THE WINDOW METAPHOR

In *Reinventing Comics*, McCloud (2000) suggested that a computer screen, rather than being interpreted as a finite surface (the desktop or the page), could be seen as a window on a larger space. A user scrolling through this space could discover what McCloud termed an "infinite canvas" or could discover the whole of a meta-panel in "whatever size and shape a given scene warrants" (p. 227).

The window metaphor is particularly well suited for works primarily designed for the small screen of a smartphone. In 2011, Casterman editor Didier Borg created Delitoon, a website for BDN, inspired by the very successful Korean system of the webtoon (a contraction of webscroll and cartoon) in France. Vertical scrolling had been used in the past, mostly in blogs-BD. However most of these short vertical strips were conceived to be seen as a whole since the size of a computer screen permitted to see the whole sequence of panels. In the webtoon and Delitoon model, in most cases one panel is seen at a time, thus creating a particular constraint in storytelling in which each drawing needs to have enough suspense to encourage the user to keep scrolling down. It is not surprising that one of the big successes of Delitoon has been an adventure story, the manga-style *Lastman* by Balak and his co-creators, Bastien Vivès and Michaël Sanlaville, which started online publication in 2013. It has been translated in English and published as a series by First Second Books in March 2015.

Among recent creative uses of window metaphor are works by comic artists in conjunction with small production companies. Such is the case of Marietta Ren's *Phallaina*, presented as the first "scrolling graphic novel" or "bande défilée" (i.e., scrolling strip; a pun on bande dessinée, drawn strips). It was launched as a downloadable app for Android and iOS in January 2016. The project was made in collaboration with the Studio Small Bang and with Les Nouvelles Ecritures-France Télévisions. It is a horizontal black and white drawing, with a length equivalent to 1600 iPads. The scrolling experience is accompanied by a musical score and delicate sound effects. Some drawings are very slightly animated and in many cases elements of the drawing seem to come to the fore through the use of parallax effects, technical choice which works particularly well in the representation of a group of whales in the underwater scenes (in Greek, phallaina also means whale). For its launch, Ren's work benefited from the fact that elements of the storyline were set up as a public artwork in a street during that year's BD festival in Angoulême. Presented as a fresco of 115 meters long (and 1,10 meters high), it was accompanied by an interactive sound design in French and in English.

Anthony Rageul, whom we referred to several times, is not only a theoretician, but also a practitioner. One of his works, *Prise de Tête* [Fuss/irritation], published online in 2009 (http://www.prisedetete.net/), even if its basic interface is a click-through slideshow, offers many moments in which the window metaphor becomes important. A simple use of this is in the change of format of Rageul's meta-panels. If most will fit on a computer screen, some are larger and one has to move through it to read it fully (and get to the click-through button). A most original use of the window metaphor comes in the chapter entitled "Dieux" [Gods]. In this case, the format of the meta-panel seems smaller than the space on the screen. Eight square shaped panels appear on the screen in two strips filling most of the upper half of the screen. For the reader to get an idea of this segment of the story, he must create a layout for the page using the eight panels, each of which being a scalable window that he moves across the space of screen, changing the rhythm of the story by the elements of the drawing that are made to appear in each panel.

THE VIRTUAL 3D SPACE

For the longest time, authors have been conscious that their characters are limited to a 2D space. As such, some storylines have evolved around this issue of flatness. There are many classic BD stories that play with this issue. A story by French author Fred, titled *Un Cadeau de Noël*, called on the reader to plant a thumbtack in the middle of the page and give the book a spin. As the hero was represented holding the center of the page, he would be saved from his pursuers thrown off the page by the swift circular motion (Fred, 1978). In a book titled *Bungalopolis* (1992), Jean-Paul Eid had a two-page story that could only be read with a strong source of light in behind so as to see the verso in transparency. This same author pushed the actual issue of 3Dness further in *Le Fond du trou* (2011), in which the storyline revolved around the fact that each page in the book has a hole in its center.

Within the BD blogging community, Vincent Giard whom we already mentioned, has also questioned the necessary flatness of the medium. The title of a short three panel BDN from his blog, dated March 3rd, 2008 pointed to this interest. In three panels, it tells the story of a floating globe in a back alley. Two panels are drawn, and the other is a touched-up photograph. Yet, in drawing one represents a sphere by tracing a circle. Who's to say that this circle represents a sphere and not a hemisphere? Hence the title *Hemisphère et boule de gomme*. This is a pun on the expression to describe something mysterious "*Mystère et boule de gomme*." The mystery is not only that there is a flying object, but it can also refer to the very nature of the object. He published on his blog in 2008 a story titled *Histoire Renversante* [Stunning/Tumbling Story]. The story was up on the blog on December 14, 2008. It was also republished on a website dedicated to works of BDN, grandpapier.org. However, the website did not integrate the GIF which is central to the effect of this story, but rather presented each drawing of the animation as a separate page. To find *Histoire renversante* with GIF, use the search engine on Giard's website and type "renversante." The story is designed to create a meeting point between two very different storylines: that of a man in contemporary surroundings coming home and trying to relax in his living room and that of a barbarian fighting a monster, walking towards a mountain hoping to find a treasure and finding a gigantic goblet. On the screen, one sees a page on the left-hand side of a grid comprised of four panels setting up the first story, with the title in the first panel. On the right-hand side is a similar grid, with the title in the first panel; however, this grid is placed upside down. In the middle is the animated GIF of a revolving cube. The cube is separated in eight chambers, one group of four such chambers continuing the right side up story, the other group of four chambers continuing the upside-down story. And the motion of the cube around an axis lets us see the moment where the two stories blend and the characters meet as the wall between where the cube is pierced. Here the use of a GIF animation, only possible in BDN, becomes a tool to question the flatness associated with the medium of BD.

Marc-Antoine Mathieu is a French BD author who has designed much of his work to tackle formal issues specifically for the book medium in a way that is similar to the oubapo authors' experimental works. These are not quite experimental comics, as Mathieu has produced many books with a returning hero, thus giving his work a broader public. Hence, he produced full stories that staged various book formal constraints such as the 2D–3D issues, reading direction, wordless narrative, various book formats, etc. In September 2011, Mathieu (supported by his publisher, Delcourt) strove to look into our perception of depths in a drawing and offered the possibility of a companion website to his book *3 Secondes* (3secondsmystery.com). The book includes a code that gives you access to the BDN. *3 Secondes* is an "infinite" continuous zoom where the reader is supposed to look for clues to solve the "murder" mystery. The first sensation given by the "normal" set speed produces a sense of vertigo. It is only by using the slowdown or backward functions that the reader can re-appropriate control and hope to find a solution to the mystery (Krajewski 2015).

MULTIMEDIA

By their very nature, multimedia works impose a different reception. In an early study on transmedia works, many of which include film/video images, Philippe Marion (1997) suggests that some media are homochronous and others heterochronous. Film and video are homochromous since the viewing time is an effect of the artwork itself.[6] On the other hand, when reading a comic, one is free to roam across the page/s at one's own rhythm. Hence, traditional comics or BD are heterochronous. Most multimedia work include large portions that are homochronous and thus create an experience that differs significantly from that of comics. In a way, a closer filiation for multimedia works would take us to works in animation, especially those that heavily use succession of stills, a classic example being the 1965 French animation, *Marie-Mathématique* by BD author Jean-Claude Forest. The National Institute of the Audiovisual in France has made available the original season of Marie-Mathématique (see http://www.ina.fr/video/CPF07004015/marie-mathematique-1er-episode-video.html).

In 2002, French BD author Frederic Boilet adapted, with graphic artist Fred Boot, two short stories he had published in book form, both about his life in Japan. Boilet and Boot presented their work using Shockwave technology under the banner "New digital manga." If *Tsuru Tsuru* (Japanese, for crane; See http://www.boilet.net/tsurutsuru/tsuru01ter.html) and *Yukiko's Spinach* (http://www.boilet.net/yukiko1_0/yukiko01bis.html) are quite different (the first is simply a still image that the viewer only partially sees in the frame with a slow camera movement giving an idea of the whole as it moves across it; the second is a sequence of drawings, at times more than one panel, with a few moments of interactivity and some animation), both intensively use still images with a musical soundtrack and, thus, generally impose a viewing time on the reader.

In André-Philippe Côté and Jean-Philippe Bergeron's *L'Oreille Coupée* (The Cut Ear; See http://lisgar.net/zamor/Fran11/oc.html), a work published online two years before those of Boilet and Boot, the interface is a succession of panels with a narrative voice-over and a musical score accompanying the action. When characters speak, their dialogue is to be read in a balloon rather than being part of the soundtrack. However, even if the reader clicks through the story, thus having some control over the reading time, the highlighted elements on the screen that act as a button to move to the next sequence only appear after a set time. In a way, the driving force between each sequence in *L'Oreille Coupée* is homochromous, with some leeway given to the reader in reading the dialogues and using the click-through interface.

The Arbiter Function in BDN

EXPLORATORY DEVICES

If the click-through function of slideshows can be said to be interactive, such interactivity is minimal. We have mentioned the use of interactivity coming from some quarters of the video game industry or in a few multimedia works. However, these works have not used interactivity in the most imaginative nor in the most pertinent fashion.

Rageul both as a theoretician and a practitioner of BDN championed more inventive uses of interactivity in order to question our habits in using a computer interface. In his doctoral dissertation, Rageul (2014) refers to a blog which included elements of interactivity. He gives the example of the entry titled *L'Ascenseur* (The Elevator) in a blog published under the pseudonym of Moon Armstrong. The interactivity functions do not seem to work anymore in these stories published in 2009 and 2010, but the blog can still be seen. In a blog, the usual format separates the entry from the readers' comments. In this case, the reader could move an elevator up and down through those comments. As an artist, Rageul used the movement of the cursor across the screen as an effective interactivity tool having an effect on our interpretation of the story. His *Romuald et le Tortionnaire* [Romuald and the Torturer], published in 2012, offers different possible interpretations on Romuald's past as he looks back on his life (see http://revuebleuorange.org/bleuorange/05/tony/). Rageul created images in which the movement of the cursor flips elements of the drawing flip from front to back and back to front as the cursor hovers on them, thus giving a different twist on our understanding of the character's life.

Including exploratory elements is not without impact on the weight of the application file. Hence most devices have stayed quite simple. This simplicity seems well suited to works directed towards children. Two recent app offerings developed in Quebec illustrate this. One was developed by the artist behind the success of Leon, the kid hero of children's books, BD and an animation series. The app is available in many languages, English being one of them: *Leon. The Adventure Continues*. Another can be found in the adaptation of three children's book by publisher Fonfon Éditions. The apps are available in French and in English. The English titles are: *Has Anyone Seen Cowleen?*, *Queen Quick-Quick*, and *Charlie Fights Back!* (see http://laboiteapitons.com/collection/interactive/). Both apps are click-through stories and offer moments of game-play. The issue of whether or not a book with an image per page (which is the case for many children's image books) is a BD has been tackled by some theoreticians (Postema, 2013). And the issue is the same in the world of BDN as these two examples show. From a technical point of view, they are quite similar. Are the Leon apps children's BDN because of their layout of multiple panels per page and the Fonfon books not a BDN? However, in this context of an evolving art form, the question seems moot.

FREE AGENCY DEVICES

Whereas most gameplay formats for BDN offer strict preset possibilities, there are very rare cases where the arbiter function does not so much control as suggest possibilities. Whether or not pushing towards such free agency devices stays within digital comics or BDN is open to debate.

An example comes in the imaginative use of the blog form. Moon Armstrong, this time with another blogger (Stéphanie Delmas), conceived of a story about two neighbors, *Voisin/Voisine*. In order to get the complete story, one must use a simple characteristic of the computer's operating system. By opening each author's blog entry for January 7th 2010 in a different window and by arranging them side by side,[7] the conflict between the neighbors in an apartment block becomes clear. However, a reader is free not to abide by the suggestion at the bottom of either blog explaining the use of the multiple windows option of operating systems. Armstrong and Delmas's story is also interesting in that it serves to question our habit in reading blog stories vertically. The co-presence of the side-by-side window both reinstates our left to right reading and questions the limit of the mediums we use, be it scrolling or slideshow in BDN or the confines of the page in BD.

The three softwares by Fonfon Éditions that we discussed in the preceding section actually all include two apps. Other than the slideshow story in which the arbiter function plays a strong role, there is also a "create-your-own-story" app. This app includes files in which one finds drawings of surroundings, or drawings of characters, an interface to write texts and in the end a button to publish the finished pages as a book, made available within the list of apps on the user's tablet or phone. In this case, the app developers leave greater space to the user's agency by fully opening the possibility for infinite variations of storyline limited only by the number of drawings available for the mix and match and the possibilities of the application.

Conclusion

BDN, as we have shown, was slower to develop than e-comics in some other parts of the world, partly due to the way the field of BD had gained its autonomy as early as the 1970s with strong legitimation institutions and a strong interest in works that had the auteur signature and partly due to the slow development of the Internet in Europe. Furthermore, a few financial failures in the 1990s cooled the potential investment by publishers. Notwithstanding this slow start, from the 2000s—and more obviously from about

2010—BDN has proven creative in the use of digital technologies to tell stories, both in the way the technology is used as a means for new possibilities in articulating a story and, to a lesser degree, as a gate into interactivity.

A quite strict parallel could be established between this market situation and the comics research in France. If France and some other Francophone countries produced a great tradition in comics (arguably the third one after the U.S. and Japan in terms of market), it also produced a great number of theoreticians of the media from the 1960s and on (Beaty & Miller, 2014). Paradoxically, universities until very recently were not a welcoming place for that high-level research. It was, and still is in 2017, rather in Art schools that research and practice meet.

Many of these researchers work outside university in various positions. Two of the most prestigious researchers, Peeters and Groensteen, to whom we have referred earlier in this essay, are prime examples of this disconnection. Whereas the former has shown an early interest for the digital medium, Groensteen has only recently given more serious attention to BDN. In fact, Groensteen (2013) devotes a chapter to it with a particular insistence on defining comics and observing how BDN holds its own against this definition. This could have had an effect on the development of BDN. However, in the recent decade, things are changing and new younger researchers are closer to new realities of the comics world. In his Ph.D. thesis, Falgas (2014) criticized a focus on the essence of BD often associated with a resistance to the new e-comics. He prefers to see BDN as a social practice and does not find in narratology and semiotics sufficient tools to describe the practice. In his perspective, "the digital era calls for its own narrative language and this language emerges by finding a foothold in the previous languages, similarly to the way BD itself was forged" (p. 24, our translation). At the same time, research is also done in art schools where obsession with theorization is less obvious and conversely connection with the market is more obvious. For example, in the Angoulême Ecole de l'Image, Thierry Smolderen, who is also a practitioner, and his students, explore the new possibilities for the young generation to whom BDN is a potentially rich, creative and economical future.

NOTES

1. French-speaking here include France, Belgium, Quebec and Switzerland but not African countries that would need another article of its own.

2. In this study, we will not be looking into the quite dynamic ventures in publishing patrimonial works of BD. This patrimonial enterprise can best be illustrated in France by the patient work of BDoubliées [Forgotten Comics], with the development on their website of the "coffre à BD" [comics chest] from 1998 and in Quebec by Mem9ire (a pun on memory of the ninth art) which has also developed a catalog of early 20th century works.

3. For some exceptions to this top-down system, see Richard Kahn and Keller (2008).

4. For this series of study, KPMG surveys most French publishers. In the case of the results presented in its 2014 survey, KPMG received completed questionnaires from almost

half of the publishers. In the case of the 2016 results, it received answers from more than two-thirds of the publishers.

5. The website was managed for the authors by Morgan Di Salvia. The main architecture of the site, but not all its original functions, among them the games, is archived at http://www.pastis.org/donjonland/.

6. Some films and TV shows, especially when adapting comics, have interrupted the flow with codes originating in comics. There are other cases also. An interesting one is a recent web series developed to teach sign language. Balloons appear on screen to accompany the shots of characters signing to one another in a dialogue. The director, Véronique Leduc, created the portmanteau word "bande dessignée" ("strip in sign language") to describe her work, thus clearly referencing BD. The series is available online at http://www.bdlsq.net.

7. Stéphanie Delmas published her blog under the pseudonym Bambiii. Delmas still maintains a blog, but the specific entry is from the blog she wrote using a different service provider. The drawings for most of the entries from this previous blog are online; however, the drawing for that specific entry is missing (http://destrucs.over-blog.com/).

The entry from Moon Armstrong's blog is archived as number 29 on his web page (http://lebloggirlydemoon.blogspot.ca/).

REFERENCES

Ahmet, M. (2016). *Openness of comics: Generating meaning within flexible structures.* Jackson: University Press of Mississippi.

Baudry, J. (2012). *Histoire de la bande dessinée numérique française.* Retrieved from http://neuviemeart.citebd.org/spip.php?rubrique72.

Baudry, J. (2016). Généalogie de la bande dessinée numérique. In P. Robert (Ed.). *Bande dessinée et numérique* (pp. 31–54). Paris: CNRS.

Beaty, B. (2007). *Unpopular culture: Transforming the European comic book in the 1990s.* Toronto: University of Toronto Press.

Beaty, B., & Miller, A. (Eds.). (2014). *The French comics theory reader.* Leuven: Leuven University Press.

Campbell, J. (2006). *A history of webcomics: "The golden age" 1993–2005.* San Antonio: Antartic Press.

Delporte, J. (2009). Les images mouvementées de Vincent Giard. In *Du9 L'autre bande dessinée.* Retrieved from https://www.du9.org/dossier/images-mouvementees-de-vincent/.

Eid, J.-P. (1992). *Bungalopolis.* Montreal: Éditions logiques (Croc Album).

Eid, J.-P. (2011). *Le Fond du trou.* Montreal: La Pastèque.

Falgas, J. (2014). *Raconter à l'ère numérique.* (Doctoral dissertation, Université deLorraine). Retrieved from http://docnum.univ-lorraine.fr/public/DDOC_T_2014_0112_FALGAS.pdf.

Falgas, J. (2016). Pour une sociologie des usages et de l'innovation appliquée aux récits innovants. In P. Robert (Ed.). *Bande dessinée et numérique* (pp. 135–154). Paris: CNRS.

Flichy, P. (2007). *The internet imaginaire* (translation: Liz Carey-Libbrecht from original 2001). Cambridge: MIT Press.

Fred. (1978). *Y'a plus d'saison.* Paris: Dargaud.

Groensteen, T. (2007). *The system of comics* (translation: Nick Nguyen from original 1999). Jackson: University Press of Mississippi.

Groensteen, T. (2013). *Comics and narration* (translation: Ann Miller from original 2011). Jackson: University Press of Mississippi.

Jeanneney, J.-N. (2010). *Quad Google défie l'Europe: Plaidoyer pour un sursaut* (3rd ed.). Paris: Mille et une nuits.

Kahn, R., & Kellner, D. (2008). Technopolitics, blogs, and emergent media ecologies. In B. Hawk, D. Rieder et al. (Eds.). *Small tech: The culture of digital tools* (pp. 22–37). Minneapolis: University of Minnesota Press.

Karajan, R. (February 2nd, 2011). Comment Dofus a dépassé World of Warcraft en France. In *L'Expansion.* Retrieved from http://lexpansion.lexpress.fr/high-tech/comment-dofus-adepass-world-of-warcraft-en-France_1372585.html

KPMG. (2014). *Baromètre 2014 de l'offre de livres numériques en France.* Retrieved from http://www.idboox.com/etudes/une-etude-tres-complete-sur-le-marche-du-livre-numerique/.

KPMG. (2016). *Baromètre 2016 de l'offre de livres numériques en France.* 3e edition. Retrieved from https://assets.kpmg.com/content/dam/kpmg/fr/pdf/2016/09/fr-barometre-offre-livrenumerique.pdf.

Krajewski, P. (2015). *L'enquête sur l'art de Marc-Antoine Mathieu.* Paris: PLG.

Lafargue, J.-N. (2010). Bande dessinée sur ordinateur (1984). In *Le dernier des blogs* [Blog post]. Retrieved from http://hyperbate.fr/dernier/?p=14156.

Marion, P. (1997). Narratologie médiatique et médiagénie des récits. *Recherches en communication,* 7 (pp. 61–88). Retrieved from http://sites.uclouvain.be/rec/index.php/rec/article/view/1441/1291.

McCloud, S. (2000). *Reinventing comics.* New York: Perennial.

Peeters, B., & Schuiten, F. (1996). *L'Aventure des images, de la bande dessinée au multimédia.* Paris: Autrement.

Postema, B. (2013). *Narrative structure in comics. Making sense of fragments.* Rochester: RIT Press.

Quesada, J. (2012, November 3). Marvel @ SXSW: Quesada opens the all-digital "infinite comics"/Interviewer: K. Phegley, *Comic Book Review.* Retrieved from http://www.cbr.com/marvel-sxsw-quesada-opens-the-all-digital-infinite-comics/.

Rageul, A. (2014). *La Bande dessinée saisie par le numérique: Formes et enjeux du récit reconfiguré par l'interactivité.* (Doctoral dissertation, Université de Rennes 2). Retrieved from https://tel.archives-ouvertes.fr/tel-01127320/document.

Rageul, A. (2016). La BD numérique, entre jeu vidéo et Net Art? In P. Robert (Ed.). *Bande dessinée et numérique* (pp. 101–107). Paris: CNRS.

Rageul, A. (2018). On the Pleasure of Coding Interface Narratives. The *Comics Grid: Journal of Comics Scholarship,* 8(1): 3. p. 1–17. DOI: 10.16995/cg.107 Retrieved from: https://www.comicsgrid.com/articles/10.16995/cg.107/.

Ratier, G. (2000–2016). Les bilans de l'ACBD. [Yearly documents published under the title *Rapport sur la production d'une année de bande dessinée dans l'espace francophoneeuropéen*]. Retrieved from http://www.acbd.fr/category/les-bilans-de-l-acbd/.

Reyns-Chikuma, C. (2016). La bande dessinée au féminin. *Alternative francophone* 1.9 Retrieved from https://journals.library.ualberta.ca/af/index.php/af/issue/view/1739/showToc.

Satrapi, M. (2000). *Persepolis. Vol. 1.* Paris : L'Association (trans. 2003).

Viau, M. (2015). *BDQ 2015 "Go west, young man!" Rapport sur la production québécoise de bandes dessinées en 2015.* Paris: ACBD. Retrieved from http://www.acbd.fr/wp-content/uploads/2016/04/Viau_Rapport-2015.pdf.

Yslaire [aka Hislaire]. (2002). *From cloud 99.* Paris: Humanoids Publishing.

Upwards and Backwards

Blurred Perspectives
on Digital Comics as Mentor Texts

TERI HOLBROOK, MELANIE HUNDLEY *and*
BILL HOLBROOK

Introduction

As Marie-Laure Ryan (2006) notes, digital technology, like print technology, has significantly impacted economic systems, politics, entertainment, and people's day-to-day social practices and relations. "But," she provocatively asks, "what has the computer done for narrative?" (p. xii). This question points to both the past and future of literature: to an enduring notion of narrative as a very human form of meaning-making "that transcends medial boundaries," but also to possible story forms yet to come where, as Ryan says, "the jury is still out" (p. xii).

This pointing is echoed in Thomas Pettitt's (Starkman, 2013) argument that when it comes to communication, humans are "moving upwards and backwards"—upwards toward information transmission methods spurred by technological developments (e.g., social media) and backwards to communication and literary practices that in key ways resemble the Middle Ages (e.g., orality and connectivity). As Pettitt succinctly puts it, "The future is medieval" (para. 5).

The question of what the computer has done for (and to) narrative affects more than scholars puzzling over textual forms and publishers wrestling with Web 2.0 impact on the business side of literature. It also affects teachers. As part of U.S. English Language Arts (ELA) curricula, teachers are charged with cultivating students as current and future readers and writers. If, as Pettitt theorizes, technology is spurring people to engage in a kind of once-and-future remixing of communication modes, then how do teachers frame what it means to be a writer? If writers, using digital tools, are experimenting with "new and strange sorts of texts" (Baron, 2009, p. x) that combine image, word, sound, touch, gesture, then how do teachers reimagine the concept of "text"? And if these "upwards and backwards" practices are happening simultaneously, what pedagogical moves can classroom teachers make so that students actively engage and enjoy, and produce digital and multimodal narratives?

These broad questions animate this essay and its emphasis on supporting students as digital text creators. Together, the authors share a commitment to digital comics and teachers as cultivators of novice digital composers. Bill is a print and digital comics artist, Teri is a fiction writer and literacy educator, and Melanie is a teacher educator and digital literacy researcher. Among us, we have published digital comics, print fiction and nonfiction, and academic articles about interactive digital narratives. We teach teachers and K–12 students how to create digital comics and other types of multimodal texts. In this essay, we blur our professional perspectives to take up notions of upwards and backwards as ways of thinking about how classroom teachers can support students as digital comics composers. We emphasize the term *composer—*students as active makers of texts in addition to appreciative readers. Henry Jenkins (Jenkins, et. al, 2009) argues that today's youth engage in participatory cultures where they learn to produce and share expressive works. While much of this creative apprenticeship occurs in out-of-school affinity spaces (Gee, 2004) such as fandoms or online publishing forums, we follow other literacy scholars (e.g., Hicks, 2013; Selfe, 2007) in asserting that schools are also sites where students grow as digital composers. Indeed, we look to teachers as facilitators who can design in- *and* out-of-school environments in which students can cultivate the skills, strategies, and dispositions crucial to the production and use of digital comics.

We do so by homing in on what are arguably old school literacy practices applied to new sorts of texts such as digital comics: teacher book clubs (Flood & Lapp, 1994) and mentor texts (see Chase, 2008; also Calkins, 1986/1994; Graves, 1994). By delving into digital comics in book clubs, teachers can engage collaboratively with the works, reading for pleasure and instructional purposes. They can foster an understanding of digital comics as a genre and an appreciation for the form as literature (see Chute, 2008). By using digital comics as mentor texts—exemplars that can be examined by novice composers for structures, strategies, and techniques—teachers and students can point out storytelling choices made by pros (Cook & Kirchoff, 2017). A rich mentor text bears "the 'fingerprints' of the authors' craft" (Dorfman & Cappelli, 2007, p. 3) and allows readers to discern the decisions creators make to achieve the text's effects, thus making those creative choices usable in students' own work. In short, by analyzing digital comics, both teachers and students can build their own repertoire of the genre's meaning-making moves.

Pulling these practices together, we model how we used a book club to engage with three interactive digital narratives, reading them for pleasure but also considering how they might serve as mentor texts for students. Through a constructed conversation (Wiggins, 2011), we examine how the creators used communicative modes—including words, images, sound, and movement—as storytelling components. To frame our discussion, we draw from two bodies of work: New Literacies and multiliteracies scholarship that argues for the necessity of students as meaning-makers in digital environments (Cope & Kalantzis, 2009; Lankshear & Knobel, 2011) and Pettitt's (2007) conceptualization of the Gutenberg Parenthesis. Together this scholarship allows us to complicate divides between traditional and "new" forms of literacy and literature so that we can better articulate the importance of supporting today's students as digital composers.

A note: We provide a brief glossary at the end of the essay to explain how we understand certain key words. Since digital comics are not only authored but also drawn, designed, scored, and coded, we use the term "creators" or "composers" to refer to teams that craft digital comics unless we specifically refer to an individual writer or illustrator. Since digital technology is inherently multimodal (Cope & Kalantzis, 2009), when we refer to digital texts, multimodality should be inferred.

Conceptualizing Texts Outside the Parenthesis

Informed by media theorists (e.g., McLuhan, 1962; Ong, 1982), Pettitt (2012) conceptualizes the Gutenberg Parenthesis as the period of cultural history between the invention of the printing press and the development of the computer. During this time, the dominance of the printed word put pressure on other communication modes, transforming how people transmitted information and developed social relations. Prior to the printing press, communication was "face-to-face (mouth-to-ear)" (Pettitt, 2009, p. 1) as people used talk and performance as primary forms of communication. After the invention of the printing press, words became disembodied, fixed, reproducible, and bounded. Not only could an authoritative text be pointed to, but the idea of an identifiable, single author was now possible. Print literacy gained primacy as a privileged cultural practice, and, not incidentally, the focus of schooling in the U.S. and elsewhere.

Print primacy was disrupted, Pettitt (2007) argues, by the invention of the computer, which ushered in cultural practices that destabilized notions of text fixity, authorship, and even the book itself. Instead of the individually authored, original, autonomous, stable, contained, canonical text of the Gutenberg Parenthesis, post-parenthesis texts are remixed, appropriated, sampled, borrowed, dispersed, reshaped, and recontextualized. These post-parenthesis practices share cultural markers with performative communications of the pre–Gutenberg era, which because of their oral nature were "re-creative, collective, con-textual, unstable…" (p. 2). For example, before print oral works were often mashups of pre-existing performances, reassembled to create a new performance with no recognized single author, much like today's remixed media (Pettitt, 2012).

Art, like orality, also functions differently outside the parentheses. The picture frame also gained dominance in Europe in the 15th century. Prior to that, narrative art was frequently limited only by the surface on which it was applied. Pettitt (2007) claims that with its closed boundaries, the frame confined, fixed, and changed the effect and function of Medieval narrative art. These assertions echo in Scott McCloud's (2000) concept of the infinite canvas, which argues that computer technologies freed sequential artists from the cramped printed page, opening up possibilities for re-imagining time and narrative in digital comics.

Pettitt's concept of the Gutenberg Parenthesis also relates to work by New Literacies and multiliteracies theorists. Faced with changes in communication technologies, literacy scholars began in the 1990s to argue that schools need to understand literacies as multiple and texts as multimodal. The influential New London Group (Cope & Kalantzis, 2009) maintains that among the changes brought about by developing technologies is a need for creative, self-motivated workers and self-governing citizens. These cultural needs push against top down hierarchies of governance and usher in "a life-world in which the balance of agency has shifted towards users, customers and meaning makers and in which diversity (not measurable uniformity) prevails" (p. 183). This call identifies the need for students to develop crucial literacy practices identified by Pettitt as being post-parenthesis. Technology allows for the production of remixed and multimodal texts that include written and oral language; visual, audio, and spatial representations; and even tactile and gestural representations (Kress, 2003). Students, to be considered literate in the 21st century, need the skills to produce such texts and the agency to deploy them with intent and effect (see Cope & Kalantzis, 2009, for a more detailed discussion). For these scholars, the question is not *when* schools should begin cultivating students in the art and science of multimodal digital composition but *how*.

Teaching Composition After the Parenthesis

Combining these two bodies of work is useful for our thinking around digital comics for several reasons. As literacy educators, it gives us a way of situating our questions about the role of print literacy in classrooms. If texts are no longer only fixed, bounded, and alphabetically dominated, how do teaching practices need to shift to make room for other understandings of texts, communication, and literacies? Additionally, this scholarship allows us to value digital comics not only as "new" but also in line with long traditions of multimodal narrative. While scholarship shows that educators stress the importance of digital media (e.g., Alvermann, Hutchins, & McDevitt, 2012) and graphic novels and comic strips (e.g., Botzakis, 2010; Carter, 2013; Cary, 2004; Cook & Kirchoff, 2017) as part of students' literacy development, the role of digital comics in K–12 students' development as composers is less explored. If digital comics are meaningful and culturally valuable texts (Dittmar, 2014) in which students engage and make meaning, how can teachers be supported to make their creation part of the curriculum?

Book clubs and mentor texts are well-known structures that can be employed upwards and backwards to teaching digital comics as a narrative genre to novice digital composers. To model these practices, we read three interactive digital narratives as mentor texts using a variation of the common teaching practice "reading like writers" (Ray, 1999), which encourages students to observe authoring techniques—or craft—when reading a work they admire. Instead of reading like writers, we read like composers, thinking about the decisions the creative teams made and how we might use similar techniques with students composing digital comics. We engaged in careful noticing, paying attention to sound, links, transitions, line, color, layout, language—expressive tools we wanted our students to develop. Using digital comics as mentor texts requires three moves by composers: 1) to look beyond basic comprehension to how modes combine to create meaning; 2) to ask questions about the choices creators make and how those choices produce effects in readers; 3) to identify craft elements that can be used in their own work. Engaging in this analysis prepares students to begin experimenting (Dittmar, 2014) with different elements of digital comics as a means of understanding and applying knowledge of digital comic forms.

We each read the apps once for pleasure and then additional times paying attention to the craft employed. Our blurred perspectives as digital comic artists, writers, teachers, and researchers fueled our conversations. To capture those intermingled roles, we decided to represent our book club talk as two constructed conversations. Understanding that teachers must connect their instructional choices with national and local standards, we selected a Common Core literacy standard to focus our observations. Since our goal was for students to create their own digital comics, we selected a writing standard, CSS.ELA-Literacy.W.11-12.3.B: "Use narrative techniques, such as dialogue, pacing, description, reflection, and multiple plotlines, to develop experiences, events, and/or characters" (National Governors Association Center for Best Practices & Council of Chief State School Officers, 2010). While all of these elements were present in the digital texts we selected, we decided for the scope of this essay to focus on how description and plotlines worked in a digital environment.

Our selection of texts was guided by our thinking about potential mentor texts. For that reason, we admittedly stepped back from adopting a strict definition of what a digital comic might be. All three apps fall within what Ryan (2006) calls the traditionalist approach to digital narrative, which foregrounds reader interactivity in digital texts that honor conventional storytelling elements. All three texts combine print, image, sound, and interactivity to develop stories within the recognized genres of historical nonfiction and detective fiction, and all three entail elements recognizable as components of comics (e.g., speech balloons, narration boxes, frames, spaces).

Each conversation below starts with an overall introduction and includes summary points that emphasize the ways each app could be used as a mentor text to achieve specific compositional moves. The introductory and summary points are in italics to set them apart from the constructed conversations. The texts are:

Cainsville Files

Author: Kelley Armstrong

Artist: Julie Dillon

An interactive detective story, the narrative allows readers to make choices that guide the main character's actions and either help her solve the mystery or condemn her to one of several dead-ends. Each screen contains an image; the app features comics elements such as speech balloons to indicate dialogue and narration boxes for exposition and decision points.

Dethany in Virtu/Noir

Story and Art: Bill Holbrook

Story and Writing: Teri Holbrook

A spin-off from Holbrook's newspaper strip *On the Fastrack*, the interactive story features a cyberspace detective. The reader makes choices that drive the narrative, which consists of two parallel plotlines. Image and print text share narrative weight. We selected this app because having the artist (Bill) and writer (Teri) as part of our team provides additional information about decision-making processes.

Operation Ajax

Creator: Daniel Burwen

Writer: Mike de Seve

A historical political thriller based on the 1953 CIA-backed coup in Iran, this app offers additional materials—newsreels, government documents, and character backstories. Image, sound, animation, interactivity, and text all carry narrative weight.

Constructed Conversation 1: Description

Description as an element of print writing attempts to create strong visuals that help the reader imagine settings, scenes, and characters. In digital compositions, description is equally as powerful, conveyed through image, sound, and other modes. In the following constructed conversation, we use the three mentor texts to illustrate how the use of images in a digital comic requires readers to understand how colors, object placements, line weights, white space, as well as movement and layers within an image combine to create meaning. Similarly, the mentor texts demonstrate how the employment of sound in digital stories asks readers to consider the roles of tempo, rhythm, melody, dynamics (how loud and soft) and silence as elements of description. In this conversation, we look into how examining modes in interaction helps digital composers build a multimodal toolkit.

Cainsville Files

BILL: At heart, *Cainsville Files* is a detective story. The lead character, Jenn, is a twenty-something former cop turned P.I. It's set up as a classic trope: the disillusioned cop who's decided the world needs her more outside the force than in. It goes back to Dashiell Hammett's Sam Spade and Raymond Chandler's Phillip Marlowe.

MELANIE: Yes, once you get into the book, you see that. But the title slide hints at something more. If we break the image into thirds, the left is dominated by the background, a forest. The middle is a black raven. The right third, a young woman, Jenn. All three are equal on the screen. My teacher move here is to point out how the number three has relevance in narratives: three sisters, three witches, three wishes. In this image, the three parts each provide a clue to the story.

TERI: Looking at the title screen, I wouldn't think detective story. I think something sinister.

MELANIE: Ravens and woods are traditional literary symbols. The raven is usually symbolic of something ominous or tricky. The woods represent nature, which could be a refuge or could be dangerous. These are the kinds of noticings I teach students to do with print texts and movies, so having them analyze digital narratives this way serves as a scaffold for novice digital composers.

BILL: The raven looks like it's sitting on Jenn's shoulder, like they're companions. But Jenn isn't a hiker—her brown blazer looks professional. The question is, professional what? The word "files" in the title conjures up investigations and records: *The X-Files. The Dresden Files. The Rockford Files.* Important stories kept in files and locked in cabinets.

TERI: But elements also lead the reader away from the detective genre. There's a turquoise glow around the figures—otherworldly. The raven's eye glows, too; I read that as supernatural. And then the programmer uses parallax scrolling so the woods slowly move from foreground to background. Spooky.

MELANIE: So thinking of this as a mentor text, I might ask questions that nudge students toward certain observations. What genres are hinted at? How do you know? Could it be a hybrid genre? What are the specific elements the creators used to indicate a hybrid of detective and horror story? In this way, I lead students to understand that visually literate readers do not gloss over the images; they read them as carefully as they read text.

TERI: Then there's the sound that accompanies the cover. Five repeating notes with light percussion. It could've been chosen to heighten the sense of drama or horror, but it doesn't do that for me. Rather, it feels more easy-going—not quite jazz, not quite contemporary, not quite blues. Focusing on the cover, teachers could engage students in a talk about multimodal composition: layout, use of color, placement of the objects, parallax scrolling, the title font, the function and effect of sound. They could even ask how another music selection or font choice could change what they experienced.

MELANIE: The story opens on an office with a desk, a file cabinet, and two empty chairs—colors are browns, tans and muted plums. Again, those colors help establish the mood and add to the scene's description. The five note musical score is repeated here—the notes are slow but the percussion is quicker, so it feels a bit upbeat. As a teacher, I might ask students how they would construct an opening scene. What modes would they include? How would the modes work together to achieve what effects?

TERI: Looking at this screen, this isn't a busy office. Business is slow. And the text confirms it: Jenn needs work. Knowing the detective genre, you can predict that someone will walk in with a

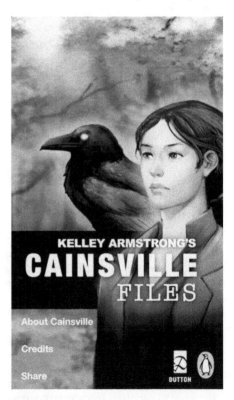

Figure 1: Cainsville Files cover (Random House).

case. It's interesting how that understanding is prompted by the image of an empty chair and clean desk.

MELANIE: But what's also interesting is how sound, image, and print together provide description and exposition. This will be a new idea for many teachers and students—that exposition doesn't disappear in digital comics but is created through layered images, sound, print, and movement. For instance a narration box reads, "So far, I've arranged my filing cabinet twice, rewritten my Rolodex, and scraped every piece of gum off the bottom of my fourth-hand desk" (Armstrong, 2013, "Jenn's Office"). The narration box serves as a visual voice-over introducing the main story and Jenn as the first person POV character. The device of a visual voice-over would be an easy one for students to replicate.

TERI: For that matter, it might also be easy for students to replicate an audio voice-over—embed sound files into the text as a way of experimenting with digital comics.

BILL: I'd like to talk about what I think were pragmatic decisions made in terms of artwork and illustration. Let's face it: creating texts that combine image, print, sound, and interactivity can be time intensive and at a professional level, costly. In a moment, we'll turn to *Dethany in Virtu/Noir*, but for that story I created over 200 full-screen illustrations. Most likely students in class won't have time to do that. But I see in *Cainsville Files* the same or modified images are used multiple times in ways that keep them fresh.

MELANIE: This is so important. Students may find that their ideas exceed their time and ability to create. That's ok. They also can be creative in making pragmatic decisions.

BILL: *Cainsville Files* could be a good mentor text to show pragmatic decision-making. Take the opening of the desk, chair, and file cabinet. The creators keep that same image throughout the entire scene, but they keep the story moving by introducing characters from the side. The reader clicks, a new character enters the room. Another click, Jenn appears to respond. This is how dialogue takes place throughout the app. Typically, a single background setting is used with characters entering from the side as they speak—which is rendered with speech balloons. You get the idea of a camera cutting from one character to the other. This is a useful strategy for students if they are working with constraints that don't allow them to create hundreds of images.

Cainsville Files *can be used as a mentor text for teaching description in digital comic. It shows students how they can make pragmatic decisions based on time and expertise and still create effective digital compositions. By thoughtfully recombining images and sound, they can establish genre, setting, and mood, as well as advance characterization through exposition and dialogue. To apply this discussion, teachers could ask students to develop multiple ways of recombining/remixing a limited number images and sounds to create new screens.*

Dethany in Virtu/Noir

MELANIE: Like *Cainsville Files*, the title slide for *Dethany in Virtu/Noir* provides clues about genre. As a reader you know certain things immediately. The main character, Dethany, is in the foreground holding an iPad. In the background is a conventional looking city skyline—black skyscrapers with lit windows. But then you notice other things: Dethany wears a fedora and trench coat. On the iPad is a picture of a revolver. Above the skyline are the outlines of computer circuits. This begins to set up an inside joke with the reader—juxtapositions between old and new. As a teacher, I'm going to draw students' attention to this.

BILL: It was important to signal right off that this was a piece of genre fiction, to let the reader know that it was not just a detective story but a noir story—so the fedora and trench coat. In print novels, the establishment of setting, character, and genre would take multiple paragraphs. The intent here was for the single title screen to do. There are also only three colors used: purple, black, and white—a decision meant to evoke the bold lights and darks of detective noir films of the 1940s and 50s.

TERI: Additionally, the music playing in the background is a mellow, bluesy jazz. This choice is intended to accentuate genre and mood—the connection to detective noir but also a liveliness conveyed in the upbeat tempo.

MELANIE: The first screen of the actual narrative continues with classic detective tropes. It opens on an office with clean desk, file cabinets, two chairs, a window with blinds.

TERI: Very similar to *Cainsville Files*, which shows how much each story draws from tropes. Bill put in an extra tip of the hat to our 1940s predecessors by including an old-fashioned candlestick telephone on the desk.

MELANIE: But Dethany is holding an iPad. Immediately the image establishes the genre and setting while pushing against genre expectations. There are other clues that indicate this isn't conventional detective fiction. The file cabinet drawers are labeled *Drive A, Drive B*, etc. The view out the window doesn't show a typical cityscape but instead computer circuitry. So the effect for me was to recognize that this story may be a hybrid genre of detective fiction and science fiction.

BILL: Yes, but more than science fiction, the story parodies technology. We made choices in this opening image to point readers toward that parody—the screen actually opens as a wireframe that fades to the filled out image of the office with Dethany holding her iPad.

TERI: In a print novel, the author could certainly describe the elements of this scene: "On Dethany's file cabinets, handwritten labels indicated each drawer's content: Drive A, Drive B, Drive C. Through the partially drawn blinds, the city's buildings slashed the night sky like the bulbous snakes of computer circuits." And that may work. But describing it through image has a different effect.

BILL: That's probably the most significant difference between conventional print-only texts and digital texts that combine image, word, and sound. With digital texts, creators decide which mode—image, word, sound—carries which content. It's not haphazard. Some of the storytelling effects are best achieved through image, others by word or sound. With *Dethany in Virtu/Noir*, we made the deliberate decision not to use the conventional graphic novel elements of speech balloons and narration boxes to convey dialogue and exposition. Instead, every time Dethany's iPad or satchel appears on a screen, the

Figure 2: To show some of the decisions he makes when visually depicting print text, Bill translated a fragment of narrative from print to image: *The house at 221 Mulberry Court is the largest and scariest house on the whole street, maybe in the whole town. Next to it is a cemetery and on the other side a cornfield. The porch is bare and uninviting. The house emits no light except for a third-floor window, where a woman's shadow is sometimes visible* (image created by author).

reader taps it to see a screen of writing on Dethany's iPad. So, for example, from this opening office scene, click on the iPad, and the iPad shows a notes page that begins: "Virtu/Noir was a rain-slicked corner of cyberspace where people go to live out their dreams of being a hero, solving a crime" (Holbrook, Holbrook & Lotshaw, 2015, Scene 1).

Teri: The narrative toggles back and forth between image and print writing. The guiding principle was not to duplicate: what was written couldn't be directly illustrated and what was illustrated couldn't be replicated in prose.

Melanie: That's another conversation that teachers can have with student writers deciding how to convey description in their multimodal digital texts: Which elements of description can be conveyed by images or sound? Which elements will you convey with words?

Teri: And why? For us, the decisions came down to wanting to honor two storytelling art forms: comics and detective fiction. Comics, of course, have their own styles and conventions. Detective fiction, both in film and print, also has conventions and styles. So each decision we made rested on which mode—word, image, or sound—best carried the effect that we wanted and how they worked together to achieve that.

Dethany in Virtu/Noir *can be used as a mentor text for teaching description in digital comics. The description is carried across multiple modes: image, words, and to a lesser degree sound. Animation in the form of fades is also employed as description. Teachers can point to specific decisions made by the creators to evoke mood, setting, and genre across multiple modes. Several scaffolding tools can be used. Students could be asked to compare similar scenes in film, print novels, graphic novels to* Dethany *to see how creators make decisions based on the medium in which they work. Storyboard templates and charts can be used to analyze mentor texts and to aid students creating original work. (See Figure 3.)*

Image/Scene	*Words/Text*	*Image/Visual*	*Sound*
Describe the image or scene you are focusing on. You may use a screen shot if you wish.	How are words used in the image or scene? What effect does it create?	How is color used? What draws the reader's attention? What effect does it create? Is there movement? Juxta-position? What kind of transitions?	How is sound used? What draws the reader's atten-tion? What effect does it create? Are there sound effects? Dialogue? Is there voice over?
	What techniques were used to create the words/text? Why? How does it help the reader?	What techniques were used to create the images/visuals? Why? How does it help the reader?	What techniques were used to create the sound? Why? How does it help the reader?

Figure 3: Example of a digital composition planning template to support students as they make decisions about words, images, and sound.

Operation Ajax

MELANIE: *Operation Ajax* is a fact-based historical graphic novel app, so it's a political thriller more than a detective story. It also uses the opening screens to establish character and setting. But there's a difference. Here the title screen looks like a game screen: it depicts a worn file folder and two action buttons giving instructions on how to navigate the app.

TERI: Click through that and the opening scenes jump right to action. The first image the reader sees is a close-up pair of wary eyes, which then dim to bring into focus a close-up of a briefcase in the hands of a running man. This image then transitions to show a third image of two men running.

BILL: How the creators handle that opening is interesting. The reader is pulled into one character's perspective like the beginning of Hitchcock's *Vertigo*. The images are tiled on top of each other, one fading as another comes into view. It gives the impression of fast-paced movement when it's really a series of still images. The digital transition feature adds the sense of movement.

MELANIE: The entire first scene is like the opening credits of a movie, with the names of the publisher and creators timed to appear with different images. After the three tiled images, there is an establishing shot of the two men running down an alley and into a crowd. The reader sees a line of protest signs, then the same pair of eyes as before, this time wide and panicked; a drop of sweat moves down the character's temple. These scenes have a sense of immediacy: we feel the character's fear even though we don't know why he's scared. So while *Cainsville Files* and *Dethany in Virtu/Noir* used images of whole rooms to establish setting, genre, and tone, *Operation Ajax* does the same with tightly cropped and rapid close-up images.

TERI: That's another discussion about creative decisions to have with students. As a narrative composer, do you describe your setting with one establishing image that gives the reader several pieces of information at once—the empty chair, the cityscape, the clean desk? Or do you limit what the reader sees and knows to a fragment at a time?

BILL: The answer may depend on the genre. For the detective stories, opening with the office set the stage for the tale of the lone PI, waiting for the case to walk in. Giving readers the details all at once lets them take it in and settle into a genre they recognize. For the political thriller, suspense built through the fast-paced meting out of details. The readers' sense of anxiety grows the more they understand—and worry—about what's going to happen next.

TERI: Sound is crucial in *Operation Ajax*. All three apps use it, but in *Operation Ajax* it's clearly an important mode. Several types of sound are used: music, sound effects, not to mention Ed Herlihy's voice on newsreels. The opening uses instrumental and vocal music, the sound of feet running, sirens, and crowd noises. Part of the description that conveys mood and tone is definitely carried by sound. Another discussion for students: given your software, how can you incorporate sound as description, and to what purpose and effect?

BILL: Yes, this is a case where sound's respected as a valued medium. It's intrinsic to the experience. For example, in the opening section, a man lights a stick of dynamite, and from then on sound becomes the main mode tying the scenes together. The burning-buzzing sound of the wick dominates the soundscape— crowd noises fade to the background. Even when the images change, the sound of the burning wick remains. As a reader, your panic amplifies as the sound continues because you know the wick is burning down. Tension is built through sound, a technique not available to creators of analog texts.

MELANIE: Color is also effective here, but it's enhanced through animation. The opening depicts violence, and selective bold color denotes that. Two bodies collide—a jagged slash of color signals the force. This technique can be used in analog graphic novels, but in a digital comic, the jagged color doesn't stay still. It moves, leading readers to the next part of the story.

BILL: Look at how white is used, too. Throughout the opening, white directs the reader's attention. The character's eyes are alarmed; we know that because the whites are large. The men's shirts are white as they run toward the crowd of protesters. The backs of the protest signs are white, drawing our attention to the protest. When the first man falls, the second man reaches out to help him up—their white-shirted arms form a diagonal line across the screen. White is used instead of verbs to describe the action.

Operation Ajax *can be used as a mentor text for teaching description in digital comics. The creators used sound and movement to establish genre, mood, setting, character, and pacing. The reader does not see the full screen immediately; with timed transitions, images and sound are layered to create anxiety and suspense.* Operation Ajax *is available as both an app and a print book. By comparing the two, students can see how print and digital environments allow creators to use modes differently and with different effects in their storytelling.*

Constructed Conversation 2: Multiple Plotlines

*Teaching multiple and parallel plotlines is increasingly a part of English Language Arts classrooms. In the following conversation, we discuss how the three mentor texts use digital features to develop multiple plotlines (*Operation Ajax*) and parallel plotlines (*Cainsville Files *and* Dethany in Virtu/Noir*). As a component of narrative construction, multiple plotlines become a tool for developing story complexity by depicting a variety of related subplots and exploring multiple points of view. A narrative develops that weaves in and out of other narratives within the singular story. For parallel plotlines, singular stories run side-by-side, sometimes intersecting at different points. The three mentor texts demonstrate how features unique to digital texts allows plotlines to play out in ways not as easily achieved in standard print formats.*

TERI: Conventionally, multiple plotlines are employed to provide different angles on the primary narrative; for example, multiple points of view composed to create a single story. Hypertext, however, allows for a branching narrative design, in which readers make choices about which plot path to follow—the old "choose your own ending" device but now more easily achieved for reader interaction.

MELANIE: Learning to read multiple plotlines used to be a complex skill that often needed teacher support. But the Internet has meant that reading across stories and plotlines is not a new practice anymore. Students are quite adept at working from multiple sources and weaving a coherent narrative—or at least a coherent story-world. Nevertheless, teaching students to compose multiple plotlines is not a normalized practice, which is why these three texts can be helpful.

BILL: Multiple plotlines play out here in a variety of ways. The most traditional from a plot standpoint is probably *Operation Ajax*. Here the story unfolds in a fairly linear fashion, with an occasional flashback or digression, but mostly the reader follows a linear path through the story. There is reader interactivity, but it's by providing the reader more information through links to additional files or background notes, not in altering the flow of the narrative.

TERI: In *Cainsville Files* and *Dethany in Virtu/Noir*, multiple plotlines are employed through readers' choice. In both apps, readers reach junctures in the narrative where they have to make decisions about which action the

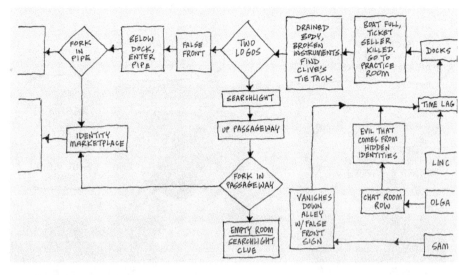

Figure 4: **Example of a flow chart for an interactive narrative featuring multiple plot lines. A diamond is used to indicate when plot lines branch off (image created by author).**

main character takes. The decision affects the direction and outcome of the stories.

BILL: The way all three used point-of-view to convey plot is notable. *Cainsville Files* and *Dethany in Virtu/Noir* use first person POV. *Operation Ajax* follows multiple viewpoints. All of them followed conventions of their genre. Hardboiled detective stories often feature a first person narrator. The reader sees the world through the narrator's eyes. If the PI follows a red herring or hits a dead end, so does the reader. That makes the use of branching logical in a PI digital narrative—the reader acts as the avatar for the detective, deciding which plotline to follow. In a political thriller, it's frequently important to shift the story among several POV characters so that multiple aspects of the same events can be explored. Branching could be used, but *Operation Ajax* keeps its complex story cohesive by not doing it.

MELANIE: In *Cainsville Files*, branching and reader choice are used to add a gaming aspect to the story. Readers are awarded points for how many branches they follow—you receive a score at the end.

TERI: That was a surprise the first time I read it. I didn't score very high, so I went back and reread it, discovered other branches, and received a higher score. So the score serves to tell readers they didn't develop the story as much as they could have.

MELANIE: I like that as a teacher. It alerts readers they haven't gone deeply enough into the story. And I like it as a composer because it gives me a way to urge readers to engage more fully—they can't just click quickly through and expect to get a rich experience.

BILL: In *Dethany in Virtu/Noir*, we created a structure that, while not a game,

Figure 5: **An example of a Decision Point screen from *Dethany in Virtu/Noir*. All of these elements can be replicated in PowerPoint (creator owned; Holbrook, Holbrook, & Lotshaw).**

played with conventions a bit. Readers come to several screens where they have to make a choice about what Dethany does next. One of the choices lands her in a parallel story with the same characters but a totally different plotline and ending. We call it the hero narrative because instead of having to solve a crime, she has to save the day. So the plot changes, the characters' behaviors are different, and the genre expectations are tweaked. The only consistency is Dethany as the POV character.

These three digital narratives can be mentor texts for teaching multiple plotlines in digital comics. Whether they are considering branching and explicit reader choice or a singular story with layers of backstory, additional information, and multiple points of view, questions of coherence and cohesion are relevant. How does a story get constructed across plotlines? What do readers need to know when? Whose point of view is depicted, and how does shifting POV change the story? These questions can be applied to print texts, but they operate differently when asked of digital narratives.

Upwards and Backwards in the ELA Classroom

Teaching in the post–Gutenberg Parenthesis (Pettitt, 2007) does not mean the elimination of print texts in ELA classrooms, nor does it mean that students do not need to know how to compose words on a page for effect and agency. Rather, it means that to be active and literate participants in their own time, students need learning environments where they can experiment with the meaning-making tools available to them in the digital age. These tools include not only the hardware and software they need to become digital composers, but also rich mentor texts that allow them to see the rhetorical moves professionals make to create new kinds of stories. The inclusion of digital comics as literary mentor texts expands the kinds of composing experiences students can have, increasing the types of stories they can tell. As detailed in this essay, digital comics illustrate the "upwards and backwards" movements possible in contemporary narratives, ones that combine multiple expressive modes in interactive structures that expand storytelling potential beyond the fixed confines of the cramped "box" of the page (McCloud, 2000, p. 222). Freed from the materiality of paper and ink, digital comics can readily combine words, images (moving and still), sounds, and links that allow for multiple plotlines, reader interaction, and additional elements that amplify the storytelling experience.

So how do teachers, having engaged in the careful noticing of craft and content that turns a text into a mentor text, actually engage their students in digital composition? What software do they use? We start our digital composition workshops with PowerPoint, which is generally available in most schools.

PowerPoint is considered by many as an aging presentation tool; however, we reframe it as a creative digital composition tool, adapting presentation features to approximate effects such as those used in the three mentor texts. The key is for composers to set aside the prepackaged templates and to break out of a rote reliance on a linear slide-by-slide structure. Instead, we encourage teachers to consider the creative possibilities of the design, sound, animation, transition, and hypertext tools that are part of the program. For example, the picture tools in PowerPoint allow for quick cropping, recoloring, and background removal. Sound effects and sound files can be easily added to a PowerPoint slide to create the immersive qualities evident in *Operation Ajax*. Images can be layered on top of one another; to mimic the parallax scrolling effect employed in all three mentor texts, composers can use the path animation tool to move background images and foregrounded elements simultaneously. Combining the image layering feature with the software's animation tools allows creators to move characters in and out of the frame. Similarly, dialogue boxes can be made visible with a mouse click or with the use of timed transitions. The hypertext feature of PowerPoint allows composers to link within the composition, rendering a linear structure unnecessary; as in *Cainsville Files* and *Dethany in Virtu/Noir*, readers can follow different paths through the story so the traditional structure of a story can be reimagined. Composers also have the option of connecting to video files as part of the main narrative or as supplemental material, replicating the structure of *Operation Ajax*. As a composition tool, this program provides numerous opportunities for teachers and students to make complex images, to add sounds and transitions, and to restructure the architecture of a story as part of classroom composition practices.

Given the increasing proliferation of digital media, it becomes an ethical call for teachers to examine the types of texts they bring into their classrooms, considering carefully how those texts support students as active creators in the digital age. Modeling how to read texts both for pleasure and as mentor texts allows teachers to support students as they move their own stories from page to screen (Goodbrey, 2013). Books, whether print or digital, are cultural tools; they help shape, reshape, and remake the stories a culture can tell. Digital communication tools are reshaping the possibilities of storytelling, positioning students as text creators that take up the question, what has the computer done for narrative?

References

Alvermann, D.E., Hutchins, R.J., & McDevitt, R. (2012). Adolescents' engagement with web 2.0 and social media: Research, theory, and practice. *Research in the Schools,19*(2), 33–44.
Armstrong, K. (2014). *Cainsville files* [Mobile application software]. Penguin Books. Retrieved from itunes.apple.com.
Baron, D. (2009). *A better pencil: Readers, writers, and the digital revolution.* Oxford: Oxford University Press.
Botzakis, S. (2010). A book by any other name: Graphic novels in education. *The ALAN Review, 37*(3), 60–64.
Burwen, D. & de Seve, M. (2013). *Operation Ajax* [Mobile application software]. Cognito Comics. Retrieved from itunes.apple.com.
Calkins, L.M. (1994). *The art of teaching writing.* Portsmouth, NH: Heinemann. Originally published in 1986.
Carter, J.B. (2013). What I know about comics and ELA education. *First Opinions-Second Reactions, 6*(1), 8–10.
Cary, S. (2004). *Going graphic: Comics at work in the multilingual classroom.* Portsmouth: Heinemann.
Chase, M. (2008). The warp and the weft: Using mentor texts to weave together reading, science, writing, and art. *Journal of Children's Literature, 34*(2), 60–67.
Chute, H. (2008). Comics as literature? Reading graphic narrative. *PMLA, 123*(2), 452–465.
Cook, M.P. & Kirchoff, J.S.J. (2017). Teaching multimodal literacy through reading and writing graphic novels. *Language and Literacy, 19*(4), 76–95.
Cope, W. & Kalantzis, M. (2009). "Multiliteracies": New literacies, new learning. *Pedagogies, 4*(3), 164–195.

Dittmar, J.F. (2014). Experiments in comics storytelling. *Studies in Comics*, 6(2), 157–165.

Dorfman, L.R. & Cappelli, R. (2007). *Mentor texts: Teaching writing through children's literature, K-6*. Portland, ME: Stenhouse Publishers.

Flood, J. & Lapp, D. (1994). Teacher book clubs: Establishing literature discussion groups for teachers. *The Reading Teacher*, 47(7), 574–576.

Gee, J.P. (2004). *Situated language and learning: A critique of traditional schooling*. New York: Routledge.

Goodbrey, D.M. (2013). Digital comics—new tools and tropes. *Studies in Comics* 4(1), 185–197.

Graves, D.H. (1994). *A fresh look at writing*. Portsmouth, NH: Heinemann.

Hicks, T. (2013). *Crafting digital writing: Composing texts across media and genres*. Portsmouth, NH: Heinemann.

Holbrook, B., Holbrook, T., & Lotshaw, J. (2015). *Dethany in virtu/noir* [Mobile application software.] Pencil Rough Productions. Retrieved from itunes.apple.com.

Jenkins, H., Purushotma, R., Weigel, M., Clinton, K. & Robison, A.J. (2009). *Confronting the challenges of participatory culture: Media education for the 21st century*. Cambridge, MA: The MIT Press. Retrieved from https://mitpress.mit.edu/sites/default/files/titles/free_download/9780262513623_Confronting_the_Challenges.pdf.

Kress, G. (2003). *Literacy in the new media age*. London: Routledge.

Lankshear, C. & Knobel, M. (2011). *New literacies: Everyday practices and social learning* (3rd ed.). Berkshire, UK: Open University Press.

McCloud, S. (2000). *Reinventing comics*. New York: Paradox Press.

McLuhan, M. (1962). *The Gutenberg galaxy*. Toronto: University of Toronto Press.

National Governors Association Center for Best Practices & Council of Chief State School Officers. (2010). Common Core State Standards for English Language Arts: Writing. Retrieved from http://www.corestandards.org/ELA-Literacy/W/11-12/.

Ong, W. (1982). *Orality and literacy: The technologizing of the word*. New York: Routledge.

Pettitt, T. (2007). Before the Gutenberg parenthesis: Elizabethan American compatibilities. Retrieved from https://www.academia.edu/2946207/Before_the_Gutenberg_Parenthesis_Elizabethan-American_Compatibilities.

Pettitt, T. (2009) Containment and articulation: Media technology, cultural production and the perception of the material world. Retrieved from https://www.academia.edu/2946203/Containment_and_Articulation_Further_to_the_Gutenberg_Parenthesis_Media_Cultural_Production_and_the_Perception_of_the_Material_World.

Pettitt, T. (2012). Bracketing the Gutenberg parenthesis. *Explorations in Media Ecology*, 11(2), 95–114.

Ray, K.W. (1999). *Wondrous words*. Urbana, IL: National Council of Teachers of English.

Ryan, M. (2006). *Avatars of story*. Minneapolis: University of Minnesota Press.

Selfe, C.L. (2007). *Multimodal composition: Resources for teachers*. New York: Hampton Press.

Starkman, D. (2013). "The future is medieval": A discussion with the scholars behind the "Gutenberg Parenthesis," a sweeping theory of digital—and journalism—transformation. *Columbia Journalism Review*. Retrieved from http://www.cjr.org/the_audit/the_future_is_medieval.php.

Wiggins, J. (2011). Feeling it is how I understand it: Found poetry as analysis. *International Journal of Education & the Arts*, 12(3), 1–18.

Glossary

branching narrative: a narrative that incorporates choice into the structure. Choosing an option or direction creates a branch of the narrative. A branching narrative is made up of multiple branches that may or may not lead to the same conclusion.

juxtaposition: two elements placed close together to create contrasting effect. Two images placed side by side can create different meanings than if presented separately.

layout: the way textual elements are arranged on a page or a screen. Layout can be used to guide readers and help create flow and meaning.

montage: a sequence of images arranged in succession

parallax scrolling: a digital technique when the background moves slower than the fore-ground to create depth and movement

sound: narration, sound effects, dialogue or music used in a text or video

storyboard: a sequence of images that includes directions, dialogue, sound effects, narrative, transitions, etc. used to plan for visual, multimodal, or video texts.

storyworld: the universe of the story. It includes the characters, setting, objects and actions that are part of the world of the text (whether print or digital).

toggle: to switch back and forth between two screens or modes

transitions: movement from one paragraph, scene, or mode to the next. Transitions are tools that writers use to move the reader from one section of a text to the next.

trope: a common convention or devise used by narrative creators that is assumed to be recognizable by most readers. For example, the trope of the poor but hardworking P.I. is frequently conveyed in detective fiction.

Using Digital Comics to Support Information Literacy

21st Century Research Skills and Authentic Composing

MIKE P. COOK *and* LUKE RODESILER

Introduction

Bryce and Withers (2003) posited that to focus on life-long learning, a school must focus on the development of information literacy skills. That is, developing information literacy skills is intimately connected to becoming an effective learner. These skills of accessing, evaluating, using, and managing information include being efficient and effective, being accurate and creative, synthesizing and managing information from multiple sources, and understanding the relevant ethical and legal issues that accompany information access and use. Information literacy, as Bruce (2002) suggested, is vital in any effort to move from "the information society of today into the learning society of tomorrow" (p. 4). Teachers must design instruction that supports students in developing the skills necessary to find any information students need or deem important, especially as they progress toward democratic citizenship. An issue of note, however, is that aside from the connection to teacher librarians, there is limited discussion of teaching information literacy in traditional classrooms (i.e., information literacy is not taught in all classrooms). Our essay responds to this need by offering two instructional approaches using digital comics to teach research skills in the English language arts classroom.

Given the importance of critical thinking with regard to 21st century contexts and information, the role of information literacy in the lives of a global citizenry is paramount. Toward that end, secondary students must become locators, curators, and managers of information, yet questions remain about how prepared students are upon graduation. Even with increased attention to information literacy in today's classrooms, students' research skills and use of academic library resources may not align with 21st century expectations (e.g., accessing, evaluating, and incorporating information in a digital world). This may be due in part to entrenched curricula and approaches to literacy, but even when relevant resources, such as school librarians, are available, finding time to collaborate and plan meaningful learning opportunities remains a challenge. Studies have found that even when able to locate and utilize research information from library resources, students still need assistance in identifying and selecting the best resources and information for their purposes (Kovalik, Yutzey, & Piazza, 2013).

It is all too easy for teachers to assume that because students grew up in the digital age they are inherently information savvy and fully literate users of information (Allen, 2007; Kolowich, 2011b; Kovalik et al., 2013). Asher and Duke (2012), for example, found that students, when searching for resources, tended to (1) conduct simple, shallow searches and (2) engage in little evaluation of the sources they encountered. A wealth of evidence (see for example Foster, 2006; Kolowich, 2011a; Mittermeyer, 2005; Percell et al., 2012; Taylor, 2012) suggests that college freshmen largely are poorly prepared to engage in the effective and efficient use of research resources. Thus, it becomes important for teachers to provide space and time for secondary students to learn the information literacy skills necessary to consume and compose research-driven texts. Digital comics offer one possible avenue for such learning and exploration by serving as mentor texts and robust sponsors of information literacy learning in relevant and engaging ways.

Defining Information Literacy

As Bruce (1997) noted, establishing an agreed-upon definition of information literacy has been difficult, in part because there have existed multiple ways of understanding information literacy as a concept. This is, to a certain degree, because information literacy, more broadly defined, accounts for a variety of skill types (e.g., information skills, cognitive skills, values and beliefs, etc.). Webber and Johnston (2000) point out the abundance of scholarship defining, in various ways, information literacy as a term. Similarly, Owusu-Ansah (2003) argued that too many definitions have been suggested and called for the field to focus less on defining the term and more on engaging in information literacy practices. That said, ultimately information literacy is about being able to effectively function in a world where we are surrounded by information and being a life-long learner. Additional components of information literacy, as discussed by Bruce (1997), are (1) recognizing when information is necessary and (2) having the ability to find, evaluate, and utilize necessary information. To drive our discussion of information literacy, we borrow from the American Library Association's (1998) definition, which features five components. Therein, students can (1) access information efficiently and effectively, (2) evaluate information critically, (3) select and incorporate information as part of their own knowledge base, (4) use information to accomplish a goal, and (5) understand the relevant issues (e.g., social, economic, legal) associated with information use.

Learning Research Skills

One important component of information literacy education is research skill development. In preparing students to do meaningful research, teachers help students foster a variety of skills. These include asking useful, relevant questions to guide the research process. As they work to effectively answer those questions, students should learn to access and evaluate sources. Part of this includes being persistent and patient in pursuing information. Through the reporting of their research, students must also demonstrate respect for intellectual property. Woven throughout each of these components of the research process are vital sub-skills students must develop:

- Recognizing bias
- Exercising determination and patience in seeking information
- Assessing information quality and accuracy
- Pursuing and referencing multiple sources for support
- Understanding the process of online searches
- Using appropriate search terms
- Synthesizing information
- Paraphrasing and reporting findings

The instructional methods we present below are intended to address these research process components and skills in ways that go beyond many traditional approaches, providing students opportunities to conduct authentic, relevant research, move from being passive consumers to active users, develop intellectual curiosity, and compose and share information with real audiences. As such, we pair the reading of digital comics with the composition of digital research texts to foster information literacy development.

Using Digital Comics to Facilitate Information Literacy and Research Skills

Digital comics go beyond the traditional notions and definitions of print comics—e.g., McCloud's (1993) "juxtaposed pictorial and other images" (p.

9)—to include movement, sound, and multimedia, or the interdependency of media. This, of course, can alter the narrative structure and content, as well as the form and method of publication. Unlike their counterparts, digital comics are not, for example, print-based or even necessarily printable (Dittmar, 2012). As McCloud (2000) noted, digital comics "...can take virtually any size and shape..." (p. 223). We believe that the close study and purposeful creation of digital comics can contribute to students developing valuable information literacy and research skills. In this section, we introduce two types of digital comics and a specific example of each that teachers might employ to build toward such important information literacy outcomes.

Multimedia Comics as Mentor Texts

To provide students multiple types of digital comics and to offer teachers varying ways in which digital comics can foster information literacy, we utilize a multimedia comic, *Operation Ajax*. Multimedia comics can go beyond print comics by including other modalities such as sound (e.g., narration or dialogue, music, sound effects), video, motion, and so forth, some of which are determined by the reader and the interactive choices they make, including going back to reread previous pages and content. Multimedia comics can also include hyperlinks to additional websites, texts, experiences, information, and archived research (in the form of primary or secondary documents, original videos and images, etc.) that supplement the narrative itself. Reader choice in multimedia comics is less about impacting the narrative and more about accessing additional/supplemental information when necessary, a notion with implications for reading engagement, motivation, and comprehension, as it can attend to gaps in prior knowledge, contextual information, and schema.

Operation Ajax

Designed as an interactive and multimedia digital comic, *Operation Ajax: How the CIA Toppled Democracy in Iran* (Burwen & De Seve, 2011) is a non-fiction retelling of the overthrow of Iranian democracy, specifically of U.S. involvement, in 1953. Using the investigative journalism report stemming from the release of formerly classified documents, the authors composed a narrative interpretation of this historical event. Part of what sets *Operation Ajax* apart from other comics, and even from many other digital comics, is the use of a variety of modalities (e.g., sound, motion) alongside primary historical documents (e.g., accessible dossiers of information about historical characters, settings, and events). Additionally, the authors utilized design elements from video games and film, such as incorporating music to establish mood and to create suspense, to create a text that is both immersive and interactive and that invites readers to experience what McCloud (1993) termed *visual permanence*. That is, rather than each image being visible for a brief period of time, readers can linger with each image until they make the decision to move on.

Ergodic-Hypercomics as Mentor Texts

For the purposes of our work, we define our second digital comic, *Tell Me Your Secrets*, as an ergodic-hypercomic, a term borrowed from new media and comic theories. Hypercomics, as Merlin-Goodbrey (2010) noted, are "comics with a multicursal narrative.... In hypercomics, the choices made by the reader may determine the sequence in which the events are encountered, the outcome of events, or the point of view through which events are seen" (p. 1). Ergodic-hypercomics go beyond the traditional pre-determined order of traditional texts (most comics and digital comics included) to include the reader by placing nontrivial narrative demands (Aarseth, 1999) upon them. In other words, they allow for reading interactivity and choices—making it a unique experience to each reader.

Tell Me Your Secrets

Also an interactive digital comic, *Tell Me Your Secrets* (Lidster & Orwell, 2016) is an adaptation of Henry Tizard's experience during World War II. The authors gained inspiration from the aforementioned *Operation Ajax* but wanted to take the idea of interactivity in a different and unique direction. Setting it apart from most other texts, including *Operation Ajax*, the *Tell Me Your Secrets* narrative is largely determined by the reader. That is, the reader goes beyond interacting with the narrative by making narrative decisions that impact the outcome of the story itself. This digital comic requires readers to actively engage in the narrative and to think like authors. Beyond the "choose-your-own" format of the story, the text also incorporates modalities such as animation and sound (i.e., voices and a soundtrack). Additionally, borrowing from Burwen and De Seve, *Tell Me Your Secrets* incorporates archived information, which serves as both context and information for readers' decision making as they move through the story.

Digital Comics as Sponsors of Research and Information Literacy

Both mentor texts we suggest in this essay, aside from being well-crafted digital comics, serve as robust sponsors of information literacy and research skill development. *Operation Ajax* and *Tell Me Your Secrets* connect with and further the American Library Association's (ALA) (1998) definition of information literacy in multiple ways. When reading *Operation Ajax*, for example, students must be able to efficiently and effectively access and engage with the dossiers of historical information to learn more about characters, events, and happenings (i.e., to connect with and comprehend the narrative). Using this information, readers are required to cast a critical eye and evaluate the information available as they progress through the historical narrative. Regarding *Tell Me Your Secrets*, because the narrative order and structure is decided in large part by the reader, students must—to effectively read this digital comic— think like authors. As such, and similar to *Operation Ajax*, students must be able to access the archived information for both contextual purposes and for the purposes of reading and making narrative decisions. Both comics also connect to the ALA definition through the use of information to accomplish a goal. Here, readers make narrative decisions in *Tell Me Your Secrets* and determine when it is appropriate to leave the narrative of *Operation Ajax* itself in order to peruse the historical documents. Students are tasked with both selecting and using relevant information to learn and to interact with the text and to use that information to accomplish the ultimate goal of making meaning from the texts.

These two digital comics also do a nice job of serving as a space for students to practice, develop, and apply the research skills associated with and vital to information literacy (i.e., those skills listed above). To be effective researchers, students have to understand that all information is biased in some way. Reading these texts, students interrogate the potential biases of the information they receive. This includes considering the authors of the digital comics themselves as well as the point of view and historical experiences they are based on. Students, while reading, must also assess the quality and the accuracy of the information. In other words, they go beyond questioning bias to evaluate the sources and the information against their own needs and knowledge. This questioning can lead to additional research, which calls for students to apply these skills in using appropriate search terms and methods for seeking relevant and useful information. Additionally, this helps students to reference, synthesize, and make decisions based on multiple sources, all important to conducting research and to developing information literacy.

Reading Digital Comics

Before asking students to compose, we argue for the importance of mentor texts. Using mentor texts in the English language arts classroom situates students as apprentices who are examining closely the rhetorical choices evident in texts crafted by experts. The study of mentor texts relies on two central elements: (1) actively analyzing texts rather than merely reading them and (2) recognizing mentor texts as presenting possibilities to emulate, not fixed formulas (Dean, 2017). Ultimately, this is about helping students interrogate texts as authors and consider the intentional moves they might make in their own writing. To achieve this, we present *Operation Ajax* and *Tell Me Your Secrets* as exemplars for collaborative analysis from which to pull ideas that might inform students' own research writing. Because we want students to explore new ways to compose and disseminate information—their own research in this case—we look to provide students with non-traditional texts, those that make use of interactivity to engage readers. *Operation Ajax* and *Tell Me Your Secrets*, as multimedia and ergodic digital comics, fit the bill nicely and model for students ways to approach the rhetorical situation, ways to organize information, and ways to include the reader as an active participant in the text.

For each mentor text, we discuss with students the various modalities and outside content the authors utilized, as well as the choice they provide to us as readers. As a class, we conduct rhetorical analyses of the texts and critique the decisions the authors made and ask a variety of questions, including the following: What elements of the texts were most impactful and useful? What other options might have been available to the authors? What ideas might we borrow and what might we avoid in our own composing and pursuit of rhetorical effectiveness? In addition to these questions, we also examine the affordances and limitations of each platform and text with regard to interaction in nontrivial ways (Aarseth, 1999), to information organization, and so forth. To help students further their thinking as readers and writers, we want students to evaluate the texts against the more traditional, alphabetic texts with which they are more familiar; here, we ask questions like how was this text different than reading another, more traditional retelling of history? And finally, we encourage students to consider access by asking them to consider whether or not access is limited in any way as a result of authorial choices.

Creating Comics— Students as Composers of Research

After collaboratively analyzing and discussing *Operation Ajax* and *Tell Me Your Secrets* as mentor texts, we turn students' attention to their own researching and digital composing. This allows students to go beyond learning a given skill or even demonstrating an understanding of a set of skills. That is, students are positioned to apply their skills in authentic ways that meet their own needs and interests. In the following sections, we share two possible research projects we might ask students to complete after analyzing these digital comics. While there are myriad options for research projects, we have selected two we feel provide students ways to stretch their rhetorical (and digitally literate) legs by composing and sharing their research in authentic, real-world ways. Additionally, the projects featured below, each culminating in the composition of a research-based multimedia narrative, could fit within any curriculum, for they invite students to conduct and present research related to authors they have already encountered and texts they have read at one time or another during the school year.

RESEARCH PROJECT 1: INVESTIGATING AUTHORS
    FOR RESEARCH-BASED MULTIMEDIA NARRATIVES

In the English language arts classroom, investigating the lived history of an author who wrote a novel, story, or poem introduced during the school year offers students an opportunity to develop research skills necessary for negotiating meaning in the present day, in a time when information is overabundant. Researching the unique history of an author such as Sherman Alexie, Toni Morrison, or Ernest Hemingway requires students to identify credible sources, gather relevant information, assess the usefulness of sources based on the aims of one's investigation, and synthesize information collected across multiple sources. An author-focused research project also allows ample room for choice, a central component of successful inquiry projects (Daniels & Zemelman, 2014, p. 260). For instance, teachers can offer students choice regarding the subject of their research, the other student(s) with whom they might work, and the sources and materials from which to draw relevant information. Furthermore, such a project gives students a chance to choose how they will organize and present their findings as they craft a research-based multimedia narrative that allows for interaction akin to that which is evident in multimedia comics like *Operation Ajax*.

Just as Joseph Lidster and Michael Orwell crafted *Tell Me Your Secrets* by weaving together information about the work of Sir Henry Tizard and important developments that occurred during World War II, a student enrolled in an American literature course could draw from research investigating the life of, say, satirist Kurt Vonnegut and create a research-based multimedia narrative to represent their findings. Students might draw from primary and secondary sources, piecing together an interactive narrative representation of Vonnegut's life, from his early days in Indiana during the Great Depression and his experience as a prisoner of war during World War II to his writing of works such as *Cat's Cradle* and *Slaughterhouse-Five*. Ultimately, this research project invites students to learn more about a self-selected literary figure while also developing valuable information literacy practices and crafting a multimodal research composition.

With a project like this, it is important that students consider the scope of the story they want to tell. Students might craft a narrative that spans the entirety of an author's life or, alternatively, presents a particularly compelling segment of the author's lived experience. For instance, sticking with the Vonnegut example above, a narrative that begins with his early days in Indiana and culminates in the writing of *Slaughterhouse-Five*, which was informed by Vonnegut's experience as a prisoner of war during the bombing of Dresden (Allen, n.d.) and is arguably his most popular novel, could make for a compelling composition. The narrative arc students settle on will likely be driven by what they uncover in their research. Have they discovered sufficient information to tell a compelling interactive story about the publication of an author's most popular novel? Or does the depth of information (or lack thereof) necessitate a narrative arc spanning all the author's years?

When conducting their research and crafting their narratives, students can look for opportunities to convey meaning through the purposeful integration of modes beyond the alphabetic. For instance, still holding with the Vonnegut example above, students adding a postscript that speaks to the satirist's cultural impact might pair the alphabetic text displayed on the screen with a soundtrack featuring a song that alludes to one of Vonnegut's works (e.g., "Nice, Nice, Very Nice" by Ambrosia, "Happiness by the Kilowatt" by Alexisonfire), purposefully using the audio track to underscore the greater point about Vonnegut's cultural impact.

RESEARCH PROJECT 2: ADAPTING WORKS OF NONFICTION
   AS RESEARCH-BASED MULTIMEDIA NARRATIVES

Adapting literature far predates contemporary trends of turning novels into films, and it is a practice with much to offer teachers and students in the English language arts classroom (Szwydky-Davis & Connors, 2018). When students are invited to produce literary adaptations of their own, they are granted opportunities to build rich understandings about multiple media, as well as the figures, themes, and events involved in the stories they deem worthy of re-telling. And when charged specifically with adapting memoirs, biographies, or other works of nonfiction, students also have opportunities to practice information literacy as they conduct research that stands to support them in building a story's historical context. Accordingly, re-conceptualizing a published work of nonfiction as a research-based multimedia narrative presents a meaningful learning experience for students.

In much the same way that authors of digital comics such as *Operation Ajax* and *Tell Me Your Secrets* made purposeful decisions about how to best use images and sounds to establish the setting or suggest the tone of a scene about historical figures and lived events, students have a host of considerations to make when adapting a published work of nonfiction from page to screen. Likewise, just as Lidster and Orwell drew from historical documents and records to tell the story of Sir Henry Tizard's work during World War II, this project challenges students to draw from research into the people and events central to a work of nonfiction as they develop research-based multimedia adaptations. For example, a student eager to adapt *Undefeated: Jim Thorpe and the Carlisle School Football Team* (Sheinkin, 2017) would conduct research into the life of famed athlete Jim Thorpe, using the award-winning work of nonfiction as a springboard to further investigate topics that include the Carlisle Indian Industrial School, the United States government's persecution of Native Americans, and the lives of Thorpe and his coach at Carlisle, Pop Warner. Then, based on their research, students must make a host of rhetorical decisions as they weigh how best to weave together alphabetic text, visual images and artifacts, voiceovers, music, and more to adapt Sheinkin's story. In that way, this project requires students to use information literacy skills to build deep knowledge of historical figures, events, and developments around which a work of nonfiction is based, and then apply their knowledge of multiple media to craft a compelling multimedia narrative.

It is important to note that literary adaptations are typically not scene-by-scene recreations. Instead, significant elements are often subject to change (e.g., Miloš Forman's film adaptation of Ken Kesey's *One Flew Over the Cuckoo's Nest* takes the narration—skewed perspective and all—out of the hands of Chief Bromden altogether). Keeping that in mind, when introducing this project, which charges students with creating a research-based multimedia narrative from a published work of nonfiction, teachers might invite students to consider the scope of their research and the adaptations that would follow. For instance, sticking with the *Undefeated* example above, students might consider where to place the greatest emphasis of the research that will inform their narrative: on Thorpe's run in the Olympics and the controversy that followed, on his athletic exploits more broadly, on the innovations of the Carlisle football team, or perhaps on the Carlisle Indian Industrial School. Whatever the focus, the scope of students' research is sure to shape the arc of the narrative to follow.

Using the Research Projects to Foster 21st Century Information Literacy

The two student projects featured above respond to 21st century information literacy concerns by offering students opportunities to go beyond consuming multimedia research-based texts to conduct their own research and embed it in their own multimedia compositions. In the first project above, we described how students can create research-based multimedia narratives about an author of interest. This allows for choice of both author and path of inquiry, as students ask unique questions and seek specific information. The research students conduct can (and should) include primary and secondary sources and positions them to make intentional choices regarding which mode(s) to use to report and represent their findings.

In the second project, students are asked to adapt a non-fiction text as a research-based multimedia narrative. This begins by reading and evaluating an existing piece of historical information. For these purposes, students can select memoirs, biographies, autobiographies, and so forth. To complete this project, students must use research and source information to create historical and informational context for their reader. Likewise, they must understand the information well enough to effectively remediate it using other modes of communication (and to pair those multiple modes together to establish a clear, coherent, and reliable informational text). This remediation process encourages students to use their research to justify the changes they make, as opposed to simply composing a re-creation.

As evidenced, both projects foster important research skills and provide students the time and space to use those skills, in authentic ways, toward information literacy development. To complete either (or both), students have to apply the range of research skills we discussed above, including being patient and persistent in searching for information; applying appropriate search terms and methods; evaluating information for bias, accuracy, and utility; synthesizing information from multiple sources; and paraphrasing and reporting findings in credible and coherent ways. Ultimately, this all builds on Bruce's (1997) suggestion that informational literacy requires us to recognize the need for information and then be able to locate and use that information for authentic purposes. Here, students determine what information is necessary and then devise methods for accessing, critically evaluating, and using that information to contribute to the disciplinary body of knowledge.

PRACTICAL SUGGESTIONS FOR TEACHERS

No matter which research project teachers opt to facilitate, it can be helpful to keep in mind a number of practical suggestions. The following tips can help teachers ensure a positive learning experience for all students when facilitating research projects that culminate in the composition and distribution of multimedia narratives inspired by digital comics.

Do it yourself. Before launching research projects like those described above, we encourage teachers to craft an original research-based multimedia narrative of their own. We offer that suggestion for multiple reasons. First, experiencing a project from start to finish—beginning with the brainstorming of possibilities, moving through the research process, and finishing with the multimedia composition—will help teachers grasp the weight of the project and identify points that might need greater attention in the classroom (e.g., the need to identify an author who lived a compelling life; the importance of considering the scope of the adaptation; the affordances and constraints of various media). Second, the teacher's composition can serve as a model for students, offering yet another mentor text for their consideration. Third, a research-based multimedia narrative of the variety described here may be new to many students who are accustomed to conducting research, writing a paper, and submitting it for an audience of one: the teacher. Seeing a strong final product in advance can help students consider what constitutes a compelling narrative and see the role that research plays in crafting that narrative, whether it is an original narrative about an author's life or an adaptation of a published work of nonfiction.

Choose wisely. The selection of digital tools to be used with any project requires many considerations. Cost, convenience, and accessibility stand among the points to be weighed, but choosing tools appropriate for the task and for the students who will use them is paramount (Reed & Hicks, 2016). When it comes to crafting a multimedia narrative that can convey a story informed by one's research, three popular options are Microsoft PowerPoint, Google Slides, and Prezi. Each allows for the incorporation of alphabetic text, hyperlinks, images, videos, and audio (e.g., voiceovers and music). Therefore, each is appropriate for the task. Moreover, most middle-school and high-school students are likely to have firsthand experience with at least one of the three easy-to-use tools, making each appropriate for the students who will use them as well.

Teach, rather than assign. Though students might be familiar with using multimedia tools like Microsoft PowerPoint, Google Slides, and Prezi, that does not necessarily mean that students are savvy users of those tools. Accordingly, it is important that we teach students to craft research-based multimedia narratives and not just assign them. Many students are sure to benefit from mini-lessons that support them in constructing their narratives. For instance, depending on students' needs, teachers might demonstrate how to create hyperlinks from one slide to another outside the linear order, how to set automatic timing, and so on. Furthermore, students can benefit when teachers provide think-alouds that illuminate their thought processes (Fisher & Frey, 2008), helping students see, for example, how one weighs decisions about the media to incorporate and where in the narrative a medium's inclusion might be most effective. Remember, too, that facilitating the multimedia composing process can be a delicate balance, one that requires teachers to negotiate providing valuable instruction while also giving students the freedom to create their own visions and see them through to completion.

Honor the process. As is true of any writing, composing research-based multimedia narratives is a recursive process. As such, students' narratives will evolve over multiple drafts, provided they have room to grow. Students are likely to experience the greatest strides when teachers offer them ample opportunities to practice techniques modeled in relevant writing-focused mini-lessons; time to develop fresh ideas and explore new directions generated in targeted writing conferences; and the chance to receive, consider, and apply feedback offered by their classmates during structured peer review sessions. Therefore, we encourage teachers to recognize students as writers and afford them the time and space to fully engage in the writing process.

Distribute widely. A central element in the joy of crafting original research-based multimedia narratives is sharing them with an audience beyond the teacher. As Atwell (1998) argued, "student writers need access to readers beyond the teacher if they're to understand what writing is good for, and if they're to write with care and conviction" (p. 102). By letting students know upfront that their multimedia narratives will be read by others, including their peers and an online audience, teachers can up the ante, nudging students to go the extra mile when conducting their research and crafting their composition to ensure a final product of high quality. To further emphasize the joys of publication, teachers can also organize author celebrations to be held in class or out, allowing students to share their final products and learn from the multimedia narratives crafted by their peers.

Keeping these tips in mind when preparing to launch research projects that culminate in the composition of multimedia narratives can help to ensure that students receive the support they need to achieve the instructional objectives, regardless of which research project teachers opt to facilitate.

Conclusion

Given the digital and global world students inhabit, the need for information literacy in a 21st century context is more important than ever. As they are constantly surrounded by multiple modes and mediums of information, they must possess the skills necessary to select, evaluate, and utilize the information available to them in order to serve as functioning and literate democratic citizens. To foster this, however, requires that teachers rethink traditional pedagogical approaches and assignments to better align with and prepare students for the ever-evolving digital world. This includes designing relevant and authentic learning experiences for students, those that task them with consuming and creating rhetorically powerful digital texts. As educators, we must move beyond the traditional academic research paradigm and consider new ways for students to act as researchers and to contribute to scholarly discourse.

One way to begin this work is to harness the power of digital comics as mentor texts for students' work. While there are myriad titles available, we discuss *Operation Ajax*, a multimedia digital comic, and *Tell Me Your Secrets*, an ergodic digital comic, as settings for learning about, analyzing, and discussing the digital composition practices available for students' own use. Part of this mentoring through texts involves critically interrogating the affordances and constraints within each and pointing out the rhetorical moves students might borrow and those they want to avoid. It is in this mentoring space that students learn the skills—the rhetorical decisions students must make and how those align with the digital comics they read—that we ask them to transfer to their own creations.

To help students develop as digital composers, we shared two multimedia research projects, a multimedia narrative based upon students' inquiries into select authors' lived histories and a multimedia adaptation of narrative nonfiction embellished by students' own research. We have also offered a variety of practical suggestions for teachers who are interested in implementing these, or similar, projects. (1) Students benefit when teachers position themselves as writers. (2) It is vital to provide the necessary scaffolding to transition students away from the traditional school research paper. (3) Helping students select appropriate digital tools is also important. (4) Teaching all parts of the project—rather than assuming that students are savvy digital writers—is key. (5) In this, as in any writing event, students gain when immersed in the writing process. And (6) to foster relevant, meaningful compositions, students need an authentic audience.

We believe the instructional examples shared here offer pedagogical promise for students and literacy instruction. Digital comics can serve as powerful literacy sponsors, and helping students to interact with these as mentor texts can aid in their development of important information literacy skills, skills needed if students are to thrive in the 21st century. Likewise, learning to apply these skills by creating their own research-driven digital texts affords students a more relevant and engaging way to use the research process to contribute to information discourse.

REFERENCES

Aarseth, E. (1999). Aporia and epiphany in *Doom* and *The Speaking Clock*: The temporality in ergodic art. In M.L. Ryan (Ed.), *Cyberspace textuality: Computer technology and literary theory* (pp. 31–42). Bloomington: Indiana University Press.

Allen, S.M. (2007). Information literacy, ICT, high school, and college expectations: A quantitative study. *Knowledge Quest, 35*(5), 18–24.

Allen, W.R. (n.d.). *A brief biography of Kurt Vonnegut*. Retrieved from https://www.vonne gutlibrary.org/kurt-biography.

American Library Association. (1998). Introduction to information literacy. Retrieved from http://www.ala.org/ala/acrl/acrlissues/acrlinfolit/infolitoverview/introtoinfolit.htm.

Asher, A.D., & Duke, L.M. (2012). Searching for answers: Student research behavior at Illinois Wesleyan University. In L.M. Duke & A.D. Asher (Eds.), *College libraries and student culture: What we now know* (pp. 71–85). Chicago: ALA.

Atwell, N. (1998). *In the middle: New understandings about writing, reading, and learning* (2nd ed.). Portsmouth, NH: Heinemann.

Bruce, C. (1997). *The seven faces of information literacy*. Adelaide: Auslib Press.

Bruce, C. (2002). Information literacy as a catalyst for educational change: A background paper. Retrieved from http://www.nclis.gov/libinter/infolitconf&meet/papers/bruce-fullpaper.pdf.

Bryce, J., & Withers, G. (2003). *Engaging secondary school students in lifelong learning.* Melbourne: Australian Council for Educational Research.

Burwen, D., & De Seve, M. (2011). *Operation AJAX: How the CIA toppled democracy in Iran.* Cognito Comics. Retrieved from http://www.cognitocomics.com/operationajax/.

Daniels, H., & Zemelman, S. (2014). *Subjects matter: Exceeding standards through powerful content-area reading* (2nd ed.). Portsmouth, NH: Heinemann.

Dean, D. (2017). *Strategic writing: The writing process and beyond in the secondary English classroom.* Urbana, IL: National Council of Teachers of English.

Dittmar, J.F. (2012). Digital comics. *Scandinavian Journal of Comic Art, 1*(2), 83–91.

Fisher, D., & Frey, N. (2008). *Better learning through structured teaching: A framework for the gradual release of responsibility.* Alexandria, VA: Association for Supervision and Curriculum Development.

Foster, A.L. (2006). Students fall short on "information literacy" Educational Testing Service's study finds. *Chronicle of Higher Education, 53,* A36.

Kolowich, S. (2011a). Study: College students rarely use librarian's expertise. *AASL Hotlinks, 10*(6), 1.

Kolowich, S. (2011b). What students don't know. *Inside Higher Ed* (August 11). Retrieved from www.insidehighered.com/news/2011/08/22/erial_study_of_student_research_habits_at_illinois_university_libraries_reveals_alarmingly_poor_information_literacy_and_skills.

Kovalik, C., Yutzey, S., & Piazza, L. (2013). Information literacy and high school seniors: Perceptions of the research process. *School Library Research, 16.* Retrieved from http://www.ala.org/aasl/slr/volume16/kovalik-yutzey-piazza.

Lidster, J., & Orwell, M. (2016). *Tell me your secrets.* BBC. Retrieved from http://www.bbc.co.uk/guides/z3b77hv.

McCloud, S. (1993). *Understanding comics.* New York: HarperCollins.

McCloud, S. (2000). *Reinventing comics.* New York: Paradox Press.

Merlin-Goodbrey, D. (2010). From comic to hyper-comic. Retrieved from *inter-disciplinary.net.*

Mittermeyer, D. (2005). Incoming first year undergraduate students: How information literate are they? *Education for Information, 23*(4), 203–232.

Owusu-Ansah, E.K. (2003). Information literacy and the academic library: A critical look at a concept and the controversies surrounding it. *Journal of Academic Librarianship, 29,* 219–230.

Percell, K., Rainie, L., Heaps, A., Buchanan, J., Friedrich, L., Jacklin, A., Chen, C., & Zickuhr, K. (2012). How teens do research in the digital world: Summary of findings. Retrieved from www.pewinternetorg/Reports/2012/Student-Research/Summary-of-Findings.aspx.

Reed, D., & Hicks, T. (2016). *Research writing rewired: Lessons that ground students' digital learning.* Thousand Oaks, CA: Corwin.

Sheinkin, S. (2017). *Undefeated: Jim Thorpe and the Carlisle School football team.* New York: Roaring Book Press.

Szwydky-Davis, L.L., & Connors, S.P. (2018, January 6). Embracing popular literary adaptations as educational tools. [Blog post]. Retrieved from http://www2.ncte.org/blog/2018/01/embracing-popular-literary-adaptations-educational-tools.

Taylor, A. (2012). A study of the information search behavior of the millennial generation. *Information Research, 17*(1). Retrieved from www.informationr.net/ir/17-1/paper508.html.

Webber, S., & Johnston, B. (2000). Conceptions of information literacy: New perspectives and implications. *Journal of Information Science, 26*(6), 381–397.

Afterword

Losing My Edge

DREW MORTON

On an abnormally warm Chicago day in March 2017, I found myself browsing the exhibition hall at the annual Society of Cinema and Media Studies conference. Boldly displayed on the tables for such heavyweight university presses as the University of California and the University of Texas were a lineup of comics studies titles: Scott Bukatman's *Hellboy's World: Comics and Monsters on the Margins* (2016), Matt Yockey's *Make Ours Marvel: Media Convergence and a Comics Universe* (2017), and Blair Davis's *Movie Comics: Page to Screen/Screen to Page* (2017) to name but a few. All I could think of was a lyric from LCD Soundsystem's "Losing My Edge" (2002).

Flashback to approximately a decade earlier—once again in Chicago—and I can remember going to SCMS and seeing one comics studies panel in the program. At the time, the preeminent academic press for comics studies scholarship was the University Press of Mississippi and their vendors had not even bothered to pack the freshly published English language translation of Thierry Groensteen's *The System of Comics* (2007). When I asked the person staffing the table if they had copies for sale, I remember getting a perplexed look and a response somewhere in the ballpark of "I thought this was a cinema conference." Essentially, up until maybe three or four years ago—just a few years after the SCMS Comics Studies Scholarly Interest Group was formed in 2011—the roster of comics studies scholars, the presses interested in them, and the list of journals eager to take on their research were pretty short. We had the *Journal of Graphic Novels and Comics, Studies in Comics,* and the same fifteen or so scholars beating the drum on a panel every other year or so. The interdisciplinary nature of comics studies did not aid the state of the conversation, as every discipline from art history to English and media studies seemed to have its own conference. Needless to say, the rich scholarly conversation that was taking part was fairly modest in scope and fragmented.

I do not begin with this preamble to disparage my colleagues in comics or as a defensive "get off my lawn" to those coming up from behind, but as a brief chronicle to document how quickly our field has flourished and expanded so we can all take a moment and appreciate the strides the field has made in the past decade. When I was finalizing my article "The Unfortunates: Towards a History and Definition of the Motion Comic" (Morton, 2015) for the *Journal of Graphic Novels and Comics* just a few years ago, the bibliography on digital comics and motion comics was scant at best. Now, imagine my pleasant surprise when I was asked to pen this afterword—such an anthology would have been tremendously beneficial to my thinking on the topic at the time I was researching it! In any case, I'd like to take a brief moment to summarize the brief history of scholarship focused on digital comics, discuss how this volume furthers the field, and pose some questions and make some suggestions to assist in the direction of future scholarship along the way.

Like cinema studies before it, the dialogue among comics studies scholars has benefited from the more theoretical work of practitioners like Will Eisner and Scott McCloud and, as many of the authors in this volume discuss, Scott McCloud's writing on the expanded/infinite canvas is a foundational starting point. Like the comics studies equivalent of André Bazin, McCloud does not see the medium's turn towards technology as being a corruption or loss of the art form. For McCloud, technology brings with it the possibility for evolution and revitalization that can be embraced creatively—although we should still realize the importance of "conceptual distinctions" between print comics and digital comics (McCloud, 2000, p. 203). In regards to the expanded canvas, McCloud (2009) notes that:

> Just as music allows for a wide range of volume, comics artists can vary panel size and shape for dramatic effect and they frequently do so in both print and online comics. On a single large canvas, those variations can again follow the needs of the story, but when a fixed page is involved, every decision about the size and shape of one panel restricts the size and shape of the next one.

Unfortunately, in the twenty years since McCloud proposed the concept and decade since he elaborated upon it, the expanded canvas of McCloud's creative imagination has largely been relegated to theory over practice. Following the lead of Jeffrey SJ Kirchoff in this volume's "Considering ComiXology's Guided View," the mainstream comic book industry seems far more interested in repackaging and remediating—in the words of Jay David Bolter and Richard Grusin (2000), representing "one medium in another" (p. 45)— print content. These remediations have taken a myriad of forms from the short lived and maligned motion comic to the tablet transpositions facilitated by Comixology's Guided View algorithm. As Scott Bukatman (2002) predicted in his essay "Online Comics and the Reframing of the Moving Image," online comics (which, in Bukatman's description, are pretty much synonymous with digital comics) are a way for "larger multimedia companies such as Dark Horse, Marvel" to try to "generate plenty of 'synergy' and 'buzz' by incorporating the 'interactive bag of tricks' associated with multimedia gaming and 'infotainment'" (p. 138).

The main motivator for the omnipresence of these mainstream low-impact remediations is obviously economics. Despite the visibility brought by superhero blockbusters, Netflix series, theme park attractions, and merchandising ranging from Superman's Gillette razors to Black Panther Build-A-Bears, American comic book sales have not come close to the numbers they had in the midst of World War II. In fact, the bestselling comics in the United States tend to be Japanese manga. As such, experimentation and innovation within the medium amongst the two majors has largely been curtailed. As Denny O'Neil noted in a personal interview, "Both comic book companies are serving as R&D arms for the movies" (as cited in Morton, 2017, p. 177).

To make matters worse, e-reader and tablet adoption rates have plateaued over the past three years. Despite a 12 percent increase in the percentage of U.S. adults who own tablets from 2012 to 2013 (from 14 percent in 2012 to 26 percent), adoption rates have been largely stagnant since 2015—hovering around 50 percent according to Pew Research Center data. Similarly, e-reader adoption rates have been stranded around 20 percent since 2012 (Pew Research Center, 2018). Mainstream digital comics have also experienced stagnant sales numbers. According to *Comichron* and *ICV2*, domestic comic sales hit $1.03 billion dollars in 2015. However, digital comics only accounted for 9 percent of that figure ($90 million), a decrease of nearly 10 percent from 2014 (Sabak, 2017). Judging from anecdotal interactions with comics studies friends, colleagues, and my students, there seems to be an almost fetishistic tie between comic book readership and the physical print object. Needless to say, if we are to find experimentation within the medium of the digital comic, it will probably come in the form of artisanal productions—although I would love to read further scholarship on digital comics that approaches the subject from an industrial analysis perspective!

What is so refreshing about this volume is its engagement with both sectors of production across a multitude of perspectives. Take, for instance, both Jeffrey SJ Kirchoff's "Considering ComiXology's Guided View" and Rich Shivener's "Re-Theorizing the Infinite Canvas: A Space for Comics and Rhetorical Theories." Both essays attempt to update and complicate McCloud's conceptualization by embracing interdisciplinary approaches. In the former, the author applies Lev Manovich's foundational exploration of *The Language of New Media* to Comixology's software in order to describe how Guided

View overlaps more with cinema and less with comics (a conclusion which I would absolutely share!). The latter, on the other hand, takes a variety of rhetorical approaches towards Randall Munroe's webcomic "Click and Drag" in order to refresh McCloud rather than throwing the baby out with the bathwater. Shivener ends his entry by suggesting that conceptualizations of play may help us better understand how readers engage with digital comics. I don't disagree with Shivener's instinct, but I would also add that we can also think of analog comics in much the same way. As Scott Bukatman proposes in *The Poetics of Slumberland: Animated Spirits and the Animating Spirit* (2012) via the work of theorists Gaston Bachelard, Roger Caillois, and Brian Sutton-Smith, Winsor McCay's *Little Nemo in Slumberland*

> is an aesthetic space ... an animated space that opens out to embrace the imaginative sensibility of a reader who is never farther than an arm's length from this other realm, a space of play and plasmatic possibility in which the stable site of reading or viewing yields to an onslaught of imaginative fantasy [p. 1].

Another interdisciplinary approach to the subject of reader activity, interactivity, and play that may be worth further considering is that of cognitive science, specifically eye tracking and what it can tell us about reception. In the past decade or so, cinema and media studies scholars have been using eye tracking technology to study viewing patterns. Essentially, audiences are given special glasses that track their gaze as they watch films in order to decode how aspects of audiovisual composition from framing and color to sound direct our attention. While the cost of such hardware and software can be prohibitive, I have long wondered where following Tim Smith and Neil Cohn's lead might take the field's conception of closure, both in analog and digital comics.

Fittingly enough, one of the other essays in this volume that resonated with me was Johannes C.P. Schmid's "Documentary Webcomics: Mediality and Contexts" because of its tangential connection to the work of Winsor McCay. McCay, in addition to being a renowned comic artist and animator, was also the father of the niche tradition of animated documentaries, which can be traced back to his 1918 short "The Sinking of the Lusitania." Like documentary webcomics, the animated documentary tradition has long challenged the Bazinian indexical linkage between reality and objective impassivity of the camera. Thus, if I can make a constructive suggestion in order to deepen this area of inquiry, I would encourage researchers to read Annabelle Honess Roe's monograph *Animated Documentary* (2013) and to engage with documentary history at large. As tempting as it is to link the digital to a breakdown and interrogation of objectivity (to put a spin on the oft-cited phrase, "Thanks Trump"), documentary filmmaking has a long tradition of problematizing that relationship, from pioneer John Grierson's (Hardy, 1966) description that documentary is the "creative treatment of actuality" and Luis Buñuel's 1933 mockumentary *Land Without Bread* to Orson Welles's 1975 *F for Fake* and the output of Errol Morris. Needless to say, I think Schmid's essay touches upon a subject with rich forms of interdisciplinary intersection and I am excited to see how it develops.

While I'm on the subject of the rhetorical and affective power of the documentary, let me add that I found John Logie's essay on the limited and idiosyncratic pool of digital adaptations of Art Spiegelman's *MAUS* (1980–1991) fascinating. Considering that the production of scholarship about *MAUS* has almost become a cliché in the field of comics studies, there has been shockingly little written on its digital incarnations—Elisabeth R. Friedman's (2012) "Spiegelman's Magic Box: *MetaMaus* and the Archive of Representation" is the only other article that comes to mind. I appreciated how Logie interrogated how the digital editions' embrace of an archival/documentary function destabilize one of the central narrative conceits of the novel. Chiefly, that *MAUS* is neither a biography of Vladek nor an autobiography of art but, as Logie notes, a possession shared between the two.

In close, I think the value of this volume lies in the intellectual waterfront the authors cover. In reviewing the essays, I was stunned by how far the field had expanded, both in terms of approach (I have barely touched upon the essays that brought out questions of media literacy and pedagogy, such as Teri Holbrook, Melanie Hundley, and Bill Holbrook's proposition that K–12 teachers use digital comics to teach students about 21st century literacy!) and with regard to objects of study (from ComiXology to an analysis of Francophone digital comics). As aforementioned, when I began writing about digital and motion comics just a few years ago, I was somewhat frustrated by how stunted the bibliography was—even when I briefly revisited the subject for "'Watched Any Good Books Lately?': The Formal Failure of the *Watchmen* Motion Comic" in 2017. Thus, it was a rewardingly surreal experience to see myself cited—to see that the dialogue was being continued—by Jayson's Quearry's essay on the phenomenology of Marvel Infinite. Narcissism aside, the joy of reading this collection has come from "Losing My Edge" and witnessing the pixelated flicker of the digital comics torch being passed. Needless to say, I look forward to seeing the future scholarship this volume inspires and I hope my suggestions for further research may prove to be beneficial.

REFERENCES

Bolter, J. David, & Grusin, R. (2000). *Remediation: Understanding new media*. Cambridge, MA: MIT Press.

Bukatman, S. (2002). Online comics and the reframing of the moving image. In D. Harries (Ed.), *The new media book* (pp. 133–143). London: BFI Press.

Bukatman, S. (2012). *The Poetics of Slumberland: Animated spirits and the snimated spirit*. Berkeley: University of California Press.

Friedman, E.R. (2012). Spiegelman's magic box: MetaMaus and the archive of representation. *Studies in Comics, 3*(2), 275–291.

Groensteen, T. (2007). *The system of comics* (B. Beaty & N. Nguyen, Trans.) Jackson: University Press of Mississippi.

Hardy, F. (Ed.). (1966). *Grierson on documentary.* Berkeley: University of California Press.

Honess Roe, A. (2013). *Animated documentary.* New York: Palgrave.

McCloud, S. (2000). *Reinventing comics: How imagination and technology are revolutionizing an art form.* New York: Paradox Press.

McCloud, S. (2009, February). The "infinite canvas." Retrieved from http://scottmccloud.com/4-inventions/canvas/.

Morton, D. (2015). The unfortunates: Towards a history and definition of the motion comic. *Journal of Graphic Novels and Comics, 6*(4), 347–366.

Morton, D. (2017). *Comics to the screen: Style, American film, and comic books during the blockbuster era.* Jackson: University Press of Mississippi.

Murphy, J. (2002). Losing my edge [Recorded by LCD Soundsystem]. On *LCD Soundsystem* [12-inch CD]. New York: DFA Records. (date of recording).

Pew Research Center. (2018). Mobile fact sheet. Retrieved from http://www.pewinternet.org/fact-sheet/mobile/.

Sabak, N. (2017). Boom! Pow! Ka-ching!: Sales of digital comics and graphic novels. *Publishing Trends.* Retrieved from http://www.publishingtrends.com/2017/02/digital-sales-comics-graphic-novels/.

About the Contributors

Mike P. **Cook** is an assistant professor at Auburn University. He has published on the use of graphic novels to foster comprehension and multimodal literacy. His writings have appeared in *The ALAN Review*, *Sequential Art Narrative in Education*, *Journal of Language and Literacy Education*, *Literacy Research & Instruction*, and the *Journal of College Literacy and Learning*.

Bill **Holbrook** is the creator of syndicated newspaper comics "On the Fastrack" and "Safe Havens," and "Kevin & Kell," considered the longest continually running daily webcomic.

Teri **Holbrook** is an associate professor of literacy and language arts at Georgia State University. Her research examines how arts-infused digital composition alters literacy education, writing, and qualitative inquiry.

Melanie **Hundley** is an associate professor of literacy, language, and culture at Vanderbilt University. Her research interests are digital and multimodal composition, teacher pedagogy, and YA literature.

Karis **Jones** is a doctoral student in the English education department at New York University, where her research focuses on writing assessment. She is a co-author of the webcomic *Story of Saliria*. Her interest in the graphic personification of Death was originally kindled by Neil Gaiman's *The Sandman*.

Jeffrey SJ **Kirchoff** is an assistant professor at Texas A&M University–Central Texas. He teaches classes on rhetoric, graphic narrative, and literary criticism. His scholarship has appeared in *Technoculture*, *Studies in Comics*, *Sequential Art Narrative in Education*, *Journal of College Literacy and Learning*, and the *International Journal of Comic Art*.

Eden Lee **Lackner** teaches at the University of Calgary and is a member of the Horror Writers Association. Her interests include nineteenth century literature, popular culture, fan and internet studies, and speculative fiction. She has contributed to *Fan Fiction and Fan Studies in the Age of the Internet* and *The Works of Tim Burton*.

John **Logie** is an associate professor of rhetoric and the Director of the Rhetoric and Scientific & Technical Communication graduate programs in the Department of Writing Studies at the University of Minnesota. His scholarship addresses rhetoric, digital media and visual rhetoric.

Drew **Morton** is an associate professor of mass communication at Texas A&M University–Texarkana. He is the author of *Panel to the Screen: Style, American Film, and Comic Books During the Blockbuster Era* and the cofounder and coeditor of *[in]Transition*, the award winning journal devoted to videographic criticism.

Jayson **Quearry** was incubated in a stew of comics and film from an early age; he is parlaying that upbringing into a doctorate degree in moving image studies at Georgia State University. His research interests focus on the intersections between cinema and comics in terms of aesthetics, adaptation, and intertextual narratives.

Chris **Reyns-Chikuma** is a professor at University of Alberta (Canada) where he teaches French culture in French and comics in English. He has published on various topics and medias, but in the last ten years he specialized more in francophone bande dessinée, mainstream and alternative comics.

Luke **Rodesiler** is an assistant professor at Purdue University Fort Wayne. His interests include the role of popular cultures in the English language arts classroom, media literacy education, and nontraditional forms of teacher professional development. His work has appeared in various refereed journals, including *English Education*, *Journal of Adolescent & Adult Literacy*, and *English Journal*.

Johannes C.P. **Schmid** is a research assistant in the project "Media-Aesthetic Strategies of Framing and Translation in Graphic Novels" at the University of Hamburg, where his MA thesis won an award. He is co-organizer of the Comic-Kolloquium Hamburg and coeditor of the volume *Praktiken medialer Transformationen*.

Jean **Sébastien** is a professor of literature and communications at Collège de Maisonneuve in Montréal. He has developed a manga and comics workshop course at the undergraduate level and has published on issues of interoperability for scholarly publications and on American literature.

Rich **Shivener** is a doctoral candidate in the University of Cincinnati's Department of English and Comparative Literature. His dissertation research investigates the composing practices and affective work of digital media scholarship, including digital comics.

Ray **Whitcher** has produced titles for *Star Wars: The Clone Wars*, the Australian comic *That Bulletproof Kid*, and *Velocity: Darker Forces*. He is producing his own independent project, *Wanton*, as part of his Ph.D. research and has previously presented at both the San Diego Comic-Con and the Design Indabas in Cape Town.

Index

www.ingramcontent.com/pod-product-compliance
Lightning Source LLC
LaVergne TN
LVHW042124070326
832902LV00036B/577